Combat Officer

COMBAT OFFICER

A Memoir of War in the South Pacific

CHARLES H. WALKER

BALLANTINE BOOKS • NEW YORK

A Presidio Press Book
Published by The Random House Publishing Group
Copyright © 2004 by Charles H. Walker

Presidio Press and colophon are trademarks of Random House, Inc.

Maps courtesy of the 164th Regiment, U.S. Army (S-2 files)

www.presidiopress.com

ISBN 0-345-46385-4

Manufactured in the United States of America

First Edition: September 2004

OPM 10 9 8 7 6 5 4 3 2 1

ACKNOWLEDGMENTS

I wish to thank the following for their contribution and insight as warriors:

Charles G. Ross

Company E, 164th Infantry, on Fiji, Bougainville, Leyte, Negros, Japan. Also fought in Korea, Vietnam. Was awarded Triple Combat Infantry Badge. Served with infantry, ranger, airborne ranger, special forces, and reconnaissance units in three wars during thirty years of service. B.S. from University of Georgia. Inducted to Ranger Hall of Fame. Distinguished Public Service Award, Humanitarian Award.

Milton C. Shedd

Company E, 164th Infantry, also regimental reconnaissance officer, cofounder of Sea World. He was called "The Walt Disney of the Sea." Founded Hubbs Sea World Research Institute. Helped create UCLA Science Center. Investment banker and chairman of Sea World for two decades.

William Byers

Company E, 164th Infantry, on Cebu, Negros, Japan. Educator before service. After service obtained MPS from Frostburg College, Maryland. Spent his entire career in public education.

William Kiker

Company E, 164th Infantry, on Leyte, Cebu, Negros, Japan. Left Japan first sergeant reserve nineteen years. College,

MBA, recalled to active duty as captain: Civil Affairs. Released as lieutenant colonel.

Zane F. Jacobs
Company E, 184th Infantry, on Cebu, Negros, Japan. Discharged to reenlist RA, discharged 1947. Reenlisted USN 1949 as aerographer's mate striker, nineteen years USN missile test center. Litton Corporation 1969–71, to Atlanta as aviation flight forecaster, USN Meteorological Technician Fleet Numerical Weather Center for nineteen years.

INTRODUCTION

This book began as a brief history of my wartime years; it was to be for my children. With the inclusion of correspondence and stories from my longtime Army friends, it began to grow far beyond my original plan.

The cadre of our 164th Army National Guard Infantry Regiment was from North Dakota. Our replacements to fill the regiment to full strength came from nearly every state in the union, and Mexico.

We stopped the enemy at Guadalcanal, in the largest land battle fought there. We continued island-hopping until the landing in Japan after the surrender.

It was my good fortune to serve on Guadalcanal, supporting Easy Company with my platoon of H Company machine guns. Later, I had the further privilege of moving to Easy Company as commanding officer.

I have failed to mention officer replacements in this memoir, especially those who took over during the heaviest fighting in the Philippines. Lieutenants Byers, Moore, Baranowski, Torgeson, and Wright took over under desperate circumstances, serving expertly.

The soldiers of Easy Company were an unbeatable team. As an octogenarian, I fully realize the honor of having served with such outstanding, wonderful men in the defense of our country.

I will always remember those we left behind.

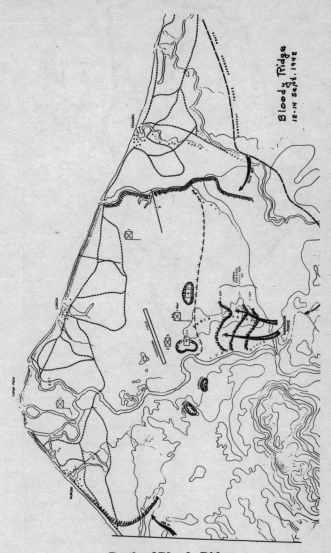

Battle of Bloody Ridge
September 12–14, 1942

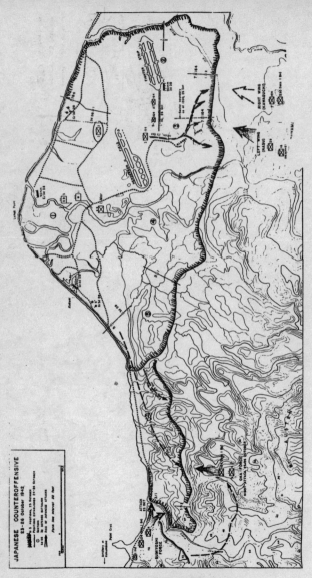

Battle for Henderson Field
October 23–26, 1942

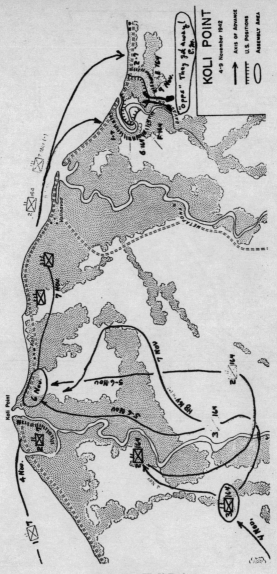

Drive to Koli Point
November 4–9, 1942

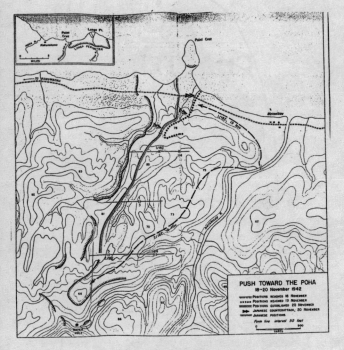

Fighting Beyond Matanikau
November 18–20, 1942

CHAPTER 1

October 7, 1942,
New Caledonia, Southwest Pacific Area.

It was nearly 6 P.M. when five Company H officers traveled the rough highway of New Caledonia to a French family farm that catered occasional meals for American soldiers. Much of the only highway running from the capital, Noumea, to the far end of the island had been hewn from solid rock; it was a real spring-breaker on Army vehicles.

The farm lay a quarter mile from the highway, with each side of the lane lined with beautiful royal palms. John Gossett, my company CO (commanding officer), and I had made the dinner reservations the previous afternoon and we had arrived at the farm just as the husband and wife were in the process of butchering a hog. The wife had been busy collecting the blood dripping from the throat-cut animal, which hung from a hoist. She'd stirred the fluid constantly as she added an additional bit of flour to make blood sausage.

Seated the next evening in an airy room next to the porch, we were each served a full bottle of wine as an aperitif. Then there came rock oysters, which we were told had been peeled off rocks in the ocean when the tide was out. They were something like barnacles, I thought, but delicious, and they were packed in chipped ice. A question arose: Where did they get the ice? Then we had a salad of vegetables, followed by fried chicken. Next was a pork chop, then a steak, and then dessert. All in all, the seven-course meal required almost two hours to consume. When a bottle of wine was emptied, it was instantly replaced with another. Surfeited by the excellent meal and wine, we were all in wonderful spirits until we heard the sound of an approaching vehicle. It had to be trouble, because only one man knew our location.

The newcomer was Dick Hamer, a lieutenant recently assigned to our heavy weapons company—the officer we had left in charge of the company while we were absent. He was excited.

"I've got real news! We're to pack up for Guadalcanal, to load on ships the day after tomorrow. You've got to get back to the company; they've dumped a pile of ordnance and ammunition upon us. I didn't know what to do, so I figured I'd better locate you all."

After we paid our hosts we headed back to our bivouac area to find the company in turmoil. We had twelve extra machine guns to degrease; two extra 81mm mortars to clean; scads of ammunition that had to be loaded into belts; and several tommy guns, Winchester 97 shotguns, and other specialty items to oil and pack.

John Gossett turned to me: "I'll run up the hill to battalion headquarters and find out the details. I'll be right back."

Minutes later he returned with a long face. It seemed that both our battalion commander and his executive officer had reported to the hospital, supposedly sick. (We were to find out later from our battalion surgeon that eleven officers of our regiment had suddenly developed pains, possible appendicitis, or other ailments.) As our regiment was a North Dakota National Guard unit, many senior officers had political connections, even down to an occasional captain. In fact, after our arrival in New Caledonia, our regimental commanding officer, a banker in civilian life, was replaced by a West Pointer. Our banker had no experience at running a regiment in combat, but what of the man from the school along the Hudson? He had no combat experience, either.

My first thought upon John's return was one of relief. Our battalion commander was a loudmouthed, uncouth drinker, a coward who covered his weakness by bluster and cursing. An additional shock came the next morning when we found he had withheld our 60mm- and 81mm-mortar training ammunition from us these past months. He had it all stashed inside a fenced enclosure behind his tent. Word had leaked down that our gasoline ration was in reality four gallons a day for each vehicle. Our battalion commander had withheld half of this in his enclosure. We would lose scores of barrels of gasoline that he had piled up; in the French civilians on New Caledonia would soon find and use them.

Also lost to us was our machine-gun and rifle-practice ammunition. The only conclusion we could reach was that our commander had withheld the supplies for demonstrations to please the big brass when they came around, demonstrations that would never take place. I never forgave him, for we went to Guadalcanal with little or no experience in firing those important weapons.

A replacement for the man was not immediately appointed, so my company commander was more or less forced to take over the reins on a temporary basis. *He* was a leader.

We packed and boxed up all night; tents were struck and cots folded. The twelve extra machine guns were readied for use and also mortars and tommy guns were checked and oiled. Crews finally finished loading many cases of loose ammunition into machine-gun belts by 4 A.M. By daylight, everyone was exhausted and asleep.

Shortly after noon a messenger arrived from regimental headquarters with orders for me to report to the 9 Station Hospital in Pieta, to be evacuated to the States. The month before I had had a bout of heart trouble after five days and nights without sleep, while we made repeated forced marches. I had been hospitalized for two weeks. I'd been released back to my unit temporarily as wounded Marines from Guadalcanal began to overcrowd the hospital.

I was determined to fight with the unit so I consulted John. "I'm going to the Canal with you!"

"Charley, you've got to go to the hospital. If I allow you to come with us, I'll qualify for a court-martial."

He mused for several moments then began to smile. "We're to load on the *McCawley,* but there's another ship going to the Canal, the *Zeilin.* I'll lend you a jeep tonight, and if you can get on that ship, good luck! Heck! I can say I don't know where you went!"

Hamer, our new officer, decided to accompany me, so after dark we drove to the city of Noumea. As it neared 10 P.M. we approached the docks to find a landing craft that was being loaded under dim pier lights.

"Hey, Coxswain! Which ship are you headed to?"

Over the sudden roar of the craft's motor, as he began to back away, he yelled, "Out to the *Zeilin!*"

"Can we catch a ride with you?"

"Sure, climb aboard. But be quick about it."

Minutes later we were at the bow of the *Zeilin.* It was inky dark, but a landing net hung within reach of the small craft. I started the climb up the net with Hamer following, but I ran into difficulty. We were not alongside a vertical wall, but at the tapered bow. Our feet swung in sharply, so that the climb had to be done almost totally by hand. Despite my full pack and rifle I managed to get to the very edge of the ship's rail before I hesitated. I called down to Hamer, "I'm about played out. How about you?" At that instant a voice came out of the darkness.

"Need some help, Mac?" A hand reached over the rail and literally lifted me over the edge, onto the deck. Lordy, I was thankful! Our hidden benefactor then assisted Hamer, and we both thanked him profusely.

He pointed. "Just go through that far hatchway; there are wardrooms along the passage."

The first wardroom door was open, and I glimpsed a man wearing dark glasses. He was lying on the bunk nearest the door. I recognized him as Warrant Officer Hall from our Service Company.

"What are you doing here, Hall?"

He tipped up his dark glasses and smiled. "They were going to send me home."

"Same here." I looked around the room and saw seven Marine officers, all about my age; they were pilots and intelligence officers on their way to Guadalcanal.

"Do you mind if Hamer and I bunk in here with you?"

A young lieutenant named Gibbs introduced himself, then presented his fellow Marine officers. "We've two spare bunks. You're welcome to them."

The *McCawley* and the *Zeilin* left October 9 for the Canal accompanied by three or four destroyers. It was to be a four-day trip.

On our second day upon the ocean, I happened to be standing by a signalman who was operating a blinker light in contact with the *McCawley*. He was scribbling on a tablet as he turned to me. "Some guy is going to be happy over this message."

A few minutes later the loudspeaker requested my presence on the bridge. I suspected I was going to be admonished for slipping aboard, but instead a smiling officer handed me a message that read: *You are the father of a healthy baby girl. Love, Lorraine.* I knew my wife was expecting soon, but to be notified in this exciting way!

The wire was addressed to Sydney, Australia. Someone there had a heart. John had managed to have it forwarded by light signal. That was my company commander, a real prince.

On the third day aboard the *Zeilin,* as I sat in the shade, leaning against a hatch cover, I reminisced about the past months spent on New Caledonia. Some good, some not so good.

While on a deer-hunting trip accompanied by our Protestant chaplain, we'd ventured some miles into the hills from our base camp. It was approaching 7 A.M. when we first heard tremendous rumbling explosions coming from far out on the ocean. I immediately abandoned our hunting plans; my platoon's antitank guns would be needed to protect Uto and Dumbea passes along our ocean frontage from a possible Japanese invasion.

As we approached my bivouac area near the Tontouta Airfield, I became aware of several Navy fighters circling to land on the macadam strip. The fighters were from a carrier that was in serious trouble, and the aircraft were almost out of fuel. The first plane crashed on the strip, necessitating the dispatch of an ambulance. The second, following closely behind, bowled into the lead plane and the ambulance. Another ambulance was dispatched, and a third airplane piled into the lot. The remaining aircraft took to the grass, anywhere they could land.

I was not an eyewitness to the accidents, and a veil of secrecy was swept over the matter so we could obtain no additional information. However, on one of my regular beach patrols with my driver, Blacky Sievers, I noted two gray life preservers that had blown ashore. On the back of each was LEX in big letters, followed by the words "Div. 10" underneath. I knew then that the carrier *Lexington* had gone down.

When I returned to the rear area I described what I had found, but everyone smiled; no one believed such a thing could happen. Some months later *Life* magazine came out with photographs of the sinking.

Near my platoon bivouac by Tontouta Airfield was an old greenhouse. Its owner went into Noumea each Thursday for his quota of wine, which he sold to the troops. He finally became so greedy that men waiting outside his door heard him pouring the wine into a bathtub, thereby doubling the quantity. They quickly cured him of that by burning down his house.

My former company commander was a heavy drinker, as was his almost-constant companion, the first sergeant. I was called to report one evening and found both well soused. My captain started to curse me about the camouflage on my four

37mm gun shields, saying, "I should beat the hell out of you, you damned young whippersnapper!"

I had taken all the foul crap he had handed out to date, but I finally rebelled at this. I challenged him, "Why don't you try?"

He did, only to end up on the ground. Then I challenged the first sergeant: "Mac, come out here and get the same!"

He was a coward, so I got in my jeep and went back to my platoon near Tontouta. The next morning at seven, a lieutenant appeared and handed me an order. It was a transfer from the antitank company to Company H of our regiment as of that day.

I was tickled pink! A month later this captain was reduced in grade to a first lieutenant and transferred elsewhere.

I was assigned to take over the First Platoon of Company H upon my arrival. The platoon sergeant, Sergeant Hoffman, was a gem. He took me through the .30-caliber Browning water-cooled machine gun from one end to the other. I couldn't understand why he was never selected to go to the officer training school in Noumea, for we were short of officers, and the man was excellent officer material. Perhaps it was because the present commander of Company H was afraid of losing good men.

Back on July 3 our battalion commander ordered all five companies to the beach area to participate in a baseball tournament on the afternoon of the Fourth. During my first few days with Company H, I sensed a current of animosity toward the company commander. In addition, I found the men also had no respect for the battalion commander.

When 10 A.M. came on the Fourth of July, every man in Company H was either drunk or pretended to be. The battalion commander arrived, red-faced and yelling, "Break every noncom in the company. I'll show the bastards."

The officers of the company were shocked, but we kept our mouths shut. Our captain did that foolish thing: he broke every noncom in the company to private.

When word of this action reached regimental headquarters, the very next morning a new captain arrived to take over command.

Immediately, Captain John Gossett reinstated every non-com. The company now had a *real* commander.

There was no bluster to this man; he spoke calmly, but you knew he meant business. He consulted with each officer in turn, asking about our education and experience. I felt a world of confidence in this man.

CHAPTER 2

When daylight came on October 13, many of us were on deck eyeing Savo Island and the mainland of Guadalcanal. The weather was exceptional. As we neared land the ships headed straight to shore, bows almost touching the beach. We were to find after we landed that the Marines held only a small perimeter, an oval perhaps five miles along the beach and two miles deep. Along this beach for miles stretched Lever Brothers coconut plantation.

Plywood Higgins boats without ramps quickly unloaded the troops. Hamer and I were able to rejoin Company H after a brief search. First Platoon was detailed to unload hundreds of cases of gelignite explosive. We had formed a pile about twenty-five feet square and four feet high when word came of a Condition Yellow. That meant Japanese bombers were on their way, arriving soon. Condition Red quickly followed.

The approaching Japanese bombers, all twenty-four of them, were difficult to spot at first, because of their high altitude. They were flying in V formations, much like geese. Apparently the enemy was focused on the destruction of Henderson Field, the main airfield on Guadalcanal, named after a Marine aviator. Under scant cover we heard bombs exploding in the distance: *Krump! krump! krump!* A minute later the bombers swung over the beach to drop a few bombs perhaps three or four hundred yards from my location. The 164th Infantry lost its first man that morning.

A second air raid began overhead about two hours later; the enemy again concentrated on the airfield. It became apparent that air raids were to be an everyday occurrence.

After Condition Green sounded we continued to work, moving gear back from the beach until five o'clock, when a large artillery shell struck the sand about one hundred feet north of me. Fortunately, a parked Bren gun carrier shielded me from the blast and fragments. More shells came in from the west, alerting crews on the stern guns of the *Zeilin* and *McCawley,* who returned fire. The enemy artillery piece was concealed a long distance back along the western shore, so I doubted that they scored any success.

Shortly after the artillery duel, we formed up to march inland. A Marine advised me, "Don't let them bivouac you by the airstrip. It catches hell every night."

As darkness fell we passed an ammunition dump that was still burning from one of the air raids. From time to time the fireworks from it were spectacular. A half mile farther along the trail we halted to bed down for the night. I promptly dug a slit trench after checking my platoon. It was dark at the time, with no moon. Somewhere around midnight I awoke to a horrendous sound. Japanese illumination shells were coming in from the sea, burning brightly with a series of loud, crackling explosions. Each explosion seemed to bounce the flares back and forth in a jerky motion. I rolled into my slit trench, but met opposition. A soldier who had woken earlier had appropriated my hole. After a brief effort to shake him out with cuss words, I gave up and sought other cover.

Illuminated in the light of the overhead flares stood a Chevy one-and-a-half-ton truck with a steel cab, only about fifty feet away. I jumped into the cab but quickly changed my mind when a large fragment of enemy shell struck the truck, shaking it violently. As I abandoned the truck I spotted a series of what looked like nail kegs; I knew it was a latrine. Just at that moment a Japanese floatplane passed directly overhead and dropped another flare to direct the naval gunfire. About one hundred yards away a parked B17 bomber burst into flames, adding even more light to the situation.

I yelled for help to tear the top off the latrine, and several men who lacked cover jumped to the task. Within seconds the deep, twenty-foot-long trench was filled with men, all reasonably safe from the shells unless we took a direct hit. The soft, mushy bottom of the trench and the vile odor told us plenty, but not an objection was heard. When the shelling ceased and daylight finally came, we threw away our canvas leggings and walked to the nearby ocean. We removed our boots, washed our legs, threw away our socks, and scoured our boots with sand, inside and out. Cruising the beach near Alligator Creek (the name was a misnomer; the creek was loaded with crocodiles), I saw Japanese arms, legs, and torsos buried in the sand: the result of a battle on August 21 when the Marines had wiped out the Ichiki Detachment of the Japanese Army.

We found to our dismay that we were on the edge of the airfield amid a litter of coconut trees whose tops had been sheared off by the shelling. A short distance away lay several aircraft, nearly all destroyed beyond repair. That afternoon we were told the main shelling had come from two battleships with fourteen-inch guns, assisted by a cruiser and several destroyers. We estimated that at least eight hundred or more of the fourteen-inch-high explosive shells had been fired, together with an equal or greater number of smaller-caliber shells from the escorting ships. Later, we referred to this as the Night of the Battleships.

On October 14 there were few American aircraft available; most of the dive-bombers had been destroyed in the shelling. Pistol Pete, a 150mm Japanese field gun, fired on the airport runway from the enemy-held west, forcing a temporary move to Fighter Strip 1, a short distance southeast of the main strip. That same day there were two more major bombing runs by the enemy, supplemented by another night of shelling from the sea. This time, only eight-inch cruiser fire came in; it was much less terrifying than the huge fourteen-inch shells.

At daylight on October 15, word came down that several Japanese transports were unloading at Tassafaronga, just ten miles to our west. As the beach curved, the ships could be easily seen. I counted four with the aid of binoculars, but later learned there were six. They had Zero-fighter cover, but

the few American planes that were capable of flying ignored
them and attacked the transports. By dusk three of the enemy
ships were ablaze, but three escaped. We learned later that
three American dive-bombers had been shot down in the action and that two thousand Japanese troops had safely landed
from the ships.

Where is our Navy? we wondered. Do we have one? Are
our admirals all cowards, or just incompetent?

On October 16, Second Battalion was ordered into the line
behind Henderson Field to relieve a unit of the Seventh Marine Regiment. Early in the afternoon, as we crossed the
main airport runway, we heard sirens that indicated a Condition Red. We hurried across the strip and stopped about
four hundred yards to the east, in a grassy area. Instead of
continuing on into the jungle, we lay on our backs to watch
the bombers approach.

Two big V formations of twin-engine medium bombers
(which we called Bettys) flew straight down the runway from
west to east. They were high, about twenty thousand feet,
and silvery in the bright sunlight. As they began their run
over the airstrip, Marine 90mm AA guns got the range. The
shell bursts were right on target, and the center lead plane in
the first formation began to smoke, then burst into flame. As
it began to dive it suddenly exploded. In a flash it was gone.
To the right of the doomed plane another also began to trail
smoke, and then evidently its bombs exploded, taking with it
the next aircraft to its right. They disappeared like magic.

Moments later the bombs hissed down and landed just
northwest of the runway. Evidently, upper air currents had
moved the bombs off target, or the leader of the flight had
misjudged. The second V formation escaped unscathed,
much to the disappointment of my platoon, who were wildly
cheering. This formation of bombers was escorted by Zero
fighters; we could hear faint sounds of fire, although it was
nearly impossible to see the darting fighter planes at that altitude. From what we *could* see, the Japanese aircraft were
taking a beating.

Unfortunately, we had too few aircraft capable of taking to

the air that day, although Zero fighters mixing it up with our Marine and Navy F4F would become a common sight.

Moving again, our Marine guide led us into the bush and along a narrow trail to our Second Battalion position. The Marines we were relieving greeted us with enthusiasm, for they were eager to get off the defensive line for a rest. As they loaded onto weapons carriers, they were all smiles.

One of my men came to me with a sheepish look, displaying a Springfield rifle. "One of those Marines stole my M1"—a Garand rifle.

Well acquainted with military thievery, I shook my head in disgust. "You greenhorn! At least he left you something to shoot with. You're stuck with it! Smarten up!" I felt like saying a lot more, but I knew the men would ridicule him unmercifully. They would not allow him to forget his carelessness. I felt he would serve as a good example.

A crude vehicle trail paralleled the edge of the jungle, approximately two hundred feet inside the bush. Company E moved into the right end of the battalion line, with my platoon of Company H in support. I placed my eight machine guns in the prepared Marine positions. Fortunately, I was able to place them a bit closer together due to the four extra guns I had been issued.

In front of our barbed-wire apron, which was about sixty yards from our frontline, Navy Seabees were packing the ground, using captured Japanese land rollers in an effort to build an emergency landing strip.

At the right end of our line was a stretch of jungle where Company E tied in with the First Battalion of Marines. This was the extreme right flank of Company E. Our link with the Marines began at the edge of this jungle, a juncture that later would earn the name Coffin Corner.

I saw only a few Marines at the juncture while placing Corporal McCarthy's water-cooled Browning machine gun in position. I walked a bit farther along the Marine line and met a Seventh Marine officer at a .50-caliber-machine-gun post. This gun was heavily sandbagged, but it had no overhead cover. The Marine officer's next words shocked me: "I

have only about eighty men left in my company; the rest of
the battalion is in similar shape. They have robbed nearly
everyone to reinforce some other sector further west. How
are you fixed?"

I told him I had four water-cooled medium Browning machine guns and four light air-cooled guns. (The barrel in a
water-cooled machine gun is surrounded by a water jacket,
which serves to reduce heating. The air-cooled machine gun
has a heavier barrel, which can be changed quickly. Spare
barrels are kept on hand at each gun.)

We walked some distance along the barbed wire that was
set up for a final protective line (FPL). In fact the dugouts we
took over from the Second Battalion, Seventh Marines were
in good shape. The barbed wire on the FPL zigzagged so that
a machine gun could be set at an angle to fire approximately
twelve inches above the ground along the outside edge of a
long stretch of wire; the adjoining machine gun crisscrossed
at the opposite angle, so that along the entire battalion front
the barbed wire was covered with interlocking bands of fire.
I complimented the Marine officer; the barbed wire and
aprons were wide and high, in excellent condition. They
would stop a wild rush of men; no one could get through the
many strands of barbed wire without difficulty, and so would
be delayed long enough to be shot.

In the left portion of my defensive line was a good field of
fire, perhaps two hundred yards, but on the right flank, near
the jungle defended by the Seventh Marines, the kunai grass
was high and as close as 125 yards. It came to me: if I only
had old King and Queen, our gray team back on the farm, together with that old Moline mower, I could easily have
widened that field of fire!

Later that evening Captain Gossett stopped by to inspect
the final disposition of my guns. He was satisfied, but I noted
he entered every gun position to check the sighting on the
FPL. He also had a few words for each man in each crew.

Due to the shortage of machine-gun ammunition, I was
forced to limit each gun to six belts while holding back a reserve for immediate delivery to any portion of the line under

attack. Spare belts and extra grenades were kept in my head-quarters tent just in the center and rear of the Company E line.

The Company H, 81mm mortars supporting the battalion were located about eight hundred yards to the rear of our line, with two extra mortars in addition to the standard four. The jeep trail behind our line extended to the juncture of Company E and the Marines. From there, farther west along the Marine line, the trail was mostly a footpath. I made sure our machine guns were securely tied in with the Marines at this junction.

My platoon headquarters tent had already been placed for me by the Marine weapons officer I had relieved. It even had a dugout with an inside entrance capable of holding four or five men. A feeder trail led from the vehicle road (sixty yards to the rear) past the corner of my tent to the frontline. Company E, 60mm mortars were located adjacent to but several yards northeast of the tent. We kept the tent side nearest the back trail open. This proved to be a blessing a few nights later.

Since we were attached to Company E for rations, our weapons platoon ate two meals each day, early morning and late afternoon. The kitchen was located near the center of the Company E line.

During daylight hours we rotated men so no portion of our defensive position was overly weakened. At night, everyone rotated two hours on duty, two hours off. We had been told the enemy favored a night attack.

October 16 was devoted to improving gun positions and barbed-wire barriers. Tall grass in front of the positions was cut to reduce cover for the enemy. Nuisance air raids became a nightly occurrence, and daylight fighter battles were watched avidly by cheering soldiers. We passed the night with no naval shelling.

On October 17, Company E sent out patrols three miles to our front. Old Japanese equipment was found, but no new tracks or signs of movement were seen. All communication was by runner or EE8 telephone. The Motorola 536 radios previously issued proved almost worthless; the excessive humidity was the culprit.

Shortly after noon, twenty bombers hit Henderson Field with fighter support. Again our cheering section showed enthusiasm; many Japanese planes were shot down.

Enemy bombers flew over Henderson at about 1400 on October 18. The various aircraft that came over at night dropped an occasional small bomb, which kept us awake. We called them nuisance raids. Frequent small explosions from Henderson Field indicated that Pistol Pete, the Japanese 150mm gun to the west, was again working over the runways and parked aircraft.

We ate pancakes on October 19 with D-ration chocolate, and C rations for the second meal. The usual Japanese bombers with fighter escort attacked Henderson Field. It seemed strange that Washing Machine Charley, our nightly sleep interrupter, was often caught by searchlights—they lit him up like a white butterfly—but the antiaircraft couldn't seem to shoot him down. Evidently the pilot could see the gun flashes on the ground and took evasive action.

October 20 was another typical day. Company E patrolled and we had bombers overhead at noon. Our pilots were shooting down a lot of enemy aircraft, both Zeros and Bettys.

On October 21 we had our first bomber raid at 11 A.M. and another at 5 P.M. Details of men dug small circular trenches along the proposed emergency airstrip on October 22. A four-foot center was left to support a machine gun. My platoon dug these positions in the rear of our wire apron. The Japanese must have had lots of aircraft: they came over several times during the day, and were being shot down in growing numbers.

On October 23, Japanese bombers flew over again, this time with fighter escort. I heard Marine artillery heavily shelling in the Matanikau and Point Cruz area, to the west. The Marines must have been having trouble there. Japanese 150mm guns shelled Henderson until noon.

October 24 was uneventful and no information came

down the chain of command. This wasn't unusual, since we were seldom given vital information. Those above probably thought we didn't need to know. Was it jealousy between the services? Perhaps it was the Marine way. But how wrong they were: we wanted to be informed; it should have been our privilege.

The commanders took our cameras away from us, and we couldn't keep diaries. Why? It seemed every officer, from lieutenant colonel to general, had been seen carrying a camera. Rank seemed to have its privileges. The men had little respect for these officers.

Evidently, from the vast amount of artillery fire near the Matanikau, the Japanese main thrust seemed to be there. I believed the Marines thought so too; why else remove a battalion of the Seventh Marines from their line next to us? In fact, we were not even privy to the fact a Marine patrol of nearly forty men had been sent to outpost a small hill one thousand yards to our right front. From there they had a telephone hookup back to their unit. Such was the lack of communication between the Marines and Army.

CHAPTER 3

It was near dusk that evening of October 24 when my platoon sergeant, Dick Hoffman, and I heard McCarthy's machine gun open fire. We also heard heavy rifle fire, then a sudden loud report that I suspected came from the Marine 37mm antitank gun. It seemed that McCarthy's gun would never cease firing, indicating he would soon be out of ammunition.

Turning to Dick, I said, "Let's grab all the ammo belts we can carry and get them down the line."

"Going to take the back trail?"

"No way! We'll go along the frontline positions; the men will be plenty trigger-happy as it is."

Each of us carried several belts of machine-gun ammunition and started down the line. Calling ahead, we warned that we were carrying ammunition toward the firefight, injecting a few choice cuss words so the men on the line wouldn't mistake us for English-speaking Japanese.

When we finally reached the rear of McCarthy's dugout, I poked my head inside to find out what was going on. McCarthy clued me in. "Japanese came along the edge of the bush in a column of twos, straight toward us. When they reached the barbed wire they stopped in confusion. At first we thought they might be a Marine patrol, but they were so close we knew they were enemy. When I yelled, 'Password!' you should have seen the cigarettes fly! Heck, most of them were smoking."

Just as we left McCarthy's position, all hell broke loose. It seemed that more Japanese had moved up to the wire. Bullets were flying everywhere. Abrupt 81mm fire was landing out in front of the wire from our Company H mortars. A Japanese mortar shell struck a tree overhead; the explosion was a big red flash. We didn't know that one hundred or more Japanese in the jungle section in front of the Marines had broken through their thin line and were in the rear of our positions. When I heard this the next morning, I was glad we hadn't taken the jeep trail!

The final protective lines worked well. Later we found enemy piled three or four deep at the front edge of our wire, stopped by constant machine-gun fire when they charged us.

Sporadic American artillery fire joined the devastation caused by the 81mm and 60mm mortars. Nothing could live in that approximately two-block-square area of impact. Company H mortars fired sixteen hundred rounds that first night. The mortar tubes were red-hot. Finally, two of the tubes failed to dislodge high explosive shells dropped into them; the shells were stuck fast. That meant the shells would soon explode in the tubes from the heat, killing the crew servicing them. The two tubes were quickly tossed into existing slit trenches and hastily covered with dirt. Fortunately, the shells did not explode, but the mortar tubes remain buried on Guadalcanal to this day.

By keeping track of the firing on the line, and the ammo we had delivered, we knew McCarthy was adequately provisioned until near daylight. Our first delivery of ammunition had been about 10:30 P.M. At about 3:30 A.M. we started out with a second load. Rifle and machine-gun fire was heavy, coming in and going out.

When Dick and I reached McCarthy's position on our *third* trip, we handed belt after belt through the back entrance before I noticed a dead man just to the left of McCarthy's position. I recognized the man.

"Mac! What happened to Flynn?"

"He caught one. Cripes, the bullets are as thick as flies on horseshit. Watch yourself!"

I reached into my pocket for a handkerchief and covered Flynn's face. Then I moved around his body to the left edge of McCarthy's position and endeavored to look out to the front. In the dim light I could see bodies and more bodies; some were heaped on the barbed wire, which sagged in many places from their weight. Suddenly, shouting came from the tall kunai grass directly across from our guns. It came from Marines who had been trapped at their outpost in front of us. They were endeavoring to get back to the American lines. Many had gone farther east to enter our lines where there was no action, but these Marines had evidently gotten lost and were mixed with Japanese troops in the kunai grass.

Out of the growing light, thirty yards to my front, three men stood up. At first I thought they were our troops. I called to McCarthy, "Who are they?"

"Why those cheeky sons of bitches!" he exclaimed. We both leveled on them, and dropped all three. Somehow they had gotten through our apron wire and had hidden in one of our newly dug antiaircraft positions. Later I judged that the yelling must have indicated that we wanted to surrender; at least that was my hypothesis. Otherwise, why would they have stood up?

As full daylight came the Japanese disaster became apparent. Hundreds of bodies lay to our front in the open grass. Our barbed wire was a shambles, and bullets were still flying. The field was a shooting gallery. It was shoot, shoot, and shoot! Many enemy, exposed by the gathering early sunlight, attempted to run back to cover. Very few made it.

As Sergeant Dick Hoffman and I moved along the line toward our headquarters tent, our attention was diverted again to the kunai grass two hundred yards to our front. Several Marines were seen; they were trying to run across the field of fire to our lines. Japanese were mixed in among them.

We yelled to the Marines to cross, that we would cover them. They all made the break, but one fell into our wire. As they reached safety, one Marine turned to run back to his buddy on the wire. He picked up his friend and struggled back with him. His buddy was conscious and actually laughing. "Hey, they got me in the leg." He looked up at me, still laughing. "I've been plugged three times. Golly! I'm entitled to three wound stripes!" Such was the courage of those Marines. I suspected some of the wounds the Marines suffered came from our own rifle fire, a case of mistaken identity.

Just as Sergeant Hoffman and I had nearly reached our position in the line I heard a Bren carrier roaring down by McCarthy's location. I found that Bob Campbell of our Company H had brought up a carrier to rescue the Marines still mixed with the Japanese in the high grass. McCarthy and two other men had jumped into the carrier, which ran across to the Japanese line, defying the odds. Armed with only one machine gun on the Bren, McCarthy held off the enemy, enabling the Marines to pile in. Their return trip was made without incident in spite of heavy enemy fire. McCarthy was later awarded the Distinguished Service Cross and the other men Silver Stars for the sortie.

Later that morning our telephone line back to the Company H mortars was cut. A detail was sent to repair the break. They found four Japanese infiltrators sound asleep beside the wire. The wire was repaired.

During the previous evening and continuing throughout the night, light, intermittent rain showers had occurred. A frantic call had gone out for help from Company A of the Seventh Marines; they needed more men. Company E had sent in their Third Platoon, and Company G, in reserve, their First Platoon, mixing them among the Marine positions. They'd passed in the rear of Company E and joined the Marines at the juncture. We were not informed of these reinforcements until the next morning. The platoon leaders of both E and G Companies were killed, as were others. The fighting was fierce, often hand to hand. The next night one of my friends from Company M and his first sergeant were bayoneted to death.

Another major detail was learned the morning of October 25: the Third Battalion, 164th Infantry, had moved into the Marine line at about 2 A.M. From then on the battle in that area took on a new dimension.

After I checked my line that morning I passed into the line

held by our Third Battalion, and was amazed to hear Japanese and Americans yelling back and forth at each other. I heard Franklin Roosevelt and Eleanor vilified by the Japanese, while our troops yelled back, "Tojo and the Emperor eat shit!" Surprisingly, one Japanese soldier spoke fair English.

Shelling had ceased after sunup except for an occasional mortar round, but sniping was constant and fierce. Everyone who had to move either crawled or crouched over, on the run.

On my way back to McCarthy's gun I stopped at the .50-caliber machine-gun position between the battalions. The men there pointed out a Japanese officer twenty feet in front of their gun. Evidently a tracer .50-caliber bullet had struck his buttocks, and he was actually burning up, slowly turning to a material like cigarette ash. I never knew a human body could burn so. He and four or five of his soldiers had nearly overrun the gun before being detected amid the noise of battle.

A second 37mm antitank gun was being cautiously installed alongside the first, as was another .50-caliber machine gun. Preparations for that night looked much better, except for our barbed wire, which was now practically gone. There also seemed to be a shortage of ammunition for the mortars and artillery.

Shortly after full daylight, we heard a twin-engine Betty approaching. It skimmed the treetops directly over us, headed toward the airfield. Big red meatballs painted on the underside of the large wings stood out clearly. Later in the day we found it was shot down by ground fire as it passed over Henderson Field. We wondered at the time what the pilot was thinking, coming in so low. Later we were told the Japanese headquarters at Rabaul had been informed by radio that our attackers had captured the airfield.

Johnny Divers, one of McCarthy's machine-gun crew, came to me with a ruptured flash hider from their machine gun. "We've used up two, and that's all we have. They get red-hot from the constant firing, then blow out. Anyone out front can spot our gun now."

"John, go back to the company CP and see Captain Gossett. If he can't get you some from the Marines, maybe you can make one out of those empty thirty-seven-millimeter casings." Later in the day we found the casings worked, but didn't last long because the brass was too soft. They blew out after only a few bursts of the gun.

The Japanese must have been totally frustrated; they made at least seven bombing and strafing attacks on Henderson Field. This was the biggest day yet, for our pilots and antiaircraft shot down nearly thirty enemy aircraft.

The ground attacks began early in the evening, mainly against the same juncture of our Company E and the Third Battalion of our regiment who had replaced the Seventh Marines. The remaining men of the Seventh Marines had been moved farther to the west. The enemy attacked in groups, and as quickly as one group was mowed down another moved up. By this time our brass realized this was the enemy's main thrust and did their best to line up every weapon. For brief, short periods the din was terrific: two antitank guns firing canister (gigantic shotguns with steel pellets), two .50-caliber machine guns, many .30-caliber machine guns, 60mm and 81mm mortars, and practically all the artillery that could be safely spared. We found later that the Japanese had committed their crack units, the 29th Infantry, followed by the 16th Infantry during the two nights of the battle. They failed with horrible losses and withdrew for another try the next day.

The third day of battle began at dusk, although sniper fire and mortar rounds were frequent during the day. Artillery fire was adjusted in front of the Third Battalion of the 164th Infantry, as the jungle was thick and the enemy hard to see. They had no decent fields of fire. A final attack near daylight on October 27 by the 16th Infantry was quickly beaten off. The 16th Regiment had little luck the past day and night. The North Dakota National Guard troops of the 164th Infantry ruled the battlefield.

During this battle on the twenty-sixth the Japanese who had broken through the line during the first night of battle became bothersome. They could not get to the airfield through a secondary line that had been established to fence them in. There was no water in this part of the jungle and little rain. They became desperate because of thirst.

On the morning of October 27, I carelessly walked to the Company E kitchen without my weapon. When I was about thirty feet from the kitchen a Japanese who had broken through the line shot at my head. A firecracker exploded in front of my nose, and I made a running dive behind some ration boxes at the edge of the kitchen. A few men sitting around the kitchen were alerted when the man wildly fired four more shots into the kitchen area from the small bush I had just passed. M1 rifles sprang into action; everyone emptied an eight-round clip into the bush. As suddenly as the action had begun, it stopped. The men who had fired from positions of leisure calmly reloaded their weapons as if they had not a care in the world. Finally someone walked over to the bush, then sauntered back. "He's dead!" the man said laconically. The distance from that Japanese to me was but thirty feet. How lucky can you get? I never forgot my weapon again.

About noon a heavy Japanese machine gun cut loose in the vicinity of the Company E command post. The fire came from an area where no action had taken place. The snapping bullets that passed by made one think. Everyone hit the deck, but a stalwart man from Company E took the Japanese gunner to task. The machine-gun duel went on for about ten minutes before the Japanese gun finally fell silent. We guessed the gunner had expended his ammunition, or it had become too hot for him.

The Japanese again struck at the sector of Company E at its juncture with the Third Battalion. The attacks were sporadic and failed to make headway. The Japanese withdrew at dawn, leaving the field to the usual snipers.

A bit of sniper fire opened the day on October 28 and Company E began to patrol again beyond the left flank. Antiaircraft positions, dug days earlier by the company, had been occupied by the enemy. Expended machine-gun brass cases were plentiful at one position that had been occupied by the gunner who had sprayed the Company E command post area the previous day.

Attacks that evening were sporadic and listless. It became apparent that the Japanese had been whipped.

CHAPTER 4

After 8 A.M. on October 29, men began drifting into the battle area to pick up enemy rifles, machine guns, sabers, and anything else of value. It seemed that every American soldier and Marine was a souvenir hunter. Many enemy helmets held a Japanese flag and most enemy soldiers had wristwatches or pocket watches. Of interest to me was the fact that many of their wristwatches were enclosed within another case for protection.

I was one of the guilty, but I collected weapons: machine guns, bangalore torpedoes for cutting wire, hand grenades, mortars and their shells, and other implements of war. These I sent back to my commanding officer, Captain John Gossett, who had the presence of mind to hide them. At noon we were required to turn all weapons over to our Service Company. Later, when I inquired about their security, I found they had all disappeared, stolen by the big shots and back-area scuts for personal souvenirs. We had been informed that each men could put his name on an enemy gun and that would be kept for him. So much for promises!

In my search for exotic weapons I found a 20mm antitank gun with bicycle handles, to be carried by four men. This was too heavy for me so I had to forgo it, but I did remove several armor-piercing shells for show. Evidently this weapon had not been in position when McCarthy made his foray with the Bren carrier. It would have made hash of that thin-armored Bren. Perhaps it had been brought up to prevent further incursions.

That night was uneventful except for sporadic shooting by

Americans, who took no chances. Most trigger-happy men had been cautioned to tighten up. Still, there were a few who were so tense they couldn't be controlled. I found that being a second lieutenant had its problems. A few men were brilliant leaders, the majority, so-so. One or two of my men were downright quirky. There were other problems. Draft boards in the States, especially in small communities, shipped out undesirables: one man was totally deaf, and another had varicose veins so bad his legs looked like bundles of grapes. I thought that the doctors who examined them should have been drafted.

On October 30 the souvenir hunters congregated; even the brass from the rear areas finally got the courage to show up, now that it was safe. Many of them brought their cameras. They got dirty looks from the men.

Air activity did not slow. I'd had no opportunity to travel much up to this time. It was only later that I realized there were so many Japanese aircraft downed that they could be found everywhere. A few crashed planes held bodies; other Japanese pilots must have used parachutes.

Pistol Pete continued to plaster the airfield on October 31, and dogfights between Americans and Japanese were an everyday occurrence. There were still many Japanese soldiers behind our lines, but their efforts were not coordinated. They harassed us in groups of only a few men.

That night, from 10 P.M. to 12 A.M., my runner, Stelck, and I were sleeping while two others had the shift. I awoke to hear Jake say, "If it moves again, I'm going to shoot it!"

Jake was a cook, sent to me as a replacement. I awoke my runner and said, "Jake is jumpy. We'd better start our shift early."

When I asked Jake what was wrong, he said, "It looks like a pig out there. There's noise in the brush."

"We'll take over; you two hit the the sack." I moved to the rear of the tent to look back toward the jeep trail. The moon was up and visibility excellent. After a few minutes I saw the pig, too, but it suddenly stood up and approached me silently. It was a Japanese soldier, his rifle with fixed bayonet at high port. He approached me head-on, hesitating momentarily, about eight feet away. As I was under the edge of the tent I was invisible to him. The password was "Honolulu." When I challenged, he froze, then slowly began to turn back.

I had my Reising submachine gun in my hands and, although I had fired it many times during the day, I had never fired it at night. When I pulled the trigger, a blast of flame instantly blinded me. After a burst of a few rounds I pulled again and emptied the magazine. I was totally blinded.

Four or five seconds went by before my runner fired his M1 rifle. We heard several men running from us, crashing through the brush. One dropped his rifle and pack as he stumbled onto one of our toilet trenches.

Puzzled, I asked Stelck, "Why didn't you open fire when I did?"

"Cripes, there were five or six Japanese right behind him."

I'd seen only the lead man as he'd approached me straight on. My runner had buck fever. My trust in him was shaken.

Minutes later, when I could again accustom my eyes to the moonlight, I saw tiny dots along the trail, almost thirty feet away. I was perplexed. At daylight I discovered that these were the hobnails on the boots of the enemy soldier, which had been shining in the moonlight. He wore the insignia of a warrant officer.

A half hour later I heard a *tap-tap-tap* in the brush behind our tent. Some distance away I heard the answer, also brushy sounds. The scattered Japanese were trying to regroup.

Cicadas on Guadalcanal made a similar clicking sound, but they started out slowly and gradually increased the tempo until almost infinity. These were definitely Japanese!

The Japanese had no lock keeper on the metal scabbard of their bayonets, so they tied a short string to their belts with a bamboo stick two and a half inches long, which they threaded through the barrel loop of the bayonet to prevent its loss. This was what they were using for signaling, this small stick tapping on the metal scabbard. Any farm boy would notice these things, especially after hearing a male partridge drumming for a mate: his wingbeats start slowly, then speed up with each thump.

Eventually the tapping sounds came close together, so Jake and I each popped a pin on a grenade and tossed them toward the sound. To our surprise several grenades went off, not just our two. The 60mm mortar crew to our north was also alert. Shortly after daylight two enemy dead were found, one a captain, the other a medic. They had a 50mm grenade launcher in their possession.

As daylight approached I stood in the doorway of the tent and scanned toward the north. As I turned east, I noticed a man furtively moving toward the Company E kitchen. Someone challenged him, and then I heard a shot. The Japanese, evidently an officer, had fired his pistol and wounded an American. Turning, he ran within thirty-five yards of me, fast through the undergrowth, headed back toward the jungle. I fired a full magazine of fifteen rounds at him as he hit the cat-claw. Later I could find no blood; I was bitterly disappointed.

Dick Hoffman admonished me later that morning, "Darn you, you shot the zipper off that mosquito bar I bought!"

I was guilty, but had no way to make it up to him. I just grinned. "Aren't you lucky you weren't sleeping under it?"

On October 29 we received a message from the Marine Corps.

SUBJECT: CONGRATULATIONS: THE OFFICERS AND MEN OF THE FIRST MARINES SALUTE YOU FOR A MOST WONDERFUL PIECE OF WORK ON THE NIGHTS OF 25 AND 26 OCTOBER, 1942. WILL YOU PLEASE EXTEND OUR SINCERE CONGRATULATIONS TO ALL CONCERNED. WE ARE HONORED TO SERVE WITH A UNIT SUCH AS YOURS. LITTLE DID WE REALIZE WHEN WE TURNED OVER OUR "QUIET SECTOR" TO YOU THAT YOU WOULD BEAR THE BRUNT OF AN ATTACK SO SOON. I'M SURE YOU ARE VERY PROUD OF THE FIGHTING ABILITY DEMONSTRATED BY YOUR UNIT AND OUR HAT IS OFF TO YOU.
C. B. CATES.

Dick Hoffman looked at me quizzically. "I wonder what Cates was thinking we were doing on the night of the twenty-fourth—sitting on our asses? Or are the Marines going to take credit for those hundreds of Japanese lying dead out in front of our machine guns?"

We talked it over and decided it was a team effort that won the battle for us. The Company E riflemen protected our machine guns; without them we would have been overrun. Our mortars, the 60mm and 81mm, put down such fire that the Japanese soldiers were destroyed almost before they could reach our wire. The artillery reached farther back, killing and disrupting enemy plans before they could be coordinated.

The constant sunshine and heat brought changes we hadn't anticipated. Thirty-five hundred bloated, deteriorating bodies created a stench that was sickening.

We had done our best to bury more than a thousand of the enemy by dynamiting a gigantic hole in the earth to the east of Coffin Corner as a resting place. Korean labor or slaves imported by the Japanese were used to move the bodies into the maw. Unfortunately, many bodies were not accessible, deep in the jungle, or even farther beyond, near the Maruyama Trail, the attack route taken by the Japanese, named after their commander.

CHAPTER 5

We were alerted on the evening of November 3 to pack up and rejoin Company H, for we were going east on foot to join Lieutenant Colonel Herman Hanneken's Second Battalion, Seventh Marines. Word came that a Japanese battalion had landed in the Tetere area and we were to assist in rounding them up. The next morning we went cross-country through seven-to-eight-foot-high kunai grass. There was no breeze and the sun was hot; we sweltered in the humid heat. Our two canteens of water per man were gone before we reached the area south of Koli Point. We crossed an open, grassy prairie that bordered heavy jungle to our left. On the way we found an abandoned F4F Wildcat; evidently the pilot had had an engine failure, but had made a perfect landing on the grass.

Fortunately a carrier with a water trailer arrived to meet us at 5 P.M. Our battalion drained every drop from the tank.

We pressed on until it was nearly dark, stopping about two hundred yards from the dense jungle. A slight breeze came to us from these woods, no doubt originating from the ocean, which was only a few miles to the north.

The men were exhausted, ready for a night's rest. As our officers gathered together we looked apprehensively at the dark jungle close by. My hearing was acute and I was sure I heard faint voices from the bush.

"John, I think I hear voices. There must be Japanese there."

"Heck!" Kenny, our executive officer, said. "I can smell them; they're Japanese, all right!"

Strange to say, Japanese equipment, especially leather

belts and goods, had a peculiar, sweetish odor—not an unpleasant scent, but not a familiar odor to Americans. Perhaps
it was the tanning process, or was it their perspiration?

John Gossett spoke up. "Regardless, we'll bed down here
tonight. Form your men into a perimeter with the machine
guns to cover us, mortars in the center. I have nothing further
to pass on since no one in the battalion has contacted me. I
don't even have a map for this operation. I guess we'll find
out what's up in the morning."

We awoke at dawn November 5 to open our last two cans
of C rations when sudden firing came from our left, just inside the jungle. One of our rifle companies had jumped the
gun and moved into the bush, only to find it occupied by the
enemy, just as we had suspected.

Normally a platoon of machine guns from our company
would be attached to each rifle company while our 81mm
mortars supplied a base of fire for the entire battalion. This
day we hadn't been assigned as yet, because the Japanese
weren't supposed to be this close. We were still not across
the Nalimbau River; the enemy was supposed to be even farther east, past the Metapona River.

First Platoon of H was to join Company E as soon as possible. Upon entering the woods we ran into sniper fire as we
were passing Company F. One of their men caught a bullet
from the sniper just as John Gossett and I passed by. John
pointed to a far coconut tree. "I saw palm fronds move in the
top of that tree over there. The Japanese is in the top."

Sergeant Shelley, of Company F, asked, "You're sure?"

"You bet I am, he's up there!"

The sergeant ran about forty yards and stopped directly
under the tree while we watched. Slowly he moved around its
base in a tight circle, then he aimed up and fired. The
Japanese hadn't tied himself in, so he fell to the ground, almost in slow motion; his rifle followed.

It reminded me of a squirrel-hunting trip back home, using the trick of placing a jacket for the squirrel to watch
while you circle to the other side of the tree.

Shelley came back to us with a huge grin; he was unfolding a Japanese flag: "Found it in his helmet."

About 150 yards away a Nambu light machine gun cut loose. We found out later that day that Lieutenant Agnew of Company G had caught a burst in the stomach. Our battalion surgeon, Dr. Schatz, crawled in and pulled him to safety. Because of Schatz's courageous action, Agnew survived. Schatz was awarded the Silver Star for his heroism.

These Japanese soldiers were not present in large numbers, but the small groups made it difficult to force a decisive fight. Their uniforms were in good condition, evidence that they were part of the battalion that had landed at Koli Point.

We pressed through this stretch of jungle and came out on the north side to face another half-mile stretch of grassy field. My platoon joined Company E and we settled to spend the night in a dry coulee. Lack of water was a problem because the day had been a scorcher. The men dug a well, using steel helmets as shovels in the lowest point of the coulee. As the men dug, the hole grew progressively wider and wider due to cave-ins. At about seven feet, water finally appeared, but what water! It was filthy, with a stink all its own; it was also filled with grit and humus, as the soil was sandy. Still, all canteens were filled and iodine drops inserted. A minimum wait of at least half an hour was required but ignored. Iodine certainly doesn't improve the taste of water!

Earlier that afternoon I had been ordered to patrol out in the grass to the north. We had gotten out about five hundred yards when we heard an airplane coming toward us. It was an F4F Wildcat, and the pilot banked to look us over. If we had been Japanese, we would have been slaughtered. We took off our helmets and waved; he waggled his wings in return.

I wanted to push farther north, to the ocean, but my section sergeants began to complain. They thought it stupid, and said so, vehemently. I foolishly acquiesced, returning with the patrol to the battalion at about 4:30 P.M. After dark a message arrived by radio. The battalion was to immediately move straight north to the beach. Company E led off with my

machine-gun platoon following. After crossing the open
field we entered a narrow stretch of jungle. There a sudden
burst of machine-gun fire ripped into our column from the
north. Then a second gun opened up. One of my section sergeants cried out, "Those are Brownings firing—our guns!"
From the cries up front we knew several men had been hit
before the firing ceased. We had run into our Third Battalion,
whose machine gunners were so trigger-happy they failed to
challenge us. I bore some of the blame because I had let the
men talk me out of doing a thorough patrol job.

The accident was blamed on lack of communication and
failure to challenge, but I never forgave myself. I became a
tough, hard-nosed lieutenant from that day on. In any case,
this order to move was made by our regimental commander,
who should have known better; the short move was absolutely unnecessary.

It was nearly 11 P.M. when we reached the beach. After set-
tling down my platoon I began digging a hole in the sand for
cover.

Our battalion exective officer Major Ben Northridge
stopped alongside. "Got a blanket, Charley?"

"Blanket and poncho, Sir."

"Then I'm bunking in the sand with you. Somehow I lost
my pack."

When I awoke on the morning of November 6, Ben was
gone, already moving the rifle companies up the beach
toward the Nalimbau River. I found my platoon had been attached to Company G for fire support and rations. What
rations? The last meal of C cans had been eaten yesterday
morning. I noticed that my two section sergeants were avoid-
ing me; I knew then that they felt as guilty as I did about not
making a thorough patrol to the ocean.

Trudging up the beach while carrying four light machine
guns, heavy cans of ammunition, and grenades became hard
work. The tide was fully in, which forced us to walk on soft,
loose sand. Again the sun began to bake us. We finally
moved inland to cross the Nalimbau River at a narrow spot.

In the center of this crossing lay an abandoned Bren gun carrier, so overloaded with ammo that the differential had failed.

We swung back to the beach as we approached the Metapona River, some one thousand yards away. Marines at the edge of the jungle shouted to us, "Get off the beach, the Japanese are shelling us with a howitzer!"

We had heard no firing, but to prevent an argument I led the platoon to the edge of the jungle where a Marine platoon was resting. A slight, short Marine lieutenant looked up at us, amazed, and said, "Where did you get those giants?"

As in all companies in our regiment, men were lined up by height for conformity. First Platoon of Company H was composed of six-footers or above. I stood six-foot-two-and-a-half myself. Jokingly I said, "Oh, we're just a bunch of North Dakota farmers."

As we turned inland, west of Gavaga Creek, I noticed four Marines hunkered down beside an 81mm mortar. We had been given no information, and I was never privy to what was planned. We knew the Japanese were near Tetere, and we were to assist the Marines in destroying them. That was all I had been told. If any plans had been made, the commander of Company G had not passed them on to me. This was like the blind leading the blind.

Company F, in the lead, was the first to encounter the enemy in a vicious fight, man-to-man. They were instantly pinned down and could not advance. The Japanese were endeavoring to escape inland, and they fought ruthlessly. Our assignment to Company G left us out of the fight, for the company was thinly stretched all the way from the ocean to Company F. Worried, I walked forward to the Company F command post for information. There I found our Company H mortar officer, Lieutenant Clark. He was unable to use his mortars for lack of direction in the heavy jungle. Just then a mortar round burst inside the Fox command post, wounding several men. I lucked out, but Clark's wounds were fatal. Fragments from the mortar shell proved it to be one of our own 81mm projectiles.

Before returning to my platoon I stopped at the battalion aid station to pick up an M1 rifle from the stack left by the wounded.

The Company F fight went on all afternoon and well into the evening before things quieted down. When daylight finally came the captain of Company G ordered me out in front to cross Gavaga Creek and close the gap. I looked at him, hardly able to believe my ears. A machine-gun platoon carrying guns and ammo, leading a patrol for a rifle company? I knew a coward when I saw one. He couldn't even look me in the eye. He knew of the losses Company F had suffered; he was not going to risk himself or his men. I was to be the sacrificial lamb. Later this captain was reprimanded severely for his act; he held it against me for two and a half more years of combat.

I led off as ordered and soon encountered abandoned Japanese equipment left from Company F's firefight of the previous afternoon. I was lead man, and fully expected to be ambushed at any moment. Visibility in this heavy jungle was limited to about fifteen feet. Eventually we encountered water and waded on. Finally it reached to our armpits. After about two hundred yards of this I heard a man yelling in the distance. There was no mistaking the voice of Lieutenant Ben Osborne, platoon leader of Company E; it was high-pitched and squeaky. It's funny how you can recognize a voice at times; this one had a timbre all its own. I yelled, "Benny! Benny! Easy! Easy!"

In the distance I heard a reply and identified myself lest his platoon on the other side of Gavaga Creek decide we were Japanese. We worked another one hundred yards east and came out of the water to find we had crossed the creek. Here, just as we reached dry land, we found a heavily traveled trail leading inland. Japanese general Shoji and his group of twenty-five hundred soldiers had escaped our trap. They had also escaped from our troops pressing in from the far side of the creek. Evidently the enemy had tried the west side, but Company F had blocked the route.

Arguments and tension among the command of this operation resulted in General Sebree relieving our battalion commander, Lieutenant Colonel Art Timboe, of his command. It seemed someone had to take the blame for the failure of this grandiose plan cooked up by the brass; a plan that had little or no chance of succeeding because of stretched lines covered by too few men.

This action of Sebree's was totally unjustified, for we had inadequate men to complete an encirclement. If Company F had not run into a massive fight, perhaps the closure could have been accomplished. Yet, General Shoji had nearly twenty-five hundred desperate men. It is highly unlikely that we could have held him with our thin line.

We followed the trail north and found the hard-pressed enemy had left nearly all of their supplies. Artillery ammunition was strewn everywhere, deemed too heavy to carry by the Japanese soldiers. Near the beach was a 75mm gun, minus a breech block. Folding boats of plywood with rubber joints lay on the beach by the dozens. About the only thing we didn't find was edible food. There were many sacks of rice, but from experience we knew it was heavily contaminated with mice and rat excreta. We were hungry, but not that hungry. I found a small pineapple, which I shared. My hunger pangs totally disappeared after about twenty-four hours without food. In the next seven days, my total food intake would be one three-hundred-calorie chocolate bar. Few of my men would fare better, although we would manage to get adequate drinking water. Whoever was in charge of this operation was derelict in all aspects. Famous schools often produce famous fools.

The village of Tetere consisted of two or three tumble-down huts. We discovered many dug-in shelters, which were reconnoitered with a hand grenade, for safety.

In the afternoon of November 12 we received urgent orders to move back to the Lunga perimeter. As we broke out to the beach we finally saw our Navy ships in the distant west. We found later they had escorted the 182nd Infantry Regiment of our Americal Division, to Guadalcanal.

Just as we rounded Koli Point we heard several aircraft approaching. Looking east, I counted twenty-one Japanese torpedo bombers skimming the waves in a long broadside line. As they passed by us I borrowed one-half of a Japanese binocular from McCarthy, who had found that portion while scrounging at Tetere.

The view was exciting. The sky was littered with black dots of AA shells from naval guns. Our Cactus Air Force was having a ball! One by one, the torpedo bombers blew up or hit the water. I was able to see the entire show until McCarthy asked for his half binocular. One aircraft escaped. It climbed slowly for altitude and turned toward the north. Moments later we first heard then saw an F4F miles behind him, going full bore. Some minutes later a column of black smoke appeared on the horizon and the F4F leisurely returned.

The long walk back to the perimeter was slow. We were so weak from lack of food that we could walk only one hundred to two hundred yards before dropping to rest. I threatened only one man; he was so exhausted he just gave up. Boosted by my threats of violence, he made it.

When about two and a half miles from the perimeter, we watched a C47 as it left Henderson Field, climbing out over the ocean. It was at an altitude of about six hundred feet when it suddenly disappeared in a white flash. From our vantage point we could see no debris falling. It was a mystery, for there were no other aircraft or any AA smoke in the area.

We arrived at the perimeter a bit before dark, greeted by our mess sergeant, who had moved his kitchen to the closest edge of the line for our convenience. We removed our helmet liners and wiped out the steel to use for mess kits. The mixture ladled into it was almost like son-of-a-bitch stew, but it tasted great, warm and filling.

To the men, the fiasco at Koli Point later became known as the Koli Point Rat Race. It did not endear us to the Marine command.

The best part followed: our supply sergeant had bags and bags of mail, a two-month supply for me, fifty-two letters! There was a problem, though: by this time it was dark and the Japanese fleet was expected at any moment. At least now we had a Navy, or part of one.

CHAPTER 6

It was a bit past 1:30 A.M. on Friday, November 13 when the show started. The big ships fired shell after shell while we watched from the beach; the projectiles could be followed readily as the missiles glowed. They arched up out of the big guns at 20- to 30-degree angles to explode miles away with brilliant flashes. It was like a giant fireworks display, but deadly. The main battle lasted about an hour, but we heard more distant shooting at dawn.

Soon thereafter, a few miles offshore, the bottom of a large ship could be seen, still floating, so close that we figured it was one of ours. Crews in small boats were picking up survivors, American and Japanese, and bringing them to the beach. I watched as they walked to the dispensary about three hundred yards inland. These men were covered with a thick, viscous tar. As they unloaded from the landing craft and walked to medical aid, there was no fight left in them, they were just glad to be alive. Many were blinded by the tar-like substance and needed to be led. The several Japanese sailors seemed despondent, harmless, their part in the war over. Strange to say, they were walking unguarded among the casualties, even helping them. Later, I found they were moved to Sydney, Australia, to a prison camp.

When I got to my bundle of letters I scanned them hurriedly and found my wife had had twins, a boy and girl, but the boy had died just before birth. I was angry because my wife had gone to the old family doctor. I had objected; I wanted her to go to a clinic, but was overruled. This doctor was so old he shouldn't have been practicing. He hadn't even known she was carrying twins.

Our perimeter was far from being out of the woods. We watched aircraft from Henderson Field fly out past Savo Island, group after group. Word came that they were after the Japanese battleship *Hiei,* which had been crippled during the previous night's naval battle. The flyers were determined to put her under. Word also leaked of a possible massive Japanese reinforcement of troops to our west sometime during the night.

The good news was that the 182nd Infantry of our Americal Division had landed safely at Kukum.

Late in the afternoon we moved to a quiet bivouac area east of the airport, about half a mile distant. I had been told that before bombs were dropped from the twin-engined Bettys you could hear the clicks of the bomb-release mechanism. About midnight, I discovered this to be true. A flight of several bombers was heard at high altitude, gradually approaching the airfield. As they reached overhead we heard several audible *click, click, click*s from far above. Seconds later we heard the growing swish of the bomb strings. Unfortunately, the bombs dropped into our new cemetery, just west of the main runway, quite near the ocean. As I looked the burial location over the next morning, I wondered how Graves Registration would ever sort out this mess. Deep, water-filled bomb craters were everywhere.

On Saturday I was ordered to the beach with Company H to supervise the unloading of gasoline drums and cargo. The fenced-off area of beach had a gate guard of Marines; it encompassed about ten acres. Cargo ships near shore dropped fifty-five-gallon drums of gasoline into the ocean and the prevailing onshore winds blew them to the beach. Our job was to roll the drums from the water, onto planking, then load them into six-by-six-foot trucks for movement inland to safety.

Just at noon LCVPs (landing craft vehicle personnel) and LCMs (landing craft medium) came in with a large number of orange crates and boneless steak meat, the meat frozen solid in frost-covered boxes. I asked the quartermaster officer at the gate where the trucks were going. He laughed. "Hell, it's all going to Marine division headquarters, where else? You'll never see a bit of it!"

I was angry as I walked out the gate to our service company, where I knew a truck driver. I asked him if he could get a six-by-six-foot truck and slip into the long line of quartermaster trucks. That afternoon our battalion shared two truckloads of oranges and two truckloads of boneless steak meat. When our regular ration issue came, we received no oranges or steak meat. The quartermaster officer was so right. At the time I was reminded of the old Army adage: The Lord helps those who help themselves, but Lord help those who get caught helping themselves!

Late in the afternoon, just before we were to be relieved, I saw a man carrying his steel helmet in a furtive manner. I stopped him and asked what he was carrying.

Caught with the goods, he dared not lie. "We've got eight barrels of one-eighty-proof medical alcohol hid among the gasoline barrels."

"When did they come in? How do you know it's medical alcohol, not torpedo fuel?"

"It's tagged medical alcohol; the barrel ends are painted white. They are all marked one-eighty-proof, too."

My mind went back to the past days at Koli Point and lack of food. Hanneken and Rupertus of the Marines and Sebree of the Army were in charge of the operation; they sure didn't supply Army troops with rations. I made up my mind. "Stash a barrel where you can get at it easily; we'll pick it up tonight." I knew there was no chance of getting it past the gate guards during daylight hours, but during the night air raids, the guards would be deep in their holes.

It worked to perfection. Our weapons carrier drove through the unguarded gate during the midnight air raid and before daylight the split had been made, all the way up to the battalion commander. My share, diluted by half with water, was stored in a gallon vinegar jug in the sand under my cot.

The next morning I was called to the end of the company street. There lay one of our men on the ground, pathetically crying that he was blind. I knew he was blind drunk, because he was a troublesome alcoholic. To top it off, along came my battalion commander with the new surgeon, together with my company commander. (Major Ben Northridge had just been promoted to command our battalion.)

The new surgeon tore into me. "Did you know the alcohol you gave those men was torpedo fuel—wood alcohol? We'll have several men going blind now!"

I looked at Ben, then John Gossett, and noted the half smiles on their faces. After all, they had each gotten a share. Even I had partaken of a few shots.

I looked at the doctor, whose name was Yancy. "That was straight medical alcohol, not torpedo fuel!"

At that instant two men walked by carrying old Jock, our supply sergeant, on a litter. Ben looked at me and winked. "Gosh, Lieutenant, it must have been torpedo fuel, old Jock's been torpedoed!"

Raucous laughter ended my inquisition, for both Ben and John turned away and returned to battalion headquarters. They were both still smiling, probably going back for another drink. Yancy gave me a final glare, but I ignored him.

The next day I was sent to patrol east toward Koli Point. When I arrived back with my men I thought it would be pleasant to have a shot with a little grapefruit juice. When I probed for my gallon jug, it was gone. Looking up at the rest of the Company H officers sitting around the tent, I asked who took my bottle. I got silly grins and denials. Realizing they were all half-drunk, I shrugged. "You are all a bunch of thieves!" My challenge failed to provoke an argument.

On November 16 we moved to Skyline Ridge, just southeast of Point Cruz. The actor, Joe E. Brown, walked along the ridge and talked to many of our men, but I was down the hill at the time, scrounging up a load of barbed wire.

Our cooks, who were not accustomed to Japanese, were jumpy. It seemed reasonable, although cruel, to play tricks on them. The men found a pair of Japanese rubber sandals with the big toe separate from the rest of the shoe. After a hard rain at night, someone put on the shoes and walked in the mud around the cook's sleeping quarters. Some gentleman pointed out to the cooks how lucky they were. Such was the humor of the men.

One afternoon I found myself in a blackjack game; by suppertime I was ahead $650. The next morning I had the company clerk get me five $100 money orders. Later, a letter from my wife expressed her shock. After all, my salary as a second lieutenant was only $183 per month. The extra money puzzled her. Had I done something of a criminal nature?

About November 18 we ran short of canned fruit and juices. I knew the beach just east of Fighter 2 was well supplied with hundreds of broken cases of food, many with the labels washed off. Such was the lousy care and policing along the beach. I took the company jeep to the beach. The driver and I were very near the end of the Fighter 2. We selected can after can as best we could until I heard an airplane coming down the strip, apparently headed for the ocean. There, fifty feet above the airstrip, was a Japanese open-cockpit airplane with the gunner standing upright, facing to the rear. He was firing twin machine guns, spraying the east side of the landing strip. When he reached the beach he swung his guns at us, the only jeep on the beach. Bullets pocketed the sand inches in front of our jeep as my driver and I attempted to roll under the vehicle.

As the airplane swung over the ocean it began to climb steadily. I wondered at the audacity of that pilot and his buddy. A minute later an American fighter pursued the Japanese. Long before the enemy plane was out of sight, it splashed. What I would have given for a camera at the time!

On November 19, First Battalion, 182nd Infantry, crossed the Matanikau River on footbridges and set up a line extending from Point Cruz to the southern ridges. That night and the morning of November 20, the Japanese hit them with everything they had. The battalion broke and moved back to the Matanikau and beyond.

At 11 A.M. on November 20, a 182nd captain and a dozen soldiers trudged up to my command post. The captain said his company was to relieve ours. When I asked him where his men were, he pointed back and said, "I just don't know. That's all I've got. They ran; I don't know where they are." He was shamefaced, but it wasn't his fault. He had green troops who had never seen a Japanese. We had been well dug in when we were indoctrinated at Coffin Corner, a distinct advantage.

Our battalion moved that afternoon down to the Matanikau River and forward to retake the 182nd's former positions. The booty we found was a gold mine, everything a U.S. soldier needed: machine guns, mortars, packs, rifles, and the prize, new sound-powered telephones. We had heard of them but had none. What marvelous things! Most everything was returned to the rear except for the new telephones.

After placing my guns in support of Company E, I moved my command post to the narrow neck of Point Cruz. From here the beach curved in to the west, offering us an excellent field of fire, much farther than our machine guns could possibly reach. Behind us, on the east side of the neck, was an abandoned landing craft, afloat, but locked onto a coral outcropping. On the beach lay the tail of a torpedo, its twin opposed propellers shining in the sun.

We prepared ourselves for the night. Dick Hoffman and I dug a five-by-seven hole in the dry sand and lined it with empty C-ration crates we found lying about. We later found the hole to be a superb trap for the giant land crabs that prowled at night. Each time, we bailed out of the hole until we could eliminate the huge, fierce creature with a club.

That first night at Point Cruz I was roughly shaken awake by Dick. "My gosh, Charley! Your snoring is calling all the Japanese within a mile! Wake up!"

Many of the men of both Companies E and H suffered from dysentery. One man had the runs so bad he refused to wear his trousers. He made frequent trips into the ocean in rear of the neck of Point Cruz.

Malaria was another problem. Atabrine pills were essential to controlling the disease, which was not only debilitating, but deadly. Some men tried to avoid taking the daily pill. In the beginning we were forced to hand-feed it in formation. I told the men that very likely it would save their lives.

Each morning and evening huge schools of mullet gathered in the shallow water. A small block of TNT usually garnered a gunnysack of fish. This was a new food item to us; John cooperated by sending us a cookstove with frying pans. Two days later we noticed a large box the size of a washing machine floating in. Lucky day! It was a crate of Mazola cooking oil. All in gallon cans! So many ships had been sunk offshore that many other items were visible, but they never made it in to us. Each morning we obtained the fish, and cleaned and fried them for practically the entire battalion. Sometimes it was difficult to maintain order, as too many men slipped away to the beach for a feed.

The second morning at Point Cruz I made my way back to our company command post through the jungle. I came to what looked like a ditch, well hidden with heavy green foliage. I suddenly froze; I had nearly stepped on a Japanese lying back against a tree. For seconds my heart was in my mouth. I looked around and saw there was not only one, but at least a dozen. They were lying in leisurely positions all around the edge of the hollow, not paying any attention to me. After a second I realized something was wrong: they were all dead and probably had been for at least a couple of days. Moving along the ditch I found a Marine lieutenant partially hidden. He had evidently killed them all, but had suffered a fatal wound himself. I moved to the footpath along the beach and reported what I had found to John. He assured me he would see to it the Marine officer was picked up by Graves Registration.

As I turned to rejoin my platoon John held up his hand. "Hold it, Chuck, I've a surprise for you." He handed me a folded paper. "You are now a first lieutenant. Maybe Kenny has a spare set of bars. By the way, I'm coming up for a fish dinner tonight. Might take a look at those Japanese. Did you search them?"

"Nope. They still have all of their equipment. Perhaps I should have, but I didn't know if any live ones were still around. It's a grim, depressing spot."

CHAPTER 7

On the third morning at Point Cruz, our battalion began patrolling toward the enemy. I was told to accompany a platoon of Company E with a section of my light machine guns. We were also told to clear the Japanese area by 2 P.M. because an artillery barrage was planned for that hour.

We took the small patrol forward about two hundred yards and struck a coulee that angled at 30 degrees into the Japanese line. The patrol was spotted and desultory firing began. It was obvious that the enemy was well dug in and camouflaged. They had constructed bunkers of coconut logs, well concealed, with fire lanes cut. We had no orders to pursue an attack, just to get information. The patrol leader decided the wise course was to withdraw with what we knew. The Japanese were not going to be rooted out without a major action.

Patrolling became a daily event, and it seemed to me that it was a waste of time. We did liven things up one day with an old Springfield rifle equipped with a Marine grenade launcher. It hurled special grenades one hundred yards or more, enticing the enemy to fire their machine guns in return. Their heavy machine gun had a brush oiler to lubricate the long clips fed in from the left side. This made it easy to locate the gun if they fired a few bursts; smoke haze rose from the gun position.

Dick Hoffman and I discussed this and came up with an idea. We now had sound-powered telephones with the small spools of wire. If we could run the line back to our Company

H 81mm mortars, we could direct the fire of one gun, using it as if sniping.

Lieutenant Clayton Kingston, our mortar officer, was enthusiastic. "I'll set my best gun and hook it directly to you. Try to stay out of the line of fire because sometimes we get short rounds." I already knew about those short rounds, especially the heavy 81mm shells, the sixteen pounders. They had folding fins to stabilize them, and often one of the spring-loaded fins would not extend due to rust. Then you heard a weird *whoosh, whoosh, whoosh,* and everyone on the line ducked, yelling, "Short! Short!"

At dawn on November 30 we awoke to see many barrels had drifted onto the beach, most in the Japanese-held area to our west. They had been intentionally dropped from the decks of enemy destroyers during the night. Even better, enemy soldiers were attempting to pull the barrels out of the water. We discouraged them during the day, riddling the barrels within range so that their contents would be destroyed or sunk. Some barrels were so far distant we couldn't reach them with our machine guns. One barrel that came in to us was filled with rice, matches, and candles.

My next patrol was in support of a Company F platoon. The sergeant running the patrol was a no-nonsense man, a real leader. We advanced up the coulee until it became necessary to look over the edge to view the enemy positions. The sergeant turned to me as he put his steel helmet on a stick. "Let's see how safe it is today." As he raised his helmet, cowboy style, a .25-caliber bullet nailed it dead center, and spun it on the stick. From the report of the gun I knew the Japanese was only a few feet away. The sergeant looked at his helmet critically, then said to me, "Lieutenant, it looks as if this is as far as we go today!"

At noon on December 6, before we could put our plan into action, a man in Company E approached his company commander and said he had been out on the last patrol and had walked all around the Japanese positions. When that word reached battalion, nothing would do but check it out immediately. I was selected to accompany a small Company E patrol with two light machine guns.

The patrol took the beach road past a small IHC crawler tractor that had been disabled by an enemy mine. The machine, evidently owned by the Marines, had been abandoned. As we progressed farther along the trail I was far enough behind that I could not see the head of the patrol.

I heard one shot. Judging from the report it came from a .25-caliber Arisaki rifle. I ran past the men of Company E until I came upon the patrol leader standing upright in shock. I bumped him, and told him to get down. Private Dowsett had been shot only a few feet ahead of him. I beckoned to two of my men who had followed me, then crawled almost to the downed man. There was a coconut tree between us.

Dowsett lay facing toward a bunker, midway between the bunker and my tree. The bunker was of heavy coconut logs about twenty-five feet away. The shot had to have come from the dark opening in the bunker. I called to one of my men for his belt. After adding mine, I attempted to lasso Dowsett's foot. A Nambu light machine gun opened up from the left flank, but the fire was not directed at me.

I called back for one of my squad leaders to bring up a machine gun to pin down the Japanese gun. The corporal crawled up with the gun, and I pointed out the general location of the enemy gun. He opened fire with all of five rounds before the gun jammed due to a ruptured cartridge. Then things really happened. Three machine guns caught us in a cross-fire and forced me to back away from my tree. As I squirmed from the high dirt mound surrounding the tree I was showered with bark particles. One enemy gunner knew exactly where I was! At that moment I could have cheerfully killed my squad leader; the fool had not checked the head space on his machine gun. It was a simple procedure: screw barrel into receiver, then back off three clicks.

"It's nearly two o'clock, the artillery fire is due. We've got to get the hell out of here!" The strident shout was from the Company E patrol leader.

We hadn't made it back to our lines before we found ourselves ducking incoming shells. It bothered me to leave Dowsett, but I knew he was dead. Evidently he had walked among the enemy positions about ten o'clock this morning. The Japanese must have been sleeping in the warm sun. Either that, or he was the bait for an ambush.

It seems strange that young men feel immortal in combat, but when the day of reckoning comes, our mortality seems fragile, only a breath or heartbeat away.

About December 14 two sailors dressed in blue dungarees, carrying old bolt-action rifles, appeared at the neck of Point Cruz. I questioned them, to find they had been ashore with a work detail, but during the naval fighting their ship had left.

Stock was a clean-cut youth of perhaps eighteen years, tall and well formed with a pleasant face. Merkle was shorter, a husky man with dark hair. Both expressed a desire to kill Japanese. Since I was scheduled for the next day's patrol, I told them they were free to come along, but that it was no party, and they might be killed. Both grinned. There was cowardice there.

The next day our sound-powered line was laid back to Kingston's mortars. We jumped off and unrolled the light telephone wire as we approached the Japanese line.

At the critical end of the coulee, one of the Company F riflemen crawled up to my right and began to fire into the Japanese dugouts. Immediately a heavy machine gun inside a pile of palm fronds opened fire, raking us. Blue smoke began to leak up through the camouflaged cover. With my direct line to Kingston, I had him fire a mortar round with a bit of extra range for safety. The shell landed about one hundred feet behind the gun.

Stock had begun to ease up the embankment, so I shouted a warning. He had a helmet liner but no steel. A rifle bullet went through the top of his helmet liner. He froze in place, head down, tight to the ground.

Our mortars had three types of shells, light, medium, and heavy. The medium and heavy rounds had both quick and delay capabilities. I walked Kingston's mortar back to the enemy machine gun and when a delay-fused round landed just in front of it, Japanese burst out the back, attempting to escape. Stock got his first Japanese that day; I saw him drop the man.

The Company F rifleman who had irritated the Japanese found another sucker. Kingston totally obliterated that machine gun with a delay round, a direct hit. We had put the fear into the Japanese; they withheld further machine-gun fire. We had accomplished what Dick and I had planned. Sniping *could* be done with a mortar if the mortar officer had Kingston's abilities. He had selected A1 ammo with no rust and no weathered cartons. It was dependable. At eight hundred yards he could put an 81mm mortar round within twenty feet of his target.

That night we had a good laugh. About 11 P.M. an enemy Betty flew back and forth along the beach for some minutes. The pilot must have become disoriented, because as he flew west he dropped bombs on his own troops. Then he turned east and flew around for some time. The next morning parachutes were found behind our lines, all loaded with medical supplies.

The stalemate gave Dick and me a lot of thinking time. We knew the Japanese had hidden guns covering the sandy beach to our front, but what if their guns could be neutralized? We both came up with the same idea. Why not crawl in the water at low tide, dropping mortar shells ahead of us, say every twenty-five feet or so, just on the edge of the jungle?

I brought the idea to John Gossett and he took it to our battalion commander, Ben Northridge, now a lieutenant colonel. They both knew of our recent success, using a mortar for sniping.

We got permission, so the next afternoon, December 17, Dick and I crawled into the water to our chests. We dropped a few mortar rounds ahead of us, then stopped every few yards or so to hook up the sound-powered line and drop more mortar shells ahead.

Finally, well past the Japanese line, we worked into the jungle through some thick mangroves and dropped more shells inland. As we reached the government road, there in front of us was a 37mm antitank gun laid out beautifully in pieces. Not a Japanese was in sight. I tried to detach the breech block, but I didn't know how to do it.

"What'll we do with it?" Dick asked.

"Let's take the carriage and dump it in the ocean."

It took the two of us to manhandle the base mechanism, but we dumped it into five feet of water amid the mangroves. I called back to my battalion commander, and told him what had transpired. I also said, "If you want to roll up this Japanese frontline, send a company along into the water. We can hit them from the rear."

His reply was succinct: "You two get the hell out of there before they catch you. That's an order!"

Dick and I talked it over and decided neither of us wanted to go back into the ocean. We unrolled more wire and had Kingston shoot our way back along the edge of the jungle. In the process we garnered two Nambu light machine guns from positions the Japanese hastily abandoned for immediate safety. One was badly damaged by a mortar shell. Those delay-fused mortar rounds dug monstrous holes along the beach. I knew the Japanese would find our wire, and we would never get away with this again. I suspected they would have trouble explaining the loss of those Nambus, too.

I was awarded a Silver Star for this stupid kid stunt, but Dick was entitled to the same. It became a bone of contention between a division staff member and I some time later (this Colonel Biggerstaff, who sat safely back in a rear area).

We had spent many days on this Point Cruz line until we were relieved on December 18. Other units took over, and forced the enemy to retreat. Curiosity caused me to return a day or two later to look over the enemy positions. The

Japanese who had shot the Company F sergeant's helmet was only twenty feet from him. His hole was beautifully camouflaged, but he was dead inside. During the preshelling a piece of shrapnel had clipped him. I took his rifle; it resides in the armory at Williston, North Dakota.

CHAPTER 8

Our battalion was moved just east of Fighter Strip 2 for a rest. The relaxation lasted just one day, when Japanese infiltrators hit the fighter strip and destroyed one aircraft and a fuel truck. After that we posted two men at each airplane at night.

A radar searchlight unit were located above the airstrip; always curious, I visited them. When the crew showed me their searchlights and explained how the radar worked, I spotted a black fused picric acid explosive charge, attached to one of the arc lights. The fuse had failed. To pull their leg, I asked, "What's that for?"

The searchlight crew admitted they had thought themselves perfectly safe and posted no guards at night.

No doubt some of our pilots on the strip were novices, as many a pilot, while taking off, triggered the aircraft's guns inadvertently. Shooting up the end of the runway became almost a daily occurrence. Early one morning as I was checking my guards, several fighters were taking off. As the last one began its run, a pilot in a brand-new P38 carelessly taxied into the middle of the runway. The fighter struck and flipped, bursting into flame as it slid along the steel matting. Fire trucks with carbon dioxide extinguishers managed to get to the pilot, but the poor man dropped headfirst to the runway when his harness was released. Fortunately, he lived. The fighter and P38 were totaled.

After a few days in this new area a lanky New Zealand sergeant came prowling by to make a swap. "I'm looking for one of those American forty-five-caliber pistols. Any chance to get one? I can give you a good, long plane ride."

This sounded interesting, and it happened we had extra ordnance we had picked up here and there. Among the lot was an old-model .45 that was in terrible condition. I struck a deal for three officers to fly with the New Zealanders. As it turned out, the Kiwi bomber unit was short personnel and were only too glad to get experienced machine-gunners to help man the side guns in their Lockheed-Hudsons.

The next morning Gossett, Hamer, and I arrived at the airfield. We were each going on a submarine hunt in three Lockheed-Hudsons. My sergeant showed me how the Lewis machine guns worked and how the drums were loaded. There were spare drums attached to the floor.

Before we took off I was given a handset, mike, and goggles; the communication was checked. The crew consisted of the pilot, copilot, rear gunner, one side gunner, and me. A rectangular hole was cut in each side of the airplane, about two feet high and three and a half feet in length. A Lewis machine gun was mounted along the center bottom edge. In the top center of the aircraft was a small hole, perhaps eighteen inches in diameter, with a small windscreen to the front.

After we were airborne, the sergeant, whose station was the twin turret guns in the tail of the Hudson, informed me, "We'll travel only about one hundred feet above the water. Japanese aircraft will see us from high up; that's what that pop case is for, stand on it!"

This made sense. Standing upright in the aircraft, I wasn't tall enough to extend my head through the small hole above. He admonished, "Be alert at all times; our lives will depend on you." When the plane leveled out at one hundred feet, the sergeant pointed to the case as he moved to take over the turret guns. Standing on the wooden crate I found the position fairly comfortable, because there were handholds to steady myself. My next information came directly from the pilot.

"Hey, Yank! We forgot to tell you that we are to skirt New Georgia. The Japanese have an airfield there. The Hudson that made this trip yesterday failed to return."

I thought he was pulling my leg, but the seriousness of his voice convinced me that it must be true. These New Zealanders would have welcomed us on every trip; they were that short of men.

After each hour the side gunner and I relieved the other. I spent the second and fourth hour watching from the sides. We flew over many miles of deep, opaque water in which we could see the bottom at one hundred feet or more. The colors of the coral were magnificent, constantly changing. I suddenly heard the pilot say, "Open the bomb-bay doors. Something is threshing in the water up ahead." I heard the hydraulics, then a disappointed voice: "Only a bloody school of fish!"

This happened twice more, each time raising our expectations. After nearly four hours of searching, we turned toward home. As we arrived over Guadalcanal we ran into a heavy rain squall that finally cleared as we prepared to land. After we had taxied to their parking area, the pilot and crew shook my hand. The pilot offered, "Anytime you Yanks are loose, feel free to join us again. We fly every day."

I waited anxiously for more than an hour for John and Hamer to return. Both greeted me with big smiles. Their pilots had swung over to the north of Guadalcanal to show them a large Japanese submarine with two midget subs, all sunk in shallow water. They were told B17 bombers had caught them on the surface.

Returning to our area we were greeted by another surprise. A Seabee group had been retrieving the mines the Marines had laid at the mouth of the Matanikau River to stop the Japanese tanks. Eyewitnesses said there had been about six men on the truck, which inexplicably exploded at the far end of our company street, blowing down trees, tents, and creating a huge crater in the middle of the road. In the bottom of the huge hole was one mangled banjo axle of the truck. There was no sign of the truck itself or the men. Why, oh why hadn't they removed the detonators from the mines? So simple! So easy! Thankfully, all the Company H men had been elsewhere.

In our everyday conversation, and for lack of something to do, we hit upon getting a 20mm aircraft cannon. Where to find it? The airport, of course. John Geroux, a mechanic from Company H, and I found just such a gun in a P400 (a low-altitude fighter without oxygen and turbocharger). The plane was propped up on gas barrels, being stripped for needed parts. The reason it was junked could be readily seen: it had at least fifty or more bullet holes in the fuselage. Evidently the pilot had been saved by the small armor plate behind him.

It took us two days to remove the gun, with no one paying any attention to us. The gun was a lot longer than we'd anticipated, almost nine feet long. It was gas-operated, requiring a hydraulic pump with a reservoir to cock it. Some Seabee welders, at a slack period, showed interest in the project. They made a pipe tripod, adding a junked .50-caliber machine-gun mount that fitted well to the gun. With homemade bicycle handle bars in the rear for control, and a rifle barrel welded on for sighting, the weapon looked formidable. We had the feed drum and Hispano ammunition.

Now what we needed was a gallon reservoir and a hand hydraulic pump. I took tools to the bone pile of junked aircraft and removed the tank and pump from an SBD Dauntless. I finished just in time to be nabbed by an irate Air Force colonel. He rode me up and down, threatening a court-martial and all those other good things. When he took me before another brass hat, I told them it was imperative we get the pump and tank. In disgust, they finally let me go.

John managed to get permission from above to test-fire the weapon, so we took it out near Koli Point. Just as we fired the first explosive round at a tree near the ocean, General Collins, of the 25th Division, cleared the corner. I believe the explosion scared hell out of his bunch! I know it did his captain flunky, who jumped from his jeep in a rage, screaming at us like a little boy. He finally calmed down when he found we had written permission to test-fire the weapon. Still, that ended our firing for the day.

Our next opportunity to fire the 20mm cannon came in Fiji, while on the New Zealand Rifle Range.

About the middle of January, while still bivouacked and maintaining guards on the aircraft at Fighter 2, I received a call to report to battalion headquarters as soon as possible. It was mighty early, as the sun was just coming over the horizon. I figured something important was up.

I found both John and our battalion commander, Lieutenant Colonel Ben Northridge, seated at a crude table, drinking coffee. Ben peered up at me through those big, thick glasses of his.

"Chuck, yesterday the Marines took an LVT [amphibious tractor] up the Lunga River on a patrol. Upon hitting a rock they tore off a track. They took along some high-priority radios we've got to recover. I'm sending you to pick them up. Hopefully the Japanese haven't found them yet."

I didn't mind helping pull other people's chestnuts out of the fire, but not the Marines'. I was still upset over our treatment at Koli Point.

"What's the matter with the outfit that left the radios?"

"All I know is that the responsibility for recovering them has been given to us. These aren't little radios, they're big and heavy. You and John figure out what you'll need, but remember, you'll have to take off as soon as possible."

During the next hour John rounded up two small inflatable boats from Service Company in which to carry the radios downriver. From what information we could glean, the radios were too heavy to pack on men's backs. We decided a twelve-man patrol would be adequate if all went well; if not, I was to destroy the radios and run like hell. That was Japanese-held territory we were invading.

By 10 A.M. we were loaded on a truck destined for the west shore of the Lunga River. Upon our arrival, the river looked placid, with only a sluggish current.

Passing the perimeter guard post on the west side of the Lunga, manned by a Marine detachment, I saw they had installed vehicle headlights on trees to cover the inward trail along the river. I thought it a good idea if it worked. The lights might serve as a temporary surprise. But where did they get the headlights and the batteries?

Trudging farther in the mud, we found ourselves getting ever closer to rough, high country. Each bend brought a change in the river; it became narrower, and with a much faster current. We kept a sharp watch now, realizing we were not far from Mount Austen, which had supposedly been cleared of enemy. To be honest, I thought the project a lost cause; surely some Japanese troops had found the amphibious tractor with the radios by now.

At a narrow, straight stretch in the river, the vehicle finally came into sight. Viewed through field glasses it was obvious the machine was a mess; the right aluminum track was off the sprockets and lay to one side.

Sending guards to explore both sides of the river, I made sure no Japanese were around. As our men covered our advance, three of us entered the river at the rear of the vehicle to find the water about five feet deep and very fast. The water temperature was pleasant, a real bonus. Inside the tractor were at least two dozen five-gallon jerricans of gasoline. In addition there were a full fifty-five-gallon barrel and a case of engine oil. With these raw materials, I wondered why the Marine patrol hadn't destroyed the radios and amphibian before abandoning it.

After inflating the two rubber boats, we loaded up the two radios. The transmitters and receivers appeared new, a type I had never seen, a bit bulky, but evidently capable of long-range use. Loading two men into each dinghy, I told them to stand by until we decided on further action.

A decision had to be made whether the rest of the patrol would walk back along the river or attempt to ride the river downstream, using the jerricans for flotation. I knew it was possible we had bypassed Japanese on the way upstream; they could easily have stepped into the jungle to avoid us. They certainly should have had patrols out watching movement at our perimeter. On the other hand, walking along the shore, we would never be able to keep up with the rubber boats; the current was too swift. They would have no protection, and be sitting ducks for even a lone enemy rifleman. I decided on riding the river.

Emptying the many gas cans and the full drum of fuel, we improvised slings using electrical wiring and other materials from the amphibian. Using the cans for flotation, we would all ride downstream together. I guessed the distance to the perimeter to be about nine miles, a bit over an hour of travel with the fast current.

The ride at first *was* mighty fast, but there were no obstacles. All we had to do was paddle enough to stay centered in the river, holding our weapons up the best we could. But at one point, while still about four miles from the perimeter, we ran into a stretch of rapids. My rear contacted an underwater rock, flipping me forward and causing me to lose my good glasses, the only pair that didn't have cracked lenses. Righting myself, I readjusted my gas-can support to find I trailed my patrol. After passing the perimeter line and nearing the ocean, we pulled ourselves from the water at about 5 P.M. We managed to catch a ride back to our company kitchen in time for chow.

I don't know what happened to the two radios after their delivery to the battalion, but I sure knew I would have liked to have kept them. When I first joined the Army, I had been a Morse code operator on the old SCR-131 radio.

Later that night I asked John why I'd been stuck with the patrol. He said, "Ben knows you're dependable." I should have been flattered, but I was too tired to care.

Later someone told me we were lucky: the Lunga River is noted for its many large crocodiles. So much for our prior planning!

CHAPTER 9

When the final push came to clear the Kokumbona and western areas of enemy, we were trucked east to the Tetere area to be in reserve, since the 25th Division had moved from there, being involved in the final drive to eliminate the enemy. Located along the beach, we immediately resumed fishing with an occasional TNT block to augment our ration issue.

One morning the driver of a weapons carrier passed by. He called to me. It was Jim Nelson, a boyhood friend from Company D whom I hadn't seen for years. In fact, I didn't know he was with our regiment. Pulling over to the side, he jumped down to shake my hand and shoot the breeze. During our reminiscences he added a pertinent bit of information: "Did you know that there are a bunch of brand-new jeeps just a mile or so east of here stuck in a swamp, maybe seven or eight?"

"How come?"

"Some outfit tried to drive through the swamp and the other drivers followed in the same tracks. I don't know where the drivers are, they just abandoned the vehicles. They must have walked back to the perimeter for help."

After we broke off our conversation, I imparted this choice information to our top sergeant. At the time both of our jeeps had suffered severe trauma. I was not surprised that evening at chow time to see our old jeeps had taken on a new sheen and tires, although their hoods, with the old serial numbers, looked weather-faded. I asked no questions.

Late that night as the sky began to darken, John had a problem. "Chuck, I can't urinate, my bladder is killing me!"

"Have you had this trouble before?"

"Heck, no!"

"Then you've got a blockage, probably a stone. Hit for the medics, they have catheters. It might be embarrassing, but they can relieve you."

I was raised by my grandfather, a country doctor. Although not interested in the medical field at the time, I drove him on his house calls for years. On these trips I'd picked up quite a bit of rudimentary information.

"Chuck, the battalion medics are still back in the perimeter. It's hairy driving back there in the dark without the use of headlights."

"You've got no choice. It's dark, but it should be reasonably safe. Otherwise maybe you can dislodge the stone enough to pass your water."

Seconds later I was surprised to see John drop down and begin bouncing his rear end hard on the ground. Somehow he must have loosened the stone, for lying sideways he was able to urinate. He never mentioned his trouble again until I visited him in the 18th General Hospital in Fiji. He described being probed to crush the stone. He was mighty grim, saying, "It hurt like hell!"

Regardless of our apparent safety from the Japanese we still sent out patrols to the east and inland. One patrol came in with information of a papaya patch loaded with ripe fruit. We found that by standing in a weapons carrier we could reach the fruit easily, for the trees stood only about twelve feet in height. The flavor was delicious, but a few of the men made hogs of themselves, and suffered the trots.

A native approached me early one morning, saying in broken English that he had a man seriously ill who needed immediate help. Having no medical doctor available I decided to see what I could do. He led me east a mile to a small shelter made of palm fronds. There I found the sick man lying on his back, obviously suffering from a high fever. It had to be malaria. He was being attended by a third native, who was carefully wetting his forehead from time to time.

The sick man half smiled at me, then reached somewhere about his person to produce an article from a San Francisco newspaper. The story was about Jacob Vouza, a native policeman I'd heard much about but had never met. He pointed at the paper, then to himself. That is how I met the famous scout and native policeman.

Being allergic to atabrine, I always carried quinine with me. Sharing half of the bottle, I held up two fingers to indicate how many I took each day. Vouza understood, but after examining the tablets, he held up five fingers.

Taking my time I fully read the article, which told of his being captured by the enemy, tied to a tree, then hacked and stabbed several times with a bayonet; he was left for dead. He had been captured with an American flag in his possession. It further told of his fortuitous escape and treatment by Marine doctors, who saved his life.

Weeks later, just before we left the island, I was surprised when told three natives wanted to see me. There was Jacob, smiling as he held out his hand. I was fortunate to be able to have my picture taken with him and his two friends. Later, I wondered how he had been able to find me, since I had not told him my name or outfit. Thinking it over, I wondered how many others, even white men, would have taken the time to go out of their way to see me.

In early January, Lieutenant Archie Dugan, from regimental headquarters, dropped by with shocking information. He said our regimental commander was evidently deranged: "He sits in the door of his tent all day aiming at a Japanese skull someone obtained for him. He raises his pistol and says, 'Bang! I got you! Bang! I got you!'" Truth or not, the colonel was evacuated; later he became a two-star general. A temporary commander was appointed, but he was replaced when we reached the Fiji Islands.

In late January we were again moved from the Tetere area back to our old position on Skyline Ridge above Point Cruz.

I noticed John was at battalion much of the time, no doubt helping Lieutenant Colonel Northridge. Kenny, our company second in command, had been evacuated sometime during December. He suffered horribly from both jaundice and malaria. It wasn't until early February that John casually mentioned, "You're running Company H now; I'm moving up as battalion exec with Ben."

I felt no different, although I had far more responsibility running a full company than managing a platoon of forty-five men. John had trained me to the point that I had no qualms; he had assigned me just about every duty in the company.

The 25th Division, with its regiments—27th Infantry, 35th Infantry, and 161st Infantry—together with Marine units, had taken Mount Austen and pressed on to capture Kokumbona. The Second Battalion of the 132nd Infantry, of the Americal Division, landed at Verahue on February 1, effectively bottling the Japanese between American forces in a pincer movement. Unfortunately, the Japanese Navy was able to evacuate the remainder of their troops on the night of February 7, after two prior lifts of troops on February 1 and February 4, rescuing a total of 10,642 men to fight again. Such was our lack of intelligence, General Alexander M. Patch and the Navy thinking that the Japanese were reinforcing their troops.

The next announcement really shook me: Company H had been selected to handle the cleanup of Japanese materials from the western area of Guadalcanal. I wondered how Ben and John had arranged it—this was a plum! It included picking up all munitions and equipment the enemy had abandoned: tons and tons of artillery shells, artillery pieces, 81mm and 90mm mortars with their ammunition, heavy machine guns, Nambus, rifles, pistols, small ammunition, and other sundry items.

We began this operation in February, using Service Company trucks and drivers to haul the heavy materials. The first day we managed to work west only about three miles. We handled load after load of artillery ammunition onto the trucks, to be hauled back to the bomb dump near Henderson Field. On the second day we found two 150mm guns with their tracked prime movers, also some Bofor 40mm antiaircraft guns that had evidently been captured from the British.

It wasn't until the third and fourth days that we found items we treasured. Evidently the Japanese had buried much of what they couldn't carry. We found concealed digging in several spots. I noted several Company H men carrying .455-caliber Webley revolvers in their belts, no doubt also captured from English troops.

Farther along the beach I found a group of men shooting fireworks out over the ocean. These were Japanese signal rockets similar to the rockets we used back home on the Fourth of July. These were huge, at least six feet in length, capable of going high in the sky. I ignored this play, not deeming the items a deep, dark secret.

On the fourth morning I heard several explosions from grenades, and worrying about stray Japanese soldiers hurried to the scene. Three of my officers were playing chicken, daring one another to see who could hold a Japanese grenade the longest after activating it. Lordy! If getting shot at wasn't enough, here they were darn near committing suicide! I gave them a chewing, but didn't think it registered. At least it stopped the dangerous horseplay.

We had one man, an alcoholic, adept at finding booze. One night after we arrived back in our area, someone reported him missing. As it was already dark, there was no chance of going west on the beach road to find him. We would hunt for him in the morning.

About 11 P.M. I was still awake, worried about my decision to wait to find him. Faintly, far down the hill, I could hear a drunken voice; a man was singing. Evidently he was climbing up our hill, as his voice was becoming louder as he drew nearer. I felt a great sense of relief, for I knew it had to be our missing man. Then I heard a strange, rhythmic *clack, clack, clack.* When daylight came, my first sergeant, Mathews, informed me the clacking sounds I'd heard were caused by two

Japanese leg bones the man had been striking together with each step he took.

We could have found much more Japanese equipment if we had wanted to dig up every patch of disturbed earth we discovered. On the other hand, it could easily have been booby-trapped.

I told John that we had found a huge pile of explosives and scores of land mines that must be blown up in place. He was interested in seeing it destroyed, so we took number-ten detonators, fuse, and prima cord with us the following morning. Five hundred boxes of picric-acid blocks were neatly stacked in a pile, approximately twelve by twelve by five feet high. Coils of leaded explosive similar to Cortex were about, so we wrapped them about the pile many times. There were oodles of small land mines that we had nicknamed tapemeasure mines. They were the size of a one-hundred-foot brass-enclosed tape measure, and had small, delicately threaded brass center caps that would crush easily with the slightest pressure.

Fortunately, these mines were not armed, as we unscrewed the tops of many to make sure the detonators had not been inserted. Piling these mines on top of the several tons of explosive, I felt sure that sympathetic detonation would occur when the main charge exploded. Fusing up, we drove back a half mile and waited for the explosion. It came like a bolt of thunder, and with it a *whir, whir, whir*ring sound. We had succeeded in seeding the immediate area with land mines. They came down like giant hailstones! We weren't worried, however, knowing they were harmless.

Lieutenant Marvin Griffen had arrived on the ship *Alchiba* just in time for that ship to be torpedoed by a Japanese submarine. He described the ordeal to us, saying the skipper had quickly run the ship aground to save both ship and cargo.

Occasionally I moved about the perimeter roads with a

passing interest in the Navy salvage crew as they patched the half-sunken vessel. They finally raised it, only to have another submarine resink it with a torpedo on the opposite side. The salvage crew was undaunted; they worked on, determined to put the ship back in commission. They succeeded.

CHAPTER 10

In March of 1943 we boarded a transport operated by the Coast Guard, our destination the Fiji Islands. Food on the ship was superb—eggs, steaks, and fresh potatoes with all the trimmings. I ate every bit, only to have it come back up within a half hour. There was only one safe place for this task, topside, leaning over the rail on the leeward side.

We landed at Suva, the capital of Fiji, on a beautiful, sunny morning, finally pushed snugly to the dock by a tugboat. First to catch our eye was a colorful Fijian policeman with his white, serrated skirt and blue jacket with red trim. His dress was immaculate; his spit and polish indicated a monumental pride in his profession.

Stepping down the gangway, we loaded into vehicles for the trip of four miles to our new quarters at Camp Samambula.

Traveling up the gradual incline on Queen's Road we met a man pushing a makeshift wheelbarrow. Riding on this barrow was a native suffering from elephantiasis. He was incapable of walking; his lower extremities and testicles had grown almost beyond belief due to parasites carried by mosquitoes.

Camp Samambula was split into two halves, a portion located on either side of the highway. Due to the hilly, rolling land the numerous buildings were set on raised posts. We entered the Camp A gate to our left, and found our company buildings were just up the first incline, on the right side of the road. They consisted of four long barracks for the platoons, also a facing warehouse for our company headquarters and supplies.

Farther up the hill, on the left, was our Second Battalion headquarters. At the top of the hill were quarters for the officers of the camp. Our Company H officers were assigned rooms facing the road, next to the mess. The mess had a bar and immediately behind it, a dining room. Adjoining the two rooms was a single large room for conferences and occasional weekend dances.

That afternoon, after being assigned transportation, my driver and I towed a water trailer to the 18th General Hospital, the nearest water point. There was no pure-water facility at the barracks, so it was necessary to haul our own drinking supply.

As a lieutenant colonel walked by, I stepped down to inquire the location of the water point. He introduced himself, then as he shook my hand, he said, "New here, aren't you? I see you're coming to see us soon."

"Why?" I puzzled.

He reached out to put his hand to my forehead. "You've got yellow jaundice and malaria. You're a sick man!"

Two days later I was in the hospital, my fever 104 and a half. I weighed in at 138 pounds, my normal weight is 175.

Officers in my ward who suffered only weight loss were given a two-ounce bottle of brandy before each meal. Supposedly it gave them more of an appetite. I never received that benefit; I was placed on a carbohydrate diet.

The hospital tried atabrine on me, against my wishes, six pills before each meal. They went down fine, but seconds later they were back up. Those small yellow pills acted like a volcano in my stomach. As I told them, quinine was fine with me. The trouble was, they gave me so many pills each day that I became almost totally deaf. It was a temporary side effect, but understanding a movie without sound was difficult.

Returning back at Samambula after a three-week cure, I found a problem. The military police in Suva had picked up some of my men. Drinking, they'd carelessly lost their hats and ties, then become belligerent. They'd been rounded up and thrown in jail. Nothing would suffice with the military police colonel, who was a West Pointer, but that I personally appear to bail them out. Knowing what they had been through, I held a certain sympathy, feeling they would soon be serious soldiers again. Unfortunately, this colonel in charge of the police had other ideas.

I stood at attention while he dressed me down thoroughly, that sanctimonious jerk. It was all my fault; I was a poor excuse for an officer, a disgrace to the military. I had no recourse; I could say nothing in my defense as he ranted and raved at me for long minutes. Finally, out of breath, he ordered a sergeant to get my men from the cells. I was shocked when I saw them; all had bruise marks around their heads and faces. The MPs had beaten them severely with nightsticks.

Dropping them at the company barracks I told Sergeant Mathews to warn the men to be on their best behavior while in town. The next morning I told them what to expect from the military police.

On Sunday, one of my drunken misfits was absent without official leave (AWOL). Sergeant Mathews made light of it and I concurred. The man had obviously gotten drunk and was sleeping somewhere. That morning I reported him as present, a stupid thing I would never do again.

This man was absent for the next week, and on the following Sunday morning, I contacted the personnel officer at regimental headquarters. Fortunately, he was a friend. I caught him at his quarters and after explaining my plight, he said, "There is no one at headquarters; get your sergeant with your morning reports and meet me there."

We sweated over those reports until they were corrected, then my friend said, "You darned fool! We could both get in serious trouble for this stunt. To hell with kindness and sympathy for your men. There is always one joker that will crap on you!"

He was right. The real problem was, many foreign ships

entered Suva Harbor daily, ships that were short of crewmen. Any man who wanted to desert could easily do so. To make the cheese more binding, my AWOL showed up the very next day. He never got another leave while on Fiji. He did get company punishment.

John and I had accumulated a tremendous amount of Japanese equipment, including rifles, machine guns, and mortars. On the training grounds I had the men erect an apron of barbed wire to demonstrate the different capabilities of Japanese and American bangalore torpedoes. We found the American version far superior to the Japanese. The explosions brought me to the attention of our new battalion commander, Colonel Dunn. He called me to headquarters to ask why the battalion hadn't been invited to watch the demonstration. The next day I was appointed to be Battalion S-3 (plans and training officer) in addition to my duties at Company H.

In this rest area, I found the job required long hours and hard work. In a combat situation the position would have been almost superfluous. I worked mostly out of the battalion headquarters building, but sometimes in my room up on the hill. Colonel Dunn was very supportive, greatly interested in training.

Being an avid reader, I studied the battalion's collection of training manuals, using the information to write scripts for the men to actually act out, beginning with small-unit actions. What I read enlightened me. I was envious of the Japanese Nambu machine gun. It had a thirty-round clip instead of the twenty rounds of our Browning automatic rifle. Why didn't the ordnance people put a bipod on our light machine gun and a stock in the rear as the enemy did? Why didn't they adapt the 60mm mortar to the same principle as the Japanese grenade launcher, for direct aiming and instant firing? Look at the enemy ammunition: it was .25 caliber, but it killed as well as our .30-caliber cartridge, which weighed nearly twice as much. We were fighting a modern war with

WWI equipment! The only thing in our favor was the new M1 rifle. Even our single trail cannon was obsolete.

A Chinese proverb says: "A wise man learns by the mistakes of others. A fool learns by his own." Unfortunately, many of my experiences were learned the hard way, but I had picked up a lot from those many mistakes made on New Caledonia and Guadalcanal.

Training began with pointers on how to take out enemy machine guns or strong points with two or more men. I gradually changed the schooling to squads in the attack, then platoon attacks, finally full company assaults. One basic rule I learned at my first outdoor demonstration: Always bring two public address systems; one is sure to fail. It was my initiation to Murphy's Law.

After training in offensive operations we moved to the New Zealand Rifle Range. This was a two-hundred- to three-hundred-yard range. Every man had to qualify with his weapon. If he failed, he had to practice each day until he succeeded. The standard bull's-eye for the two-hundred-yard range was used at three hundred yards. Four of the Company H men were shooting offhand at three hundred yards with almost perfect scores. They were remarkable!

One afternoon John Gossett appeared, so we moved our 20mm cannon to the range. We fired a single explosive round at an empty steel barrel on top of the range wall. The first shot hit it dead center, throwing it beyond the pit. Upon its recovery we found a two-foot hole in the center; the remaining steel was perforated with numerous small holes.

John asked, "What will it do on full automatic?" The huge feeder drum on top held nearly one hundred rounds.

Leveling it on the right edge of the abutment, we opened fire. I judged the firing rate at about six hundred rounds per minute. After a brief burst John shouted for us to stop. He was smiling. "Better quit, you'll destroy the entire range wall."

It was true; we had removed a truckload of dirt from the range with that short burst. Sadly enough, we turned the gun over to the ordnance outfit, as it needed a shortened barrel length to be practical. We had no means to correct that. It was shipped back to the United States for testing. We heard nothing further.

Kingston, the Company H mortar officer, and I arranged for a demonstration of the Japanese 90mm mortar. Prior to the exhibition we found the base propellent charges wet, the fulminate primers ruined. I unloaded the powder from each shotgun shell in turn, dried it, and with a drill reset a .45 ACP case to the base of the shotgun shell for a primer. Then the powder and wads were reinserted. The booster charges in the fins were still good, made from a sort of semiblue plastic or perhaps a waterproofed silk.

The battalion was seated upon a ridge with the mortar set below, firing parallel to the ridge, the shells to land in the ocean. We fired two rounds without nose detonators and all went well: the projectiles landed far out into the ocean. We put a detonator in the next round, and when it was fired it pooped out of the tube one hundred feet or so, falling flat to the ground. Thank goodness, it failed to explode. The battalion was about 150 feet from the line of fire at the time; a few men took off over the hill, while most just hit the deck.

Things simmered down and we fired a few more rounds, all performing to perfection. We tried another round with a detonator—you guessed it! It flopped and the crowd thinned out. We were pushing our luck.

I called off the firing, but Kingston still wanted to shoot one last live shell. Moving the battalion out behind the mortar, we watched the final firing. Kingston left all the booster increments on the tail fins when this round was dropped into the tube. Massive flames shot from the tube; the report was the loudest I had ever heard from a mortar.

Over two minutes passed and no explosion was heard. Impatient, the battalion began to walk back toward the highway. I figured it for a dud until much later, when we heard the explosion. The Japanese rated the maximum range of their 90mm mortar (Model 97) at 4,155 yards, but I believe this was an error. It should have been *meters,* for this projectile far outreached our 81mm mortar.

On another training mission I ordered a case of lady-finger dynamite (similar to giant firecrackers) from Service Company. They mistakenly sent out a crater charge, a forty-pound chunk of 60 percent dynamite. I was about to send it back when Colonel Dunn questioned, "Will that dynamite go off if shot at with a rifle?"

"I'm sure it will."

"Give it a try."

It was set back on another ridge about two hundred yards from the crowd. One rifle bullet dead center sure set it off. There was a tremendous explosion! When we returned to headquarters that afternoon, the 18th General Hospital called, giving me hell. The Section 8 (shell-shocked) men in their ward had gone berserk, and they'd had trouble calming them. In the future we were prohibited from using explosives in that area.

A river-crossing mission was planned for each battalion by regimental headquarters. The selected stream was 130 feet wide with clear water, a strong current, and a depth of about thirty feet. Our battalion drew first turn so we selected a spot with gently sloping banks. Along the near bank were brushy sticks about five feet in height that would serve as material for bull boats. These were made by cutting the brush, forming a ring on a tarp, then rolling in and securing the sides. With a few men swimming across the river with a rope tied to one end of each boat, it was simple to move the other men and the equipment across the stream. By wetting the slanting riverbank under big tarps, we drove a jeep, even a six-by-six truck, onto these tarps. Tying up the tarps to the sides, we safely crossed the jeep and the truck.

Unfortunately, one bull boat was tugged too hard and spilled a mortar and its ammunition into the deep water. Diving from a stationary boat, I managed to get down to the mortar, but the current was so swift I had no chance to tie the rope to any part. Other swimmers tried, but had no luck either. I took my jeep out to the R&R camp, which was run by an officer from Company E. He found an old native Fijian, who had tortoiseshell diving goggles, and his son. Ben told me the man was a fisherman.

Taking the man back to the river crossing I explained what had happened. This old man went down with a rope, staying down a long minute. He not only tied to the mortar, but the ammunition. In three dives he recovered everything. I was in a quandary as how to reward him, but he refused any money. Finally I gave his son five dollars. They were happy when I returned them home.

We had nearly finished and were packing up to return to Samambula when an Indian Sikh with a huge turban approached me, gesticulating wildly with both arms. According to him we had cut his entire tapioca patch, totally destroying his crop. As someone who had come from a farm, at first I was embarrassed; the tapioca stalks had looked much like dried-up nettles to me. I told him to see Second Island Command for compensation, but by now I figured he was a liar, putting the screws to us, as the material we had cut appeared dead and dry.

I had a chance to meet Captain Edward Cakobau at the Grand Pacific Hotel on a Saturday afternoon. He was the company commander of Company C, of the Third Fiji Battalion. Later I met his cousin, George, who commanded Company A. We three became good friends and I was invited to George's home many times. There I met his wife, Adi, and Gus Saffings and his wife, Marge. The girls were very talented musicians; they both played jazz piano, singly and as a pair. Gus could play any stringed instrument.

I received my captain bars shortly after our arrival in Fiji, together with another officer, Fred Flo. A celebration party was held for us at the 18th General Hospital. Upon the conclusion of the dinner, everyone decided to play bridge. I had to admit my ignorance, as I had no interest in the game. I would have preferred poker; it was more my style.

In July the Cakobau family put on a special party for me called a *Meke*. I was late because of a staff meeting and didn't arrive at their home until after dark. Their yard was lighted by lanterns of every color; they even had a native orchestra. Adi, George's wife, took me by the hand to meet my companion for the evening. The girl was embarrassed, having been brought especially from MBau, the island of the chief, for the occasion. She seemed about sixteen years of age, very pretty, but obviously out of place at this adult party. After a few minutes of polite conversation, I mingled elsewhere; I could tell she was relieved.

Dances were held periodically at our officers club, with special arrangements for bathroom facilities for the ladies. Our barracks was formed like a big H, with a central passageway with a washroom on one side and toilets on the other. The several water closets had wooden doors with no locks. When a dance was held, all officers and male guests used the lower facilities down the hill. Our regular facilities were available only to the ladies.

Nearing midnight on a dance night, I was still working on plans for the next day when suddenly I heard a woman screaming from our toilet area. Racing out the door I turned into the latrine area, first man on the scene. A drunken officer stood at the open door of a toilet urinating on an Army nurse who was sitting on the pot.

I grasped the man's shoulder, locking on his epaulet, to fling him across the concrete floor to the urinal side. He was of slight build, a lightweight, with a small mansard mustache under his nose. Other officers joined me and a captain rescued his nurse-date. She was mighty shaken!

Glancing at the stunned man on the floor, I perceived he was a bird colonel. I had never met the man before, but I instinctively knew he was our new West Point, regimental commander. I silently slipped away.

Most weekends when free, either George Cakobau or Gus Saffings and I fished, using dynamite for bait. On one occasion George and I went up the coast about thirty miles to fish in a tidewater river. We scored with several huge fish in the twenty-pound class. As George removed their heads, a Fijian boy came by, asking for them.

Toward dusk, George turned to me. "Hey, let me drive your jeep."

"Where are we going?"

"To get some supper."

I was agreeable and sure enough he knew the location of a small village. They treated him like the king he was. Up until then, I hadn't realized that George was a grandson of King Cakobau, the past ruler of the Fiji Islands. (Later, after WWII, George became Sir George Cakobau, governor general of the Fiji Islands. My wife and I visited him and his family in 1978, at Government House in Suva. We had a lot to talk over, but had to be discreet; we had both remarried.)

Dinners were held each Sunday night at the Grand Pacific Hotel just below Government House. The English civilians showed up in force with their wives, dressed to the nines. Several wore uniforms of their past association with the British military. Our dress uniform was chino cotton with black tie, hardly competition for those so grandly appareled. At first we received haughty frowns from the dowagers, but persistence paid off; we were soon accepted.

The semi-outdoor bar attached to the hotel was always crowded. Officers escorting their nurse-dates had to pass through this section to gain the walk outdoors to the lawn and oceanfront. Many devious smiles and smirks were cast as the couples entering the bar from outside were forced to run the gauntlet of drinkers to enter the hotel proper. Occasionally a nurse wearing a white skirt would come inside with heavy grass stains on her rump and back, while her escort's knees and elbows also showed heavy stains. At this sight, loud cheering and clapping were heard, the couple suffering much embarrassment. Good tips, we all thought!

Our monthly pay had to be picked up at the finance office in Suva. At a long desk, checks were alphabetically arranged in groups along the thirty-foot counter. Just because Congress had declared an officer a gentleman didn't deter some officers from thievery. One or more removed checks and cashed them in town, the merchants thinking all was aboveboard. The next month we were ordered to place our thumbprint on the back of our check before leaving the finance office. This stopped the thefts.

I was invited to a poker game one evening, but had only $20 on my person. Someone remarked, "It will take only twenty minutes to lose it."

He was right! In that same game a new officer was caught cheating. Captain Al Weist, an expert at poker, trapped him. A few days later this officer managed a transfer out of our battalion. A good thing too, for he had been ostracized by all.

Edward Cakobau invited me to go along to the island of Ovalau for a weekend. We were to meet at Londoni on Friday, to catch a motor sailer at the dock. When I arrived at noon I was fed at his Army camp, then a letter of apology was handed me. It seemed Edward's company was to maneuver as enemy against units of one of our Americal regiments.

Although I was no longer fully associated with Company H, a half dozen men from that unit arrived by truck. They had booked passage on the sailboat, having reservations at the hotel in Ovalau. Knowing them all, I shared the beer they carried. When we landed at the dock in Ovalau, several were loaded.

I was booked at the Gentleman's Club, a refined private club for the upper echelon of prosperous Englishmen. This club had a fine, old-fashioned bar; the entire building had stood for ages, signs of old prosperity readily apparent. Outside, a group of elderly men were bowling on the grass. I was graciously invited to participate, but begged off, knowing they had their own groups. I could see the relief on their faces when I declined.

Wandering along a cricket field I met the Company H men speaking with several Fijian girls. The girls were trying to entice the men into playing field hockey with them. One or two girls disappeared for a moment, coming back with four other girls carrying several hockey sticks. These sticks were about four feet long, hardwood, with a crook at the bottom end.

Fijian girls had walked and run all of their lives; they were physically far more fit than our men. They played the men out in a matter of minutes, running like deer. They loved to reach out to trip the men with their sticks; they didn't play fair! It was the roughest I've ever seen men treated by girls. When everyone tired of the game, dates for the Saturday evening dance were arranged.

I attended the dance and stupidly accosted a drunken soldier from a tank outfit. His shirt was out of his pants and open down the front; he had slopped beer on his clothes.

I said, "Button up your shirt and act like a man!"

In a rage he hit me, and of course, it was easy to deck him. Immediately two MPs appeared. Thank the Lord, a man who worked for one of the trading companies stepped forward, explaining he had witnessed the entire thing. I turned to the MPs asking, "If you are policing this dance, where were you when this man made an ass of himself?" They played dumb, but I knew they had been drinking.

Back at Camp Samambula I attended a meeting at battalion headquarters the following Monday night. The new regimental commander was there to question me about striking an enlisted man. I could read the writing on the wall; he was out to get me, he knew who I was! He said, "I'm going to send an officer over to Ovalau and thoroughly investigate you."

I had no answer other than to say, "That tanker hit me and I hit him back!" Thinking it over, I decided my remark to the two MPs was what had created the problem. They had reported the incident to cover themselves.

The regimental commander picked Captain Tom Conlon to investigate me. Evidently he didn't know Tom was a friend of mine. When Tom asked me what had happened, I said, "Look up the man at the trading company, he'll tell you what transpired."

Tom had a fine three-day vacation and vindicated me fully. When he went to Island Command to get his payment of expenses and per diem, he was told our regimental commander had no authority to authorize the trip. Such is life.

Colonel Dunn initiated a new policy for company commanders. We were to meet each Saturday morning at 10 A.M. to inspect all five company kitchens. Just before noon he held a critique of each kitchen, before delving into other general problems.

His last subject hit us like a bomb. Gonorrhea was exceptionally prevalent among the whores around Suva. Each company had several men incapacitated with venereal disease.

Colonel Dunn began to quote some startling figures: "Captain Kloster of Company F must have a very high moral influence on his men, far greater than any of you other commanders. He has only seven men in the hospital with the disease. Stimson, you have twenty-four, Walker, you have the same. The rest of you are not any better off, either!"

We were puzzled, knowing Kloster's men were as horny and attracted to women as the rest of the men in the battalion. However, we couldn't argue with the statistics; figures are figures.

Later, a day or two before we were to leave Fiji, the truth came out. Our surgeon came to me, smiling. "I've solved the mystery of Kloster's high moral fiber. I just got a requisition from Company F for three hundred packets of sulfa wound tablets for their jungle aid kits. Those damned medics in Kloster's company told the men to take all twelve of their wound tablets with a canteen full of water if they went whoring. It would prevent them from getting the clap. It's damn lucky some of them haven't died from crystals in their kidneys. That's one of the dangers of sulfa pills."

We company commanders breathed a sigh of relief, and hoped Colonel Dunn got the word. If he did, he never let on.

When we left Guadalcanal, Colonel Ben Northridge had been transferred to a camp in the Southwest United States.

He was to impart his knowledge of jungle fighting to new soldiers.

At this particular military camp they had a soldier free-ride station near the gate. Ben picked up two soldiers from the East Coast, one of whom sat in the rear seat of his car. Down the road some distance, the man in the rear crushed Ben's skull with a large wrench. The two men were deserting. Stopping at a curve in the road, they hauled his body into the desert, leaving him for dead.

A truck driver on a night schedule spotted something far out in a field as he made a curve in the road. He stopped his vehicle, knowing something was wrong. He found Ben barely alive, and got him to a hospital. Ben survived, but the blows did massive damage to his brain. He was, to me, one of the finest officers I ever met, kind, but firm. He had been a schoolteacher prior to the war.

Early in December 1943 we were warned to prepare for a move to Bougainville, in the Solomon Islands. Just a few days before Christmas we were notified to load aboard ship the very next day.

The word traveled like wildfire in Suva. Shortly after 7 P.M. that evening, my city friends showed up to say their farewells. George and Edward Cakobau were both with their units above Nausori, but George's wife, Adi, Gus and Marge Saffings, plus many others came out. They brought flowers and bottles.

The party began swinging at about 9 P.M., continuing until daylight the next morning. Our company officers and many of the battalion officers took turns dancing with the girls. Adi and Marge traded at the piano, while Gus accompanied them with his banjo. It was a grand send-off, enjoyed by all. Before the night was over empty bottles littered the floor of the officers club.

After loading my friends back into their cars at dawn, I returned for transportation to the dock in Suva. Aboard ship, shortly before the supper hour, we were surprised to hear

Tokyo Rose, saying, "All of you boys in those ships about to leave Suva, Fiji, are doomed to die."

I knew there were spies in the pay of the Japanese. In New Caledonia, the Vichy French owner of the local radio station was caught red-handed. His code was adapted to music he played, according to our information. Knowing the many wonderful and patriotic people of Fiji, I wondered who could stoop so low. It seemed money could corrupt, or was it pseudo patriotism?

CHAPTER 11

We landed Christmas Day, 1943, on Bougainville and quickly moved ashore. The Marines had again been the advance force here, landing on November 1.

My S-3 responsibilities were few; the main work rested with company commanders to care for their men. As we marched inland we passed elements of the 37th Division. To my surprise, I was hailed by a soldier from my hometown. A few hundred yards farther I was again stopped; this man was a friend from Bathgate, North Dakota.

Our first encampment was crude, upon a side hill, a mighty poor location. Finally, after a week of boredom, we were moved to a new bivouac area recently abandoned by a Marine unit. At the tail end of each company street was a small, clear river, about thirty feet wide and four feet in depth, a branch of the Piva River. The current was slow, excellent for bathing.

I dearly wanted to get back to a company command, any company, preferably rifle. My chance came sooner than expected; I was to take over Company E. I had worked with them on Guadalcanal and knew many of the men. They were a National Guard unit from Williston, North Dakota. Many of the men in the company had been the Class A basketball champs of Dakota in 1940. It seemed every high school boy in the state, in whose town a National Guard unit existed, augmented his income by enlisting. I had done so in 1937.

Before leaving the Second Battalion headquarters, I consulted with the mess sergeant, Annard Dale. He had his ear to the ground, and told me the Company E kitchen food was poorly prepared. He advised, "Tell them to shape up or go back to the line." He also confided, "If you need replacements, I'll get good men for you."

My first talk was with the top sergeant, the mess sergeant, and the cooks. Things improved immediately. Good food is the most important thing to soldiers. It must be the best possible.

I knew the reputations of the present officers of Company E; they were all well qualified, with past combat experience. A new officer, Lieutenant Charles Ross, had been assigned to the company just before my arrival. He was sharp and eager to learn.

Officers come and go. Suddenly I received several seeking temporary quarters until assigned to other companies. Eventually all were assigned elsewhere. Rotation home was slow, based on a point system, a minimum of eighty points required. Even so, the selected few were supposedly drawn by lottery and there were about three thousand names in the pot.

I lost a fine first sergeant, Sande, to rotation, so promoted Joel Fedje to the post. He was superb officer material. Later, when we ran out of officers, he refused a commission, citing his care for the entire company.

Some officers at regiment managed to get a forty-five-day leave to the States, but to my knowledge, no line officers were selected. Perhaps we were judged expendable. I soon found there were favorites at headquarters, the bootlickers and the ones who played badminton with our regimental commander.

One of my officers became so broken up over the sudden death of his mother he moped and cried for days. The Red Cross helped me send him home. I didn't need faint hearts! He would have affected the morale of his platoon. In his place I received Lieutenant Paul Clemens, a Texan, a remarkable man and fine soldier.

Before we found a generator to power electric lights for the company, the 155mm rifles across the road snuffed out our nightly candles each time they fired. Happily, Pete

Sherar, one of our officers, was selected to spend time with Special Services; he trained the division boxing team. He was also adept at scrounging, getting us a brand-new Easy washing machine and a five-kilowatt generator from the Seabees. We traded Japanese weapons for them, also getting a water pump for the washer and the shower facilities.

Setting the wringer-washer by the stream at the end of the street, we rotated a crew to wash clothing daily. We also organized a lumber crew to cut trees for boards. The use of men for this task was prohibited, so it had to be done surreptitiously. On weekends we bribed the sawmill operator at division with beer, running the machinery ourselves, thus getting framing lumber and boards for our tents, all of solid mahogany. At one time we were the only company in the battalion with a hundred-watt lightbulb in each tent, a laundry, showerheads, and raised, framed tents with board floors. The men also hung a lighted sign along the road: "Easy City, Population 187." A mystical number we never reached because of casualties.

We got a new battalion commander, Lieutenant Colonel Samuel Gee. He organized a huge garden; company details cleared, planted, and cared for the future produce. Weeks later we enjoyed fresh vegetables and sweet corn. Lieutenant Sherar and I also started a tomato patch in front of our tent that was successful.

A huge training area was cleared, requiring an enormous amount of work. The 245th Field Artillery, our regimental support, often lent us their crawler tractors and trailers. We found the new area loaded with chiggers, which had to be removed at the conclusion of each day's training. Those who neglected to do so suffered itching and open sores. Later, at an old Japanese bivouac area west of the Torokina River, another regiment of our division found these chiggers or lice, infected with the deadly scrub typhus. Some men died of it.

At the north end of our battalion, next to Company E, which I came to call Easy Company, was a 90mm antiaircraft unit. To our west, just across the road, stood four 155mm rifles of a black artillery unit. On our south was the 245th

Field Artillery. We became accustomed to frequent artillery fire. The Japanese fired a 150mm gun quite often, but usually their shells were directed at the airstrips. From the distant flash on the horizon at night, and the sound of the gun, we estimated the Japanese gun to be five miles to our west.

We began routine patrols to scout out the Torokina River area. We found Japanese telephone lines crossing the river in the vicinity of hills 250 and 600, which we cut, removing all the wire we could. Their wire was easy to spot, a bright yellow. It became risky to cross the Torokina. We did, but with caution, using covering fire. The jungle was thick, with no trails except the so-called East-West Trail. It ran inland, paralleling the coast, established by natives many years earlier. This trail was firmly blocked by the enemy. It wasn't until a few days after the attack of the Japanese troops on March 8, 1944, that we traveled it with a vengeance.

A new commanding officer was assigned to Company H, a young West Pointer just out of school. He had evidently gone directly from graduation to the infantry school at Fort Benning to earn his first-lieutenant's bars. Lieutenant Dick Hamer, the Company H commander, with his previous Guadalcanal combat experience, was set back from company commander to executive officer since his promotion to captain had not come through. This was an obvious WPPA (West Point Protective Association) scam. Sad to say, due to his lack of experience, this new officer was killed on his first patrol.

About noon on February 28, I was called to battalion headquarters and told to ready Easy Company to recover the body of Lieutenant Richard Combs, who had been left dead under enemy fire. Under strict orders, we were never to risk men's lives to recover a dead man. But this was different—this was a West Pointer!

Easy Company left the Company B front perimeter line along with a forward observer from the 245th Field Artillery, Max Kerlanski. He was assisted by two men carrying his 612 radio. Our departure time was 1 P.M.

I was informed that the 245th Field Artillery would fire intermittently at the top of hill 250 to keep the Japanese heads down. At about 2 P.M. we approached the bottom of the hill. Suddenly, four rounds of 105mm shells came in on us, one exploding in a tree just thirty feet overhead. Max and I were just below that tree. The remaining three rounds cleared other trees, impacting about fifty yards to our front.

Kerlanski immediately put the two sections of his radio together, to order a cease-fire. Meanwhile, I found two of my men seriously wounded. When Max asked who had changed the fire order from the top of the hill to the bottom, he got no answer.

Combs lay on open ground, in full view of the enemy above. The distance to him was about 150 feet from our jungle cover. Dick Hamer, Combs's second in command, had accompanied us on this trip. It looked like suicide to go out in the open to pick up Combs, but it had to be done.

Thinking it over, I said, "Dick, let's take off our sidearms and jackets; maybe they'll let us pick him up."

He agreed, so we shed our upper clothing and moved into the open. Why they let us retrieve Combs's body, I'll never know. They were either compassionate, or sleeping on the job. Both Dick and I were pretty dicey about it, expecting to be shot at any moment. It only took a minute—we hurried!

On my 300 radio I was told to send Combs back with my wounded, but to stay out with Easy Company until the next day. I puzzled over this as it was only two miles back to our line; there was no legitimate reason to keep us out in the jungle. Why did they want us to stay overnight?

The next afternoon we entered the Company B line and a forward observer from the 245th came to me; he was nearly crying. He said, "I didn't do it! Please believe me! Your regimental commander stood beside me and ordered me to fire at the bottom of the hill. I told him your patrol was nearly in that position, and it would be too dangerous. Your bird colonel said, 'I gave you a direct order!' "

It was then I realized why we had been left out that night. The short rounds could be explained as a mix-up if a little time expired—I might forget about it. What could I do now?

Absolutely nothing! That regimental commander knew the result of his order. He had stood near the radio when we called for a cease-fire and explanation.

What was this colonel thinking, after being warned by an experienced artilleryman? It brought up two questions. Why was my company selected to recover the body? It should have been the duty of Company H to do so. Did this man seek revenge on me—for my manhandling of him when he urinated on the army nurse? No doubt he had found that I was the man responsible for his degradation. This colonel later became a two-star.

Normally, weapons companies in a combat situation wouldn't be asked to do patrol work, although I often had while I was a platoon leader of Company H, on Guadalcanal. However, except in one questionable case—my run-in with the Company G commander on Guadalcanal—these were all squad and section patrols in a stalemate situation, such as at Point Cruz.

West Point Protective Association mentality put Combs above Hamer at Company H, in a promotion situation. No doubt the man was well educated and indoctrinated, but he had absolutely no combat experience. He should have been worked into the system gradually, not pushed up the promotion ladder. It was his first patrol in enemy territory and he'd wanted to do his best. He attempted to take that well-defended hill with a small patrol. We rifle companies had never been ordered to take 250. If we had been so ordered, we would have accomplished it, but with a severe loss of men. I know how shocked we were at this unfortunate occurrence. What had happened was almost criminal, and it spoke for itself. A fine man with a brilliant future was lost.

Late in February, Colonel Gee took the company officers on a trip along the 182nd Infantry line to familiarize us in case we were required to reinforce any of their units. We were in battalion reserve at the time.

On hill 260 the artillery had a tree outpost of eighty to one hundred feet above the jungle. Someone asked if anyone

wanted to go up for a look. Curious, I volunteered, not bothered by heights. Hoisted to the top, I was disappointed, seeing nothing but the tops of trees. In fact, it was difficult to
trace even the outline of the Torokina River. The only benefit
I could see was that a more accurate azimuth could be taken
on the Japanese 150mm gun's flash when they fired at night.
It might aid counterbattery fire.

We continued south along their line until we reached the
adjoining Company B of our First Battalion. I noted that the
apron wire in front of their positions was complex, with a
gate to allow passage of patrols.

Behind Company B, which was located along a draw, was
another ridge about 350 yards north of the 182nd Infantry's
hill 260, paralleling it, but set off. The next day we were
moved to this ridge as backup, in case our frontline was penetrated. We dug in securely with all battalion weapons, including a 37mm antitank gun. From this high ground we had
a perfect view of much of the Torokina River to our west,
also of hills 250, 600, and 1,111 to the south.

Fortunately, an earlier patrol had captured papers disclos-
ing the date of an imminent attack. When it finally came at 7
A.M. on March 8, we were prepared.

At that hour several enemy howitzers opened fire on us
from hills 600 and 1,111. Another fired from the far side of
the Torokina River. As it was a bit overcast, each time a gun
fired, its position was disclosed: we could see every flash.
The 150mm gun far to the west began firing steadily, hurling
shells into the area of our artillery. The firing from hills 600
and 1,111 looked like rapidly blinking lights. There must
have been at least eight cannon in action.

For some reason Colonel Gee was not present, but our regimental executive officer was. He walked confidently back
and forth along the ridge since the fire was not falling on our
backup line.

The Japanese gun firing from the river was within range of
our 37mm gun. The crew yelled to me, "Can we return the
fire? We can reach that gun just across the river."

I said, "Hop to it!"

They fired four or five rounds before the executive officer ran down in a tizzy. He had turned pasty white; I could see he was scared stiff.

"Who gave them permission to fire?"

I wasn't dodging. "I did! Those Japanese are firing at us; we shot back!"

"Stop it right now! I won't have it! I won't have it!"

I knew then and there he was a coward. His carefree walking ceased; he disappeared into a hole farther up the slope, and he didn't come out. The rest of us had a good laugh.

Regretfully, I told the gun crew to cease fire. Their words were brief and loud: I hoped the exec heard them.

As the result of the few rounds fired by the 37mm gun crew, the Japanese howitzer by the river was silenced, probably saving lives in the rear area. The position of the 37mm was such that it couldn't be seen from hills 600 and 1,111 for counterbattery fire. The 37mm gun crew was fully safe.

Minutes later I received a phone call from regimental headquarters, telling me to get back to my company bivouac area. It was being heavily shelled by the 150mm gun.

· Upon my arrival I found our mess tent and kitchen totally destroyed. Our supply tent was gone, the area littered with broken rifles and equipment. Our artificer, Joe Lauer, was digging frantically into the mess with a shovel. Just as I asked him what he was up to, a 150mm incoming Japanese shell struck between our two rows of tents. It landed about thirty feet from us, tearing a big groove in the sand street. It failed to explode, ricocheting away with a *whoosh-whoosh*ing sound. Across the road men were shouting; a truckload of 155mm powder bags was blazing, set afire by the Japanese gun.

I finally realized Joe was attempting to dig into their dugout. He yelled, "John is hurt bad. I can hear him, he says his rear end is torn up. Can you get a medic?"

The entire area was apparently deserted. If anyone was available, he had to be in a hole. I ran to battalion headquarters, knowing the location of the large medical dugout. Shouting down the hole, I asked if a doctor was there. I heard loud arguing, then a voice said, "They're still shelling out there."

Then another voice said, "He won't come out until the shelling stops."

I blew up! "If he doesn't come out, I'm going to toss a grenade down there!"

Moments later the doctor was bodily ejected from the dugout. Grasping his jacket, I put him on the run to our company area. The poor guy was white as a sheet and trembling like a leaf; he was terrified.

By this time Joe had Johnny Wells, our supply sergeant, out of the dugout. His one buttock was a bloody mess.

While the doctor and Joe worked over Johnny, I checked my tent and found only a little damage: just a big hole in my sleeping bag made by a large piece of shrapnel.

Returning to Sergeant Wells, I found him in good hands. The shelling suddenly ceased, allowing the few men in the area to come topside.

When I returned to the ridge, the executive officer had disappeared. I hoped he felt thoroughly ashamed of himself, but doubted it. Much later, in the Philippines, I had a repeat performance of his cowardice. After the war he was discharged from his position for lying about his college education.

It seemed my unorthodox treatment of the surgeon was too much for him. His mind wouldn't adjust to the reality of combat. He was evacuated after this episode, but I did not hold him in contempt. Neither did I have scorn for a new officer of my company who shot himself in the leg the day after I arrived back on the ridge. Men do have a breaking point. It isn't everyone who can stand the constant stress of battle. I was fortunate, able to disregard immediate danger to do what had to be done.

CHAPTER 12

A sudden Japanese attack was launched on hill 260 in the 182nd Infantry sector at daybreak on March 10. Wild, vicious fighting trapped the observer up on the tree platform; Company E of the 182nd took heavy losses. Flamethrowers, mortars, artillery—everything went but the proverbial kitchen sink.

At the same approximate time General Kanda with a Japanese force attacked the 37th Division (which held the left half of our perimeter line) in two different areas. The fire of the entire corps and division artillery was concentrated on Kanda's troops.

On March 11, while the fighting on hill 260 continued, I was ordered to patrol upriver to hill 250, then back to our battalion sector line. Upstream, we found the Japanese still occupied hills 250 and 600. Retracing our steps downriver to the approximate juncture of the 164th and 182nd patrol sectors, we stopped to take a break.

A patrol of about twenty men wearing helmets arrived, just out from the line. They were 182nd Infantry and I spoke with the leader near the edge of the river. I don't remember the conversation, except that his patrol turned back toward home.

Lieutenant Jim Pfeiffer, of Easy Company, had led his platoon well into the 182nd Infantry sector as there were no definite maps or definitive points to identify. Calling to me, he pointed out a group of enemy crossing back and forth on the almost dry riverbed in the rear of hill 260. Wounded Japanese were being carried piggyback to the west while ammunition and other supplies were being carried east, up on hill 260.

We approached within easy rifle range and Pfeiffer's men shot seven enemy in the open riverbed, which at this point was about 450 feet wide. In an effort to obtain the identity of the enemy unit, Lieutenant Pfeiffer, Sergeant Disrud, and Corporal Catalfamo of Easy Company were wounded. Because of overhanging trees I was unable to use our 60mm mortars.

Calling on the 300 radio for 245th Field Artillery fire, I was disappointed to learn they could shoot only in the 164th Infantry sector. After a long, agonizing wait, an officer answered from the other end, ordering me out of the sector. Here we had the opportunity to possibly stop the fighting on hill 260, but were stymied by bureaucracy. The impression I got was that the 182nd Infantry would do all the fighting in the 182nd area, and didn't need any help. I also got the impression that this was almost a private war.

Upon our patrol's return to the lines I was met by Colonel Dunn, who had now been assigned to the 182nd Infantry. When I explained the facts, he felt as disgusted as I. He asked me to present the circumstances to General McCulloch, a pompous man who was evidently running the hill 260 show. (The Americal Division commander had sent his executive to run the hill 260 operation.) This general had a private tent complete with tables and maps in the rear of the 182nd line. He dressed me down, saying in no uncertain terms that I had no business in the 182nd patrol area and pooh-poohed all ideas I had about crossing the Torokina River and cutting off the Japanese supply line. He caustically informed me that I was only a civilian captain, while he was a graduate of West Point!

His discourtesy, while I was doing my best to be polite, made·me later realize my naivete. Attempting to explain a simple solution to a general is stupid.

The next morning I was ordered to meet with several Silver and Birds, and two carrying Stars. I blew my cool. I was sick of red tape and incompetence and told them so. I

added some pertinent remarks about graduates of the great
school along the Hudson, of alcoholism and cover-ups.

When I left that meeting I knew I would be up for a court-
martial but didn't give a damn. But it never happened.
Perhaps my honest anger shamed them. Instead, a wonderful
thing happened. A young lieutenant colonel, Jim Taylor,
from the 245th Field Artillery, came up and put his hand on
my shoulder. He said, "Charley, not all West Pointers are
pricks. The next time you want artillery fire, you call me; I'll
see you get it!"

From that time on, whenever on a patrol, I asked for a forward observer from the 245th Field Artillery. I fondly remember a few: Lieutenant Kerlanski, Captain Fall, and so
many others whose names have slipped by these past years.
Later, in the Philippines, the 245th did a great job for us.

My bitterness stemmed from the feeling of being ham-
strung by our own brass, who didn't really comprehend what
was going on out in the field. They wanted us to do the job,
but kept us from doing it by a set of meaningless rules.

Really, what rules can there be in war? And to get three
good men wounded for nothing—what a kick in the rear!

Constant artillery attacks were made on hill 250, but they
were futile; the enemy simply moved to the other side of the
peak for safety. A 90mm antiaircraft gun was moved to the
nose of the ridge behind Company B, and timed fire was
placed, with shell bursts just over the edge of the ridge. This
may have disheartened the Japanese, but they didn't abandon
the hill.

A day later I witnessed about eight SBD dive-bombers at-
tacking hills 250 and 600. Suddenly one aircraft broke away
from the circling group and crashed into the jungle about
two miles west of 250. Another aircraft flew by in front of us.
The front toggles had apparently released, but a bomb hung
at a 45-degree angle from the rear mounts. The pilot was
shaking the plane violently, trying to dislodge the bomb.
When the air show was finally over, we had lost one aircraft
to enemy ground fire.

On March 13 it was our company's turn for the daily patrol. I sent Lieutenant Charles Ross, with his platoon, up the Torokina River on what was normally a routine task. The same day Lieutenant Colonel Samuel Gee took us company commanders on an inspection tour of the 37th Division line in case Japanese general Kanda's force made a breakthrough.

As we followed along the various regimental lines of the 37th Division, we noted it was quiet; not a shot could be heard. The jungle to our front was decimated; an area of at least a half mile square had been totally demolished by the massive artillery barrages. Grumbling could be heard from men along the line as we passed: "Those bastards are going to draw fire on us!" Other vociferous comments followed as well. Crossing one bare stretch, Colonel Gee suddenly turned to me, saying, "Where is your gun, Captain?"

Normally I carried a scope-equipped M1 rifle, but due to the walking involved had substituted a belt and a .45-caliber pistol hidden under my untucked jacket. Sliding my hand up my leg I grasped the unseen pistol and thrust the muzzle against his stomach.

"Here, sir!"

He froze for seconds, then said, "Point it away, it might go off!" He wasn't afraid, but he was mighty surprised. Truthfully, I couldn't have made that draw again in one hundred years!

Upon our return I found our company alive with excitement. Charles Ross's patrol had caught thirteen enemy swimming in the Torokina River and had wiped them out. They had felt so secure in numbers that they had left no guard. All of their equipment on the riverbank had been recovered by his platoon. The best part—not a man was wounded or lost.

Word came down that General Kanda, defeated, was heading west, attempting to gain the East-West Trail by circling in the rear of hills 1,111 and 600. Our battalion moved out, Easy Company to take hill 600 as soon as possible.

I picked up a mortar observer and a platoon of machine guns from Company H, as well as a forward observer from the 245th Field Artillery. We reached the top of hill 600 with little difficulty, and from there had an excellent view of Mount Bagana, the active volcano. This advantageous height enabled us to see both east and west forks of the Torokina River.

Company G, under Captain Forrest Stimson, went up the east fork of the Torokina to where General Kanda was expected to cross the river. Sure enough, at about 3:30 P.M., leading Japanese scouts began crossing the river, then larger groups pressed forward.

Our artillery observer opened fire, churning the water to a froth. After a short delay, more men attempted to cross. Again the artillery blasted them. Company H mortars entered the fray, but it was almost maximum range for them.

Suddenly I got a battalion call from Stimson: "You won't believe what's coming across the river now; a Japanese is leading a white horse!"

Even without my field glasses I could see the horse in the distance, midway in the river. It was General Kanda's personal horse! I had a hard time accepting the fact that a general in any army would be so arrogant and conceited as to bring his personal mount miles and miles through dense jungle, where every bit of feed had to be hand-carried by his men. This was outrageous, a total waste of manpower. It brought to mind the wastrels of our military schools with their so-called privileges and special flunkies to wait on them.

As darkness fell an American came up our hill with a Japanese prisoner. The American told me he had spent several years in Japan and spoke the language fluently. His prisoner was supposed to show us the location of the artillery pieces on hill 1,111, and possibly talk the Japanese soldiers there into surrendering.

All that night intermittent shelling of the river crossing and nearby jungle continued. Some of the shells seemed to pass so close to the top of our hill that we could almost reach out to touch them. I asked our artillery observer about short rounds. He shrugged and shook his head: "The shells you hear are clearing us adequately."

When daylight came the remaining Japanese had evidently cleared both forks of the Torokina and were well on their way toward the East-West Trail. There was one other way to cut them off; that was to take a shortcut up Pendleton Creek, to our west. They had to cross the creek somewhere. The next afternoon Easy Company was ordered to relieve Company G and push up the creek. At this time our battalion commander was Major Bill Meline. Somehow we had lost Lieutenant Colonel Gee in the shuffle.

As we began our push up Pendleton Creek, we lost our 245 forward observer to another unit. We had our 60mm mortars, but in heavy jungle they were worthless: the shells would become armed as soon as they left the mortar tube, and explode overhead when going through any foliage. This lack of an artillery observer cost us the life of a man that day.

It drizzled steadily; everyone was wet and miserable. Those who wore glasses could barely see, as the small-billed fatigue caps were not waterproof and lenses were either constantly wet or fogged up. Steel helmets would have shed the rain, but they were not only heavy but impractical in heavy jungle. You couldn't hear well while wearing them, and your life often depended on your hearing.

By 2 P.M. we found the SBD airplane that had crashed just days ago. It had burned, although the tail surfaces and cockpit were intact. The horizontal stabilizer was riddled with .50-caliber-bullet holes. The pilot was missing, having probably bailed out at such a low altitude that his chute failed to open. His passenger had burned in the rear seat with the aircraft. His body had shielded his partially burned billfold, which was in his rear pocket. It contained his name and address, a $2 American bill and a $2 Canadian bill. His home address was Bismarck, North Dakota.

When this information was passed to the men, one of them stepped forward. "He lives just across the street from me. I didn't know he was on Bougainville!"

After bagging up the remains of the man I radioed back information about him, and serial numbers of the aircraft.

Pushing on in the rain, our lead scout received Japanese fire at 4 P.M. The trail there was very narrow with a gentle bend. Upon being shot at and missed, our man retreated some thirty feet. I spoke to him, asking if he could again get near the position where he was fired upon. I wanted to set up a base of fire and flank the trail block. I told him specifically to stay off the trail and not take chances. He said, "Okay, but take my pack so I won't be encumbered." I took his pack.

If I'd had artillery support I would have backed off 150 to 200 yards and called for concentrated fire. Here, as in many other places, our mortars were useless. This was heavy jungle, difficult to penetrate.

Turning, the scout went around the corner of the trail standing upright, while I implored, "Get down! Get down! Get off the trail and crawl!" There was a single shot, dropping him in the center of the trail.

Sergeant Jacobson ran forward to recover him just as a heavy machine gun opened up, the bullets throwing mud in our faces. Jacobson ran back, hopping on one foot; a machine-gun bullet had penetrated his shoe and cut around the inside of his heel. The bullet stuck there was hot!

The machine gun fired more bursts, which struck in the mud all around us. My radio operator, Private Amore, fearing for the safety of his new 300 radio, shouted to me, "What will I do with my radio?"

I lost my temper. "Get your damn head behind it! Maybe it will save your life!"

We were in a poor place for maneuvering. The creek was on our right and the jungle to our left was nearly impenetrable. As darkness descended, the rain continued. There was only one alternative, we moved 350 yards back to the crashed-airplane site to bivouac for the night.

I awoke about midnight, frustrated and shivering, worried about the next day. I determined to cross the creek and bypass the trail block if possible. Wet and cold, I moved clothes and all into Pendleton Creek, the water of which was almost

95 degrees. (It came from a hot spring of volcanic origin west of the active volcano Mount Bagana.) Finally warm at last, I stepped out to roll up in a soaking-wet blanket and managed a little more sleep.

At dawn I crossed two platoons to the opposite side of the creek and advanced upstream, hitting Japanese about a mile farther on, just as they were setting up an ambush. Lieutenant Charles Ross's men killed the machine-gunner.

We approached the machine-gun position cautiously, knowing there were other enemy nearby. Upon our advance we found a noose of vines that told us someone had tried to snag and pull the gunner from the trail.

Finally in contact with Third Platoon, under Lieutenant Pete Sherar, across the creek, we found they had recovered our dead man, and that the Japanese contingent had hastily abandoned their trail block. This must have happened when they heard our firing upstream, on the opposite side of the river. Their block had been well dug in, with a circular defense of about ten to twenty men. Our artillery would have been the answer.

It was overcast, still drizzling steadily when darkness came. Moving inland a couple hundred feet, I set up a perimeter defense for the night. On the edge of this line I began cutting the tall, wet grass to eliminate the usual chiggers. Someone walking by stopped to ask, "What are those two men doing over there?" He pointed to a low spot below me, perhaps twenty-five feet away, covered with tall grass. I glanced over and saw nothing. "Oh, Roush has probably put out an outpost." The man nodded and continued on.

Moments later another man stopped. "Who are those two men over there in the grass?" This time I stood up, but still could not see the two men. They must have ducked down. I said, "Get Sergeant Kerbaugh, be quick!"

In seconds Kerbaugh was there, and aiming a bit to my right, opened fire with his Thompson.

Grabbing my rifle I ran parallel to the grass to cut off the two men I now knew were Japanese. Charles Ross followed me. Crouching, I could see a man's hands through the leaves, about fifty feet from me. He looked to be holding the breach of his rifle. Hesitating for a sure shot, I heard his rifle bolt click—only it wasn't his rifle bolt. He had popped a grenade and tossed it in the vicinity of Kerbaugh. When it exploded Ross and I could hear men shouting. Just as Ross stood upright to check his men, another grenade exploded in the same location. Ross got a fragment in his leg.

That smart Japanese had popped a second grenade under cover of the first explosion. It was a new lesson for me.

We failed to find the bodies of either Japanese, but did recover a rifle dropped by one; evidently he was wounded. It was a short carbine type I had never seen before, with a nine-inch, triangular bayonet that folded under the barrel.

Recovering my pack, I found one of the grenades had landed alongside it. The blade of my prized knife had been blown from the handle; my pack, blanket, and poncho were shredded.

All said, it was a disappointing patrol, ending after seven days of rain. Ten men were slightly wounded by grenades and rifle fire, and one man was lost. For a month I was teased unmercifully about bedding down next to the Japanese.

Upon an examination of the damage done to our supply tent during the shelling by the Japanese 150mm gun, it was discovered that our ten new sniper rifles were totally destroyed. However, our supply sergeant, John Wells, had stored the ten scopes in a .50-caliber-ammunition box. They were safe, but there was a problem: they were Weaver 330, three-power scopes. How some high ordnance officer had authorized the purchase of these told of his ignorance. In addition, the so-called sniper rifles that had been destroyed were 1903-A1s. Some had only two lands and grooves cut in them; to any good rifleman, they were junk.

The mounts on the damaged rifles were fine, so we removed them, traveling to the Seabees to have them welded on to M1 rifles. They were secured on the left side and zeroed for three hundred yards. A bullet drifts to the right in a barrel with a right-hand twist, lands, and grooves. This was partly compensated by the left-side mount of the scope.

Lieutenant Sherar found that we could order training equipment through a branch of the Special Services, so we ordered a public address system with two speakers. It operated on either six- or 110-volt current and had a phonograph. We received it in about three weeks, resulting in the men writing home for phonograph records. They vied for its use every evening. Glenn Miller was the favorite.

I was surprised one afternoon when an officer of the Navy presented himself at my tent. It was Bill Guy, an SAE fraternity brother. We both had lived at the frat house in Fargo (prewar) while attending the state college. He looked at me with a mischievous grin. "How did you get to be a captain when I'm only a lieutenant junior grade?"

I gave him my stock answer. "Heck, Bill, they had to promote me, everyone else was killed. Say, what is a Navy officer doing running loose?"

"I'm off the destroyer *Porter*. She left me ashore, took off with the fleet during an air raid. They'll be back to pick me up."

He expressed an interest in our patrol work, wanting to know more about the jungle, so I took him in a jeep across the Torokina River. Climbing up the far side, there was a snow-white Japanese skull on a post, equipped with a helmet tipped at a jaunty angle.

Bill was a bit shocked, saying, "My God! What's that?"

I laughed. "Why, that's a good Japanese soldier."

Since the regimental headquarters company was originally from Fargo, North Dakota, Bill had many friends there. He expressed an interest in visiting them, so I dropped him off. After the war he became the governor of North Dakota, serving twelve years. Quite adequately, I must say.

Shortly after the battle for hill 260, our battalion commander called the company commanders and his staff together. We were going on some sort of orientation trip. To our surprise we crossed the Torokina River on foot, moving west a quarter mile or so. Stopping there, we were to hear his words of wisdom. This was a man who had absolutely no personal experience with Japanese soldiers.

To make matters worse, just two days prior to this outing, a company from our battalion had crossed the river, running into a major firefight. They had an officer killed. We were all antsy, knowing this was an unhealthy place to be. It made no sense. Was this man trying to show his bravado? To me, it was a grand show of stupidity. You just didn't cross the Torokina with only your battalion staff. There were lots of enemy still active in the area.

On another occasion the same gentleman had decided we needed night training. My company was ordered to go out from the frontlines along the jungle trail to hill 250, then proceed downstream to the junction of the 164th Infantry and 182nd Infantry intersection. Finally we were to proceed back into the perimeter. This was on a totally moonless night, dark as pitch.

Leading off, holding to one another's jackets, we made it to the bottom of hill 250. Stopping there, we took a break of perhaps fifteen minutes. Proceeding downriver, we kept to the trail on the bluff, rather than walking along the riverbed. Finally we arrived back at the perimeter at about 4 A.M.

That morning I was told one of my men had found a Japanese pistol while on the night maneuver. I was curious: Just how did one find an enemy pistol in the dark?

Upon speaking with the man, he said, "When we took the break at the bottom of hill 250, I sat down on a lump. It was then I discovered I was sitting on a pistol."

I asked, "What condition was it in? Was it rusty?"

"Spotless! Here, I'll show you." It was indeed!

I knew then that we had been close to trouble. We had no doubt interrupted a small party of Japanese that were disconcerted by our large numbers. How the pistol was dropped is conjecture, but you didn't find clean, spotless Nambu pistols everywhere.

Another first hit our company. Sergeant Carmichael was bitten by a poisonous centipede. It had climbed into the blankets on his cot. His ankle swelled immensely, and the pain was terrific. After his recovery the skin of his foot peeled like a bad case of sunburn.

CHAPTER 13

In July 1944, several of the men expressed an interest in firing the so-called Japanese knee mortar. As we had acquired these weapons and much ammunition on various occasions, we decided to try it out in the open area of the Torokina River, just below the forks. This Japanese Model 89 grenade launcher, 50mm, was never designed to use on the knee. The recoil would instantly break your leg.

It was a simple weapon, a tube with rifling, the range depending upon the angle it was held and the amount of barrel used. The firing pin actuated up and down in the tube, with ranges indicated on the outside. The farther down the barrel the firing pin was lowered on the Acme threads, the longer the range, and vice versa.

The 50mm grenade itself was approximately six inches in length, rounded on top with a flat base. The discharge primer was in the center of the base with surrounding discharge holes to propel the grenade into the air. At the time of discharge, a copper band near the base of the shell expanded to firmly grip the lands and grooves in the mortar, giving it longitudinal spin for stability. Small holes under the copper ring allowed the propelling gas to expand the ring when the missile was fired.

The nose detonator of the round was protected by a safety, pull-type split pin; the detonator was easily removed by unscrewing it in the opposite direction of the rifling in the tube.

We fired the first of several rounds without nose detonators and found the small, so-called mortar a handy-dandy weapon. It was quick, easily portable, and effective. It weighed only ten pounds. It was a simple, foolproof, deadly weapon. I often wondered why the Japanese didn't use it more effectively; perhaps they had insufficient grenades.

We all agreed that we needed such a weapon, but it wasn't until months later that our 60mm mortars were equipped with a trigger base. That new base was an improvement; still, you had to be fully exposed to fire the weapon. The Model 89 could be fired from any position: foxhole, direct fire, or even from a tree.

Walking the trail along the fork of the Torokina, I chanced upon a 50mm dud projectile. Deeming it harmless, I casually picked it up and tossed it into the nearby water. An explosion came that nearly bowled me over. It taught me a valuable lesson. Don't touch a dud shell! Evidently the detonator struck a rock in the bottom of the stream.

Some time later the men found a dud 105mm shell (ours) in our bivouac area. When I called bomb disposal, an officer, a Native American, arrived. He looked at the shell, then whistled. "Stay away, I'll have to put a charge on it. One-oh-five duds are deadly; it's a good thing no one tried to pick it up!"

Looking in the rear of his truck, I was shocked. There on an old wool blanket lay several artillery 150mm projectiles and Japanese bombs; they were rolling loosely in the pickup box. This guy lived mighty dangerously!

It reminded me of a Japanese bombing raid near the Lunga River on Guadalcanal. A large bomb had fallen next to the tent of several officers, driving deep into the ground. Fortunately the bomb had failed to explode. A bomb disposal crew had dug very deep in the ground to recover it. The crew chief had cheerily told the tentmates, "You guys are lucky! This is the first dud of this type we've ever recovered!" The fortunes of war: Win some, lose some!

While on Bougainville we were subjected to an earthquake every couple of months. The ground would move in a slow, undulating motion, causing pots and pans in the kitchen to fall to the ground. This usually lasted from five to as many as twenty seconds.

On one patrol up the Crown Prince Range, the rocks began to tremble. Although we could see no movement, the mountain groaned and grated as massive shifts were made. The sounds were much like those from that old radio show "Inner Sanctum." Quite eerie!

It soon became apparent that each company would be subjected to a ten-day patrol each month. Our 164th Regiment, and no doubt the 182nd, began exploring the East-West Trail, pushing the remaining Japanese west, bit by bit.

Often during the slack periods, between these long range patrols along the Crown Prince Range, we made short forays. It was on one of these jaunts that we patrolled up the west fork of the Torokina River to the base of the active volcano, Mount Bagana.

I managed a J3 airplane ride. This was purely a pleasure flight. The pilot took me over the edge of Mount Bagana at eight thousand feet to show me the litter of boulders in the central cone, which was about three hundred yards across. From ground level at the perimeter line, the volcano looked pointed, with no indication of a crater.

At one time during a recent earthquake, Bagana had mildly blown its top. Several of us had watched black specks high amid the clouds of steam. My pilot informed me that those black specks I saw were rocks the size of automobiles tossed in the air by the steam pressure. I believed him.

Our patrol to Bagana was uneventful; we saw no signs of movement in the area. Coming down the west side of the slanting plateau, we came across an area littered with monstrous boulders, perhaps eight to twelve feet in diameter. They had evidently been spewed from the volcano during previous massive eruptions. It was then someone shouted, "Hey! There goes a native!"

We had always endeavored to bring locals into the ANGAU (Australia, New Guinea, Auxiliary Unit) compound run by the Australians. They pacified and fed these people talking them out of their most deadly weapon—that bow with long arrows. But what arrows! They were about three and a half feet in length with many thorns extending back about ten inches from the poisoned tip. The poison looked much like the luminous paint on old alarm clocks. Once the arrow was inside a person, it was impossible to extract.

I had two sets of bows and arrows lent to me by a friend, Warrant Officer Bruce Watterson, of the Australian Army. He was one of the ANGAU bosses. He wanted $25 for each set, and foolishly, I failed to buy one. I didn't think it would arrive at home, that some SOB would steal it, as so often happened to anything sent back to the States.

We hunted high and low for that native, knowing he was within a forty-acre spread. He was never found; he probably hid under a massive boulder and covered himself with smaller rocks.

Just as we reached the forks of the Torokina River on our return trip, we did meet two native male adults with a small boy, perhaps ten years of age. They made no effort to escape us and appeared friendly. The boy carried their fire, a small woven basket that held a burning material. While I endeavored to speak with the two men, one stripped a piece of bark from a rotting tree. There exposed to sight were several large, white, fuzzy grubs. Stuffing a handful into his mouth, the grubs squirmed in his lips. They must have tasted good as he licked the remains away with a smile. I watched, fascinated.

I found they were working for ANGAU, trying to get other natives to come into the compound.

Proceeding downriver to the 182nd sector, we found no sign of enemy in the area. It appeared that the Torokina River was finally free of Japanese.

Earlier, in May, we had received another new officer, Lieutenant Milton Shedd. This put us in officer overstrength, but Lieutenant Sherar was unavailable to us, being on special duty, managing the division boxing team and Special Services. Milt mixed well with the officers and was well liked by his platoon. When we officers matched off in the evenings, putting on boxing gloves, I rued the solid punches Milt handed out.

The following is from Lieutenant Milton Shedd's letters, sent to his wife after he was assigned to Easy Company in 1944.

It never ceases to amaze me how much is done to make things comfortable out here for the fighting men. If the Japanese knew how high our standard of living is, I'm sure they'd throw up their hands in disbelief and then in amazement. What's the use of all this? Tojo must not be such a hot shot if he can't give us half the things the Americans have.

The weather here isn't nearly as hot and bad as I thought it would be . . . the ground is sandy and dry, although it rains almost every night . . . conventional storms. At night it is cool enough to use one wool blanket . . . must go look at a training site where we practice making an assault and mop up, following tanks. We will be firing live ammunition. After that we are going fishing. . . .

It's raining harder than I've ever seen it rain before. Our tent in this rear area is flooded . . . the water is running in streams in every direction . . . it's getting nice and cool though. We are going to the front for the night. P.S. May 24 . . . the problem ran smoothly.

It is 8 a.m. and we are waiting for class to start. Each student sits on a box containing two 4.2-inch high explosive shells weighing about 30 pounds apiece. Our lecture is on vesicant gases, mustard, lewisite, and nitrogen mustard. The area around our camp has been cleared of all vegetation except for the great massive trees which are quite numerous. These trees, mahogany, etc, for the most part have a tangled mass of roots and vines. Each tree has its own little clan of lizards which grow fat eating the local bugs.

Just finished a good dinner . . . we had fresh roast pork,

the first meat that wasn't canned since I've arrived on the island. We usually have pancakes or mush, or both for breakfast, red dog (mixture of ground up dried beef and hot dogs) for lunch and either red dog or fish for dinner. Today we had fresh celery. Every few days we get fresh greens, onions, etc. Of course, dehydrated potatoes, corn, peas and carrots are always present, as is canned fruit. It gets tiresome eating the same old thing day after day.

I've been out in the jungle for four days. I saw lots of Japanese, all dead and pretty well rotted away. I wasn't scared, but tingly, the same sensation I have when I am tracking a buck or waiting for a big goose to fly overhead.

I've been conditioning myself to become a better swimmer. Last Saturday we went swimming, the sea was rough and waves high. I could see cross-currents sweeping through the surf, but people were swimming. The rip tides were very strong and in two instances as we drove along the beach there appeared to be dark brown rivers flowing out to sea. I could not touch bottom and worse still, found myself in a current taking me out to sea. I wasn't a bit scared as I had complete confidence in my ability to get back to shore.

Suddenly I heard someone hollering for help. Another boy near me struck out for the man; he was about 25 yards away. He had a lot of guts trying to save the drowning boy as he was not a good swimmer. The drowning man climbed on top of him and down to the bottom they both went. I didn't want two drowning men on my hands, so told the other fellow to go in and send out a boat if he thought he could make it. We were about 200 yards out and the current wasn't slackening at all. I found out his name when I tried to calm him down; he was in a bad way, completely exhausted and scared.

I told him to listen to reason, asking him his name and where he was from. He said Bob, from Idaho. I told him to put his right arm around my waist and relax. I kept him afloat with his head above water until he said he was better. By this time we were now about 500 yards out and I became a little uneasy. I could see 50–100 men on shore watching, but not doing a thing. By this time the current subsided and although I was getting tired, I started dragging him slowly back toward shore. The rising swells helped a lot. We rode a few more swells together and when I saw a big wave coming, I told him we'd try to ride it in separately. I made it in about 30 yards farther than he, thinking the wave would finish me. It swirled, tumbled and dashed me madly. When it passed I could touch bottom, but I never expected to see Bob again.

There the plucky devil was, again shouting, Help! Help! Help! I got to him and it was easy from then on.

When he caught his breath he asked me who I was. I said, Lieutenant Shedd. He said, "Gosh, a lieutenant! Thanks, thanks a lot for saving my life!"

After my patrol up the Numa Numa Trail I was asked for information concerning what my battalion commander did that night (to help him get a medal!). Actually he did no more than most privates in our company, and less than any man on my patrol. I told him I had no information, very politely, referring him to other officers that were involved. The number of medals doled out to the brass is out of proportion to that given to enlisted men. The officer that called me was quite disgruntled with what he got from me.*

I will miss the gang at Easy as they are a fine bunch of men. . . . I'll miss them all, especially Lieutenant Ross.

A small problem occurred between Company F and Easy. One or two Company F men were stealing from Easy tents. Thankfully, I was informed and actually witnessed a Company F man running from one of our tents. At the time the tents were very close, almost back to back. I spoke with the captain of Company F. He couldn't see trouble coming if he had four eyes! Being raised in farm country, I knew a

---

*Note: Lieutenant Shedd became Reconnaissance Officer Shedd on September 5, 1945, when Lieutenant Pete Sherar was finally returned to his duties with Easy Company.

fence was the solution. It would be much like apron wire, stopping all running back and forth except at the open ends of the company streets. I had a five-strand barbed-wire fence built between Easy and Company F tents, and this stopped all further trouble.

In June I received orders to report to regimental headquarters; Colonel Gee wanted to see me. (He had taken over command of the regiment from Crump Garvin in April.) Evidently word of my fence had preceded me, some officers thinking me ridiculous.

Colonel Gee came right to the point. "Why did you build that fence between Company E and Company F?

I said, "Colonel, I've lived and worked on farms. We fence in bulls from the beef cows until breeding season; we fence in our horses and other farm animals, all to eliminate trouble. I spoke with the Company F captain about future trouble. He just didn't give a damn, so I took the matter in hand. There won't be any more stealing."

He looked at me thoughtfully, then asked, "How would you like to take over the Antitank Company? There seems to be little leadership there."

"No, sir! I was in that outfit once and was mighty glad to get out. I tangled with the captain, who was later reduced in grade to a first lieutenant. I got sick of drunken, misfit officers. Don't get me wrong, I like a drink, but I don't drink on duty. I want nothing to do with the Antitank Company. Easy is a top rifle company; they are great soldiers and have dedicated officers."

He gazed at me for a few moments, then said, "Okay, that's that! You may as well return to your unit."

Word that a large portion of the Japanese fleet had moved to Rabaul Harbor from their bastion at Truk brought a quick response from the fighters and bombers on Bougainville. We soon got word and watched anxiously as scores of B24, B25, F6F, Corsairs, P38s, and other aircraft made trip after trip north.

They must have gotten a hot reception, for the B24s usually left in groups of eight to ten. Many returning groups were down to four or five. We watched one returning B24 point out to sea, several men bailing out at the last moment.

Stopping by the airport that afternoon, my driver and I watched a B25 make a wheels-up emergency landing, tearing up a long strip of metal matting. The aircraft made a perfect, soft landing on its belly, then began a turning twist as it slowed on the runway. It finally stopped about a hundred yards from us, the crew exiting frantically to run from a possible explosion or fire. After running one hundred yards or so, the widely scattered crew stopped to look back. Since no fire or explosion took place, they sheepishly walked back to the aircraft to collect their gear. We didn't know if the plane had dumped its bomb load, but we could see heavy flak damage about the fuselage.

That evening, just before dark, John Gossett stopped by, saying, "Let's go over to the strip and watch them come in at dusk."

We stopped our jeep near the west (incoming) end of the active runway as several F6Fs landed, one by one. Apparently the last one to touch down had an engine failure just short of the runway. It just quit flying, dropping like a stone, crashing about two hundred yards short of the strip. It immediately burst into flames. We felt helpless, not being able to assist in any way. Ammunition in the fiery wreck began to explode as we watched. A feeling of deep depression hit me at the moment. It took some time for me to realize: That pilot was doing his job just like the rest of us. We all take our chances in war.

CHAPTER 14

As Easy was scheduled to move up the Laruma River for our next patrol, I managed to get an orientation flight with a pilot named Rosen. He wore shorts, carried no gun, and had no emergency rations in his small plane. I thought it almost foolhardy at the time and told him so. He just shrugged his shoulders and smiled. The Cub J3 strip was narrow and short, hewn from the jungle near the ocean by Seabees.

We flew up the Laruma River fifteen miles, circling over our future position on the northwest side of the river. On the return flight I spotted a narrow trail leading up a high mountain, and indicated to Rosen that I would like to look it over. Our eyes led us up to the top of the mountain, where there was a village. The several nipa huts were apparently deserted. The trail upward could easily have been defended at several points. After all, these people were headhunters and raided each other's villages. Somehow, it reminded me of my grade school books of the Greek defense at Thermopylae, or was it Troy?

The flight lasted about an hour, convincing me that fighting in the Laruma Valley would be no picnic. General Kanda had come out of this valley in his attempt to surprise the 37th Division. There was no flat territory here; everything seemed straight up and down.

Fiji's Third Battalion had moved to Bougainville shortly after the New Year. I renewed my acquaintance with George and Edward Cakobau; we soon began visiting back and forth. Whenever beer or booze was available, we shared and celebrated; I even became acclimated to their tea with lemon.

On one of my visits to the Fiji battalion I took Lieutenant Charles Ross along. He and Captain George Cakobau hit it off, immediately cooking up a plan for Charles to accompany George on the next Fijian patrol. (At the time Easy Company was recuperating after a ten-day patrol to the west.)

On June 23, while in heavy jungle, the Fijians ran into machine-gun fire from a strongly held Japanese position. Several men were wounded and the remainder pinned down. A Fijian corporal named Sukanaivalu crawled forward twice to rescue wounded, then was himself hit hard. The firing became so intense that Charles found grenades thrown by the enemy were landing behind him.

Corporal Sukanaivalu, realizing he could not be rescued, called out to his squad to abandon him. Finally, to stop further rescue attempts, he purposely rose up to take more machine-gun fire. He was posthumously awarded the first Victoria Cross to be given to a British Colonial soldier in the war. To say the least, Charles was greatly impressed with the Fiji Third Battalion.

On another occasion I was invited to George's company for an evening dinner. The aperitif was beer, lots of it, with a monstrous bowl of spicy conch chowder. George's mess sergeant was Indian, an accomplished cook. Most of his Company A men were fishermen with experience. They had made outrigger canoes immediately upon their arrival, never lacking for Neptune's bounty.

The party went on the better part of the night and finally I could barely stay awake. I finally said, "I've got to take Easy up the Laruma Valley tomorrow. We're to relieve a company of the One hundred forty-fifth Infantry."

George laughed. "Yes, and you'll sweat out all that beer on the way too! It'll be hot as hell!"

He was right. Before noon, trucks moved us to the river through the 37th Division sector. From there it was a long, fifteen-mile walk upriver under a scorching sun. We bedded down for the night on the northeast side of the river near a crew of 4.2 chemical mortars (our fire support, as we were out of range of our artillery back in the perimeter). I visited them to find they had a 300 radio on our frequency; I was also informed the mortar rounds were the equal of 105mm artillery shells. They had plenty of ammunition and assured me of immediate fire as needed.

Battalion wanted a small group for a patrol to scout up-river toward Igarue, on the Numa-Numa Trail. I picked Lieutenant Shedd for the job. He had joined Easy early in May, taking over the command of a platoon with confidence. I knew he was well liked by the men; I also knew he was exceptionally capable.

It was quiet that night. Early in the morning the remainder of the company crossed the river on a huge, slimy log easily six feet in diameter. My executive officer, Harry Mork, proceeded to fall off the log into the river, amid shouts of amusement from the men. The look of chagrin on his face as he stood in the fast-moving current, submerged to his chest, was the epitome of frustration.

Attached to me at the time was a platoon of machine guns from Company H; their commanding officer, Dick Hamer, had come along. The uphill climb to the unit we were relieving was nearly vertical, requiring the constant use of both hands. By 11 A.M. we arrived at the top of the ridge to find the unit of the 145th Infantry already descending past us. No doubt they were mighty glad to be replaced. One of their officers stopped to tell me they had lost a sergeant while trying to take the next hill; they had been unable to recover his body.

Dick Hamer and I walked the crest to determine the best locations for the machine guns. Looking across at the hill to our northeast, I figured we could take it easily by concentrating our firepower, using smoke for cover. Hopefully, we would be able to recover the 145th sergeant's body. Two men from our battalion intelligence showed up with a 20-power spotting scope. I put them both in a forward hole to look for

Japanese positions. Maxwell, one of the two men, came to me just before nightfall.

"Hey, Captain, take a look through the scope." There, well down on the forward slope of the hill, was a camouflaged position, with a log across the front. A pair of Japanese eyes could be seen under the edge of the log. He was looking directly at us, the range about two hundred yards.

Maxwell turned to me. "Can I borrow your scope rifle? I've never shot at a Japanese."

I said, "Sure, take it, but since he's on the forward slope, he's been there all day. Someone will relieve him soon."

As if on cue, a man came over the hill to exchange positions with his buddy. The man on the forward slope evidently heard his signal; deeming it dark enough to be safe, he stood up. Maxwell dropped him.

His relief panicked, running back up the hill, stopping behind a tree on the skyline. Portions of his shoulders showed on each side of the tree.

Maxwell was puzzled. "He's hiding behind the tree. What should I do?"

I laughed. "Shoot through the tree. That bullet will go through at least two feet of solid oak."

After he shot, the enemy soldier slowly crumpled in a heap at the base of the tree.

The following day was spent planning covering fire for the next noon's attack. That afternoon two more men came up the hill to our position. Each had a dog. One animal was a German shepherd, the other, a nondescript mongrel. I was informed they were messenger dogs, not trained to attack.

Shortly before our jump-off, I sent Lieutenant Charles Ross with his platoon down the left side of our peak to cross below and cut off the retreat of the Japanese when we pushed them off the hill. He was accompanied by one of the dog handlers, with his dog.

I had removed the plug from my M1 and equipped it with a conversion plug to fire smoke grenades, figuring smoke would cover our advance until we were within hand-to-hand distance. I also called the 4.2 mortars for smoke in the draw

Landing six miles north of Dumaguette, Negros

George "Dick" Hamer, standing on a new fighter with
an in-line engine, Atsugi airport, Japan

Sunken Japanese
transport,
Guadalcanal

Hamer and
Gossett beside an
antiaircraft gun,
Guadalcanal

Walker at Camp Samambula, Fiji

Walker with a 7.7mm Nambu

Dumaguette theater converted to a hospital

Dumaguette airfield, with J3 strip at an angle. This field was mined, and when a P38 pilot landed to see a buddy, his plane was destroyed.

Walker with a Japanese 150mm gun at Guadalcanal

Walker at Cape Esperance, Solomon Islands, in front of a *Kinugasa Maru* lifeboat

Philippine landscape behind Cabu City, Cabu

Air strike on Negros, inland from Dumaguette
about twelve miles

Pete Sherar, Walker, and Harry Mork at Bougainville

Dumaguette landing, Negros, south of Japanese airfield

Easy officer homes for a year in Bougainville

From the Avenging 2nd, left to right: Lt. Roush, Lt. Sherar,
Lt. Landeck, Capt. Walker, Lt. Shedd, and Lt. Ross

to our left, to conceal our advancing men. They failed to tell me they had only white phosphorous shells, no HC smoke (which is harmless. I was not to know this until after the attack was over. Two of my men received burns from the phosphorus, fortunately, not life-threatening.).

At the last moment I heard loud shouting in the rear. Anxious to jump off, I turned back to check it out. An enlisted man said loudly, "I'm not going on the attack unless an officer goes first!"

I was so disgusted I grabbed the man by his sleeve. "You and I are going to be the first men up on that hill! You're coming along with me!"

Everything went as planned. The machine guns chewed up everything until we reached the top of the opposing hill. I fired several smoke grenades as I went up the forward slope, disappointed at the little smoke they emitted.

We had competition getting to the top of the hill; it seemed everyone wanted to be the first. On the summit lay a Nambu machine gun, which I grabbed, as my M1 rifle had to be hand-operated for each shot. There were at least eight to ten full magazines lying nearby. Slipping on a clip I took several more, then ran forward about 150 feet over the ridge in order to shoot down at the adjoining saddle and lower ridge. Lieutenant Paul Clemens and seven of his men followed me.

To my sorrow I found the Nambu wouldn't fire; it had a ruptured cartridge in the chamber. Evidently its Japanese owner had not taken proper care of it. The chamber was rusted.

At that moment dust kicked up all around us. Somewhere from our front a Nambu began peppering. As we hit the deck Sergeant Victor Anderson was lucky enough to find a large hardwood stump for cover; the rest of us dropped into the best places we could find. I landed tightly locked against a newly dead Japanese soldier, my face within five inches of his open mouth. Flies were already starting to buzz in and out.

A second machine gun, this time a heavy .31 caliber, opened up. We were so pinned down we couldn't move.

When the .25 Nambu stopped for another magazine, Anderson leaned around his stump and rolled off eight rounds from his M1. Lieutenant Clemens faced downhill, his head a foot behind and above my buttocks. A tight Nambu burst punched in the dirt between his head and my rear, missing us both by inches. (Thank goodness Nambus fired a tight pattern!)

Clemens spoke up grimly. "Chuck, better keep your ass down or you'll get it shot off!" (Where does a man get a sense of humor in a situation like this?)

We were pinned for nearly ten minutes while they fired literally hundreds of rounds at us. Something had to give, and that was me.

I yelled to Anderson, who was firing intermittently as the Japanese machine-gunner changed magazines.

"I've got to make a break and get us mortar fire. Can you cover me?"

"Best you get up behind me when he finishes the next magazine."

I took off while Anderson fired rapidly, crouching tightly behind him. Tapping him on the shoulder, I said, "Okay, I'll make the break when he quits firing next time."

The Japanese was a little quicker at loading, as bullets were kicking up in front of me as I raced up the hill. Clearing the top, there sat a complacent group: my executive officer, Mork, Dick Hamer, and my radio operator. I was damn mad! I looked at Mork.

"Why in hell didn't you call for mortar fire ahead of us? You knew that was the thing to do."

All eyes turned to Corman, my radio operator. He looked guilty as hell.

"I lost the base section of the radio antenna during the attack; the radio won't work."

"Like hell it won't, where is the rest of the aerial?"

Shamefaced, he produced it.

"Give me your handkerchiefs!"

Wrapping the antenna with the handkerchiefs for insulation, I picked up the handset and held the aerial to the post.

It worked to perfection. (Thank the Lord I had been trained as a radio operator back in 1937, and knew a little.)

Within moments 4.2 mortar fire was slamming the Japanese in the saddle. The balance of my crew walked back over the hill in safety, with only one man wounded. We had no fatalities, we had been lucky. Yet one man had the stock of his Browning Automatic Rifle (BAR) shot off.

I had the second dog handler send a message to Ross, telling him to return. This dog was gone only a few minutes, then it came back, still carrying the message. Moments later the German shepherd from the patrol showed up. The dog carried a message that read: *Saw your dog, but he was timid, wouldn't come to us. What do you want? Send our dog back with the message.*

This was done, then someone suddenly said, "Hey, Cap! You've got a bullet hole in the front of your pants, right by your balls!" Sure enough, one slug had gone through while I was running up the hill. Everything must have been swinging just right!

Someone found the body of the 145th Infantry sergeant; it was sent down the mountain. Our sojourn lasted only another day; we were pulled back before we could progress farther. The walk back down the Laruma was just as tiring as the walk upstream. We found the wreck of a Cub J3 in the riverbed; it hadn't been there before. The pilot had walked away; he'd probably had an engine failure.

I learned a lesson the hard way: Don't get caught on the forward slope of a hill. It can be deadly!

CHAPTER 15

Lieutenant Milton Shedd's patrol had worked around the right flank of the enemy. Due to the rough terrain he had trouble with men who played out, having to leave five of the weakest on a ridge, a future rendezvous point. His native guide took Milt and his six remaining men close to a small village where they could hear Japanese chopping wood while shouting back and forth. His men had made a dry run of a similar situation previously, so positions were assigned and the men made their approach. One shack held three sleeping men; six were eating in front of the shack and two more were chopping wood. Other Japanese moving about brought the estimate to twenty-five total. Throwing a grenade, Milt followed it with six more. The enemy was bunched up, screaming amid the firing of Shedd's guns. A heavy Japanese machine gun opened up, but was silenced by grenades. Shedd's guide was the only man wounded, and from an American grenade. Milt moved out before losing men. By his estimate, they killed or wounded at least twenty enemy.

Here is Milt's version:

I had a severe time restriction on my mission and was about an hour short of my objective when several of my men played out. I picked five of the weakest and left them at a rendezvous point in case of trouble. Our native guide took the remaining seven of us to our objective. At the time our weapons consisted of two Browning automatic rifles, one Thompson, one carbine, three M1 rifles and 33 grenades. I was glad I ordered three grenades carried per man, but there was much dissension about it.

We rested at our hidden perimeter point so as to reach the enemy when all would be in from their search for food, and might be congregated in preparing for their evening meal. It was close to 4:00 P.M. when we commenced our stalking of them. They had lived here for months unmolested; they had no security! We could hear them chopping wood and hollering when 200–300 yards away. We approached their position on the back side, away from the main trail. I cautioned the men to be extremely quiet. A BAR and M1 covered our crossing the deep, steep gully only 70 yards from the Japanese. When nearly at the bottom I slipped on a wet clay band and landed on my rear. I sat there for what seemed like hours, but was only seconds, with my carbine trained on the facing bank above, listening, but the enemy kept right on chopping and singing. I was not only scared, but embarrassed as well. We made it up the bank which oddly enough sat about ten feet higher than the Japanese shacks.

It was quite a sensation to find yourself in a field manual situation. When I saw those enemy going about their every-day business of getting ready for supper, I felt like I did when sighting down on my first deer. I appreciated all my hunting experience and participation in organized athletics. Those past situations helped me control that runaway feeling in my stomach.

What to do? I lay and watched them for five minutes thinking about what course of action I should take. No, I didn't conscientiously make an estimation of the situation and draw up a five paragraph order. After I had looked, I made up my mind and told the men what we would do. Luckily the platoon had dry run a similar situation only a few days previous, so we were all of the same mind.

I guess under proper training conditions a man thinks in an orderly manner and he unconsciously follows a plan of systemized thinking when under stress. We were all in position to see from the reverse slope of the bank. We couldn't be seen because of the dense vegetation, but neither did we have a good field of fire. I placed my men with the right flank M1 and BAR up on the line first to cover our final approach and withdrawal in case things went wrong. The rest followed into position as soon as the two right men had moved into place. Because of obscuring vegetation the first line I formed was not adequate. We had to move farther down the forward slope to where the bank dropped away. The men moved forward individually, crawling sometimes in plain view of the enemy.

The actions of the men showed the results of good discipline and combat experience. They would do their firing only if positively detected or on my signal, which would mean the throwing of grenades. I had collected eight of them, and all during this phase of the operation held one, pin pulled, in each hand. Our final line was the ideal. We looked down onto their position with 100% visibility. I had taken 15 minutes to work up to this point and we were more than ready to start the fun, but we lay in observation for a minute or so while the men picked out their targets.

The village was situated in a clearing. The enemy was completely in the open and the farthest was only 40 yards. I could see three Japanese sleeping in shack #1. The side toward me had a large window. A group of six was eating in front of shack #2. Two more were chopping wood. Others would occasionally show themselves, moving from one hut to the other. In all, there must have been nearly 25, or the better part of a platoon. I had cautioned the men to lay their magazines in front of them where they could get at them easily. I pointed at six enemy eating, and then the three sleeping. My BAR man nodded, then grinned.

I was dumbfounded and in a trance as I sat there, realizing what we had stumbled onto and accomplished without being discovered. I threw one grenade and then the other, following these with six more. Everything happened at once. The confusion and noise was terrific. Above the sound of our firing could be heard the Japanese screaming. For better than a minute the shooting was done by us. There were only seven of us, but then an enemy machine-gun opened fire. I don't know where the first burst hit, but the second hit the bank only a few feet below us. The gun was located only 30 yards away and was silenced immediately by grenades, BAR and M1s. At this time one of my men was hit and began sobbing, but the sound stopped as he pulled himself back over the hill. It was our native guide, hit by a fragment of our own grenades.

There is no fair play in soldiering. You shoot enemy in the back without warning. You allow them no protection. What is cowardly in kid games is good tactics to a soldier.

CHAPTER 16

About this time someone in the United States smartened up, copying the Japanese Nambu light machine gun. We received bipods and shoulder stocks for our light machine guns. In addition we got new trigger bases for our 60mm mortars. This enabled us to drop a mortar shell in the tube, place the tube over a shoulder, then back the base firmly to a tree. Sighting with a small strap-on sight, the mortar could be fired by jerking on a lanyard. This gave us direct fire on known gun positions. It wasn't the best solution, but it was an improvement.

We received orders that every man must learn to swim. In Easy we had about eighteen nonswimmers. An abandoned engineer's gravel pit was selected as a pool, with a twenty-foot platform erected to simulate a ship's side. The best swimmers in Easy were selected as instructors; they completed their lessons in just over a week. Every man in the group could jump off the platform and swim across the lengthy gravel pit. As one man said to me, "All it took was confidence. I was always afraid of water!"

I was dissatisfied with our hand grenades, and after the Third Fiji Battalion left Bougainville, my source of supply for Mills bombs more or less dried up. I was fortunate to get a few grenades from ANGAU.

Obtaining open-topped steel barrels, we experimented with the grenades, first centering one in the steel barrel. It left few holes, not fragmenting small enough. The big chunks were killers, but there were too few of them. The Japanese fragmentation grenades were far superior, showing good patterns. It only takes one small piece of iron inside you to kill.

I crushed a block of TNT, powdering it to fill a U.S. grenade. Substituting a number-ten detonator for the standard one, we blew it. It was a marvel, far superior to both standard U.S. and Japanese grenades, and probably as good as the Mills. It made us all wonder, did our ordnance people back in the States experiment? Or did they just get kickbacks, plus wining and dining by the manufacturers? Our grenades were designed for WWI.

Another sore spot was lack of grease paint. Our surgeon, Nathan Somberg, handed out gentian dye that was used for staining microscope slides, as much as he had available. It worked, but faded with our excessive perspiration. Carbon black would have worked, even charcoal; mud and water were only a temporary fix.

Many times at night flares would have been useful, but the battalion never seemed to carry them. Colored smoke grenades were also in short supply, and hard to obtain. They could be used to call for emergency fire, or to mark a position.

It became obvious to the men of Easy Company that stealth and surprise were the answer to jungle combat. The means to strike at close quarters with ferocity, then escape before the enemy could react, became a hard-and-fast rule. We laughingly referred to it as: *He who fights and runs away, lives to fight another day!*

Nearly every man of our supposed 187-man company knew the others by their first name. Friendships developed. Each man knew the abilities of the other men in his squad or platoon. Knowledge of weapons was important, each squad seeking a balanced team. Each man knew his life might depend on the ability of his comrades. Men lacking in experience were taken in hand, especially in weapons training. They paired up, supporting one another, providing covering, interlocking fire. Easy soon became a team!

Standards for patrol were set, since patrols sometimes

were long, seven to ten days. Three canteens were carried, two with drinking water and one with white gas for the cook-stove. Usually every sixth man carried a small Coleman gas stove. Its supply of fuel was determined by the length of the patrol. A full belt of ammo was carried; those with M1 rifles also had one clip of tracer (red tipped), one of armor piercing (black tipped), and one of incendiary (blue tipped), each located in the back pockets of the belt. Many carried gun oil, compasses, field glasses, and an entrenching shovel or pick mattock. In addition, a jungle aid kit with salt tablets, water purification tablets, and a Carlisle (large bandage) for severe wounds were attached to the cartridge belt. The men also carried a combat knife and mosquito head net. Because of the weight of this belt, olive-drab suspenders were worn for support. The chest rings in them also supported two hand grenades. In addition to one blanket and a poncho per man in the jungle pack, the men carried their entire rations for the patrol, together with a round for the 60mm mortars. (This was not always the case, the number of mortar rounds depending upon the situation: Was artillery fire or 81mm mortar fire available?) In most cases the men carried at least seventy pounds.

On trail blocks we dug in, camouflaging our positions. Movement after dark was limited: no lights, no smoking, just quiet, patience, and the exchange of guard duty.

In addition to regular patrol equipment I usually carried a small block of TNT, along with a number-ten detonator and six inches of time fuse. For an instant foxhole, we would dig an eight-inch-deep hole with a knife, insert the TNT block with detonator and fuse attached, light the fuse, and crawl back fifteen feet or so with our heads down. We had about a twenty-second wait. The explosion would usually dig a good-size hole in most earth. The material deflected up, so we were safe. *Do not try this in gravel or rocky ground!* I demonstrated this technique several times and many men carried that small block. It was also a mighty fine fishing tool.

To a combat soldier, knowledge of explosives is a must!

Booby trap know-how is a lifesaver, but so is safety training with explosives.

In June 1944 a U.S. immigration officer showed up. He was dressed nattily in a white shirt with black tie and trousers. He was brief, to the point. "Captain, I want you to call out all the Hispanics in your company for a formation."

As it happened, we had about twelve, all excellent soldiers who took their soldiering seriously. I knew many had joined the army for the pay. Sergeant Fedje gathered them out front. Many were nervous as cats, expecting to be shipped back to the States and deported. The immigration officer smiled at them. "Since you are all soldiers in the United States Army, you are also all citizens of the United States!"

He went down the line to take the names of the grinning and happy Hispanics, their apprehension gone. He had given them their fondest wish, full citizenship in the United States.

Lieutenant Sherar came back one evening with news we could scarcely believe. He asked, "Any of you want to bed an Army nurse? It will cost you two hundred dollars a crack, and I'm not punning."

I questioned, "What Army nurses? There aren't any on the island."

He laughed. "But there are. They come in now with nearly every ambulance flight from the Hebrides."

This was news, but of course we had little to do with the airfield. I asked, "Do those nurses stay overnight?"

"Darned if I know, I just heard that one or two of them are putting out for cash."

It was nearly a month later when Sherar managed to get a copy of the "Stars and Stripes" Army newsletter. It was the first issue I'd ever seen; he'd picked this up at Americal division headquarters.

Now it was official—two Army nurses stationed on New Hebrides were charged. One had sent home nearly $50,000 in money orders, the other, about half that amount. Talk about business acumen!

CHAPTER 17

Our many contacts with the enemy on patrols paid off in experience. We were improving our killing tactics without serious loss to ourselves. In late summer of 1944 Easy Company was ordered out to X block, about thirty miles west of the Torokina River. We were to patrol vigorously for the enemy.

I was fortunate to get the aid of Warrant Officer Bruce Watterson, from ANGAU, with four of his New Guinea police boys to assist.

By this time engineers had built a road across the Torokina, terminating at the former position of a Japanese 150mm gun, about five miles to the west.

Bruce was a tall, thin, ruddy-faced Australian who had been a plantation manager in the Lae, Salamau area of New Guinea. He explained that the natives there raided one another's villages periodically for women and other gain (they were so-called headhunters). The Australian government attempted to stop these depredations by forming groups of local military police. Bruce's men spoke only pidgin English, with expressions such as: "Two fella ten, three men across river." This translated to a total of twenty-three enemy, doubling the ten by two and adding the three.

I never became proficient speaking with his men, but I knew they understood what I wanted them to do. They were indoctrinated to hate the enemy, and were sometimes a bit too bloodthirsty for my taste.

• • •

Moving on foot from our truck drop, we traveled four or five miles west before we came to a steep, smooth rock coated with a slippery mold. At its base lay General Kanda's horse. It was no longer white in color, but had turned a light brown, almost a sorrel. Every rib could be seen; the poor animal must have starved to death.

Pressing farther on, we approached a perfect spot for an ambush. This setup had been bypassed by our most recent patrols, but it had been used to good effect by the Japanese on Company I, Third Battalion, not long ago. Our men had been killed, including the battalion surgeon.

We had gotten off to a late start that day, so bivouacked a few miles short of X block. About 11 P.M. that night I heard a man begin screaming; it was Sergeant Jacobson's younger brother. He had been bitten in the shoulder by a centipede. These six-to-ten-inch-long many-legged critters can move as fast as a rat, and inject a poison through two protruding horns that is instantly, terribly painful. To quiet him until morning, morphine had to be administered. When daylight arrived he was sent back to the perimeter, escorted by two men.

The company holding X block left immediately upon our arrival. I was surprised to find an EE8 telephone line had been run to the high ridge—it was operable. I had seen the line along the trail, but had figured it unusable since it lay in water and mud. Not knowing of this phone line in advance, I had placed two 300 radios and spare batteries with three-men crews on mountaintops we had bypassed, to relay messages back and forth. They were to operate on even hours for contact.

Our 300 radios had, so to speak, line-of-sight capability. In thick jungle they were only good for one to three miles, but from one mountaintop to another, with no foliage or cliffs between, would transmit and receive ten miles or more.

Bruce was an able scrounger and had the ANGAU facilities at his beck and call. He phoned back to a friend, arranging for extra rations, an ax, and other materials, all to be brought up by native carriers organized by the ANGAU group.

The carrying party of over fifty natives arrived two days later. One of the natives approached Bruce with a tin container. Bruce removed the lid and grinned, then held out the can to me. Inside were six eggs.

"We'll eat a high-on-the-hog breakfast tomorrow morning! We've a can of bacon, also that pancake flour you chaps carry."

He put several natives to work making a nipa hut for us. Two days later we had a well-built ten-by-fifteen-foot shelter with windows to the south, completely rainproof, all made from sago palm leaves and bamboo framing.

I noticed two of his police boys were missing. He had sent them out to scout for Japanese farther to the west. He was jocular about it. "They'll be back in a day or two. If there are Japanese nearby, we'll know just how to hit them."

We discussed air supply drops, using our artillery J3 Piper Cubs (also called L4s). When I called back on the phone to the artillery headquarters, the pilot wanted to know how to find us. He said, "It's all mountains and jungle, I'll never spot you." Bruce spoke up. "Tell him we'll cut a clearing on the ridge."

He put a native crew cutting huge trees to clear an open spot. We got the first drop on the fourth afternoon, but it was badly damaged when it hit the ground. The padding was not adequate. A later drop was more successful.

Bruce's scouts returned the fifth morning. I listened as he spoke with them, noting the sudden smile on his face.

"Charley, the Japanese have a trail block about six or seven miles to our west. Evidently they feel secure, as some of the enemy went higher up the mountain range to cut palm centers for eating. My men could hear the machete strokes. They say we can intersect the trail they're taking, then break into their camp from the side door." He looked up to the sky. It was beginning to rain; it had been a dour, disheartening day.

"It will be a tough climb in this weather. What do you think—leave now or in the morning?" He looked at me questioningly.

"Let's go now, but we'll have to wait until near dark to tap that upper trail. We sure don't want to meet any Japanese returning to their camp."

Gathering the officers, I told them the plan. Within a half hour we headed out to the west. The trail was typical jungle: mud, roots to trip over, and constant rain. Several miles out the scouts stopped; a confab was held with Bruce. He turned to me. "It's a hellish climb up to that upper Japanese trail. It's nearly straight up, slippery as hell."

I knew the men were soaked and would soon get cold at this altitude. "Let's get at it; at least we'll keep warm until we bed down tonight. We'll sleep just above the enemy when we reach the trail."

Climbing the almost vertical rock wall in constant rain was difficult. Men occasionally slid back as much as twenty feet, but there was no bitching—only silence, with sharp whispered quips exchanged back and forth. We reached the trail between the Japanese and their meager food supply just before complete darkness. From the fresh tracks being washed from the muddy path, we knew the Japanese had already returned downhill to their camp.

Bruce and I discussed grabbing a prisoner as they came up the trail in the morning, but decided against it. He said, "My boys won't take prisoners, they only want to kill Japanese."

I agreed with him, knowing the enemy executed every American they captured. Cautiously I led the way downhill, wanting to be fairly close to the trail block, no farther than 150 yards if possible. I doubted they would be active since the heavy drizzle persisted. (From past experience our men wearing glasses had waterproofed the fronts of their caps with candle wax.)

Sleeping conditions that night were deplorable, but exhaustion helped. Also, we had two hours on guard and two hours off. By this time Easy soldiers were experienced and tough fighters. There was strict discipline; not a sound was heard, everyone tense with expectation. I was mighty proud of the men. They were aggressive, a team.

Before leading out the next morning I had a 60mm mortar

crew go back up the trail with instructions to fire a few rounds just below the enemy camp as soon as we opened fire. This would put an additional fear in the Japanese, I hoped.

Bruce suggested I send one of his police boys along with a squad down the hill to our west, to seal the outlet trail there. Unfortunately, when the shooting started, the young policeman, not wanting to miss the firefight, forgot his mission and led the group into the scrap. The escape trail was not blocked.

Bruce and I led off; we hadn't gone one hundred yards when around a bend in the trail we saw a Japanese soldier standing by a tent. He had his back to us while he spoke with his buddies inside. We could hear them talking. He wasn't thirty feet from us, hunched over against the steady downpour of rain. I believe we could have walked up and touched his shoulder, our steps on the soggy trail were so quiet.

I motioned a BAR man up alongside us just before Bruce and I each tossed a Mills bomb into the tent opening. We dropped flat until they went off, then the BAR man poured twenty rounds into it.

A mass charge was made down the hill by the entire company. So many grenades were thrown that I worried about our own men being wounded. Two or three Japanese did escape to the west, at least one of whom was wounded.

I stopped alongside an enemy soldier I thought dead, going through his pockets with my knife. He suddenly rolled over to face me, a grenade in his hand, his arm extended. Startled, I reacted, killing him. It was unnecessary, for he had nothing solid upon which to pop the primer on his grenade: the ground was all soft mud. Whether he had fallen and knocked himself out, or was sleeping, or even playing possum, is conjecture. He had not been wounded.

We knew our reconnaissance platoon from Second Battalion, under Lieutenant Buie, could possibly be in the area ahead of us. (They had taken a side trail.) Lamentably, the Japanese had cut off the main trail just 150 yards short of Buie's patrol, crossing the river to the west.

We found Buie's reconnaissance unit well concealed, but

disappointed, ready to ambush the enemy as they retreated from us. We crossed the river to further check the Japanese, and found the trail split just on the west side of the stream, the northeast trail leading to the coast at Kieta (about fifteen miles) and the southwest trail (our escaping Japanese) leading to the ocean on the opposite side of the island.

On the way back to X block early in the afternoon, we stopped to search the bodies we had left. I found a clean sock filled with garlip nuts, all shelled. They looked like almonds and were delicious, growing on the trees here and there in the mountainous region. They were difficult to shell, but the work had already been done for me. I shared.

On the way I spotted a lone mountain apple. It was the size of a peach. Bruce clued me in on what was edible in the jungle. Sago palm was not only excellent for building nipa huts, it was porous in nature, honeycombed with a gummy material that looked like yellow sugar. If you boiled pieces of the wood, the sugary substance dissolved, and after boiling off the water, you had a material much like candy. And of course Bruce recommended the grubs, saying they were nutritious. A case of mind over matter.

Arriving back at X block, the men were bedraggled and worn. I was forced to lay down the law about swimming in the river below the block. Our men were always to swim upstream of the natives who were constantly bathing in the river. The reason: the natives thought nothing of defecating in the water, thus transmitting their diseases downstream. Many of the natives were infected with amoebic dysentery, to which they had a certain tolerance. Our men would eventually die from it, unless treated. About ten days later, approximately five Easy men came down with the parasite. Everyone in the company was forced to crap in a paper cup for microscopic examination of their feces. One or two of the men admitted they had broken the rule, for which they suffered the consequences—massive doses of chemicals injected deep into their buttocks with hypo needles nearly three inches in length.

CHAPTER 18

On the seventh day on X block, Bruce sent out one of his policemen, Constable Saga, with another man to see how far the Japanese had moved. On the morning we were to be relieved, they returned, saying twenty-five Japanese lived in a village just fifteen miles or so southwest of us.

I called regimental headquarters asking for permission to stay out with eighteen or so volunteers. The okay came, but I was to send the remainder of the company back to the perimeter.

Bruce and I left the next morning at daylight, headed for the Japanese camp. My supply sergeant, John Wells, was one of the volunteers; he had never been on a patrol while in Bougainville. I took along two mortarmen with a trigger mortar, and eighteen rounds of ammunition.

It was still daylight when we reached the Japanese camp, located on the west side of a fast, noisy mountain stream. Bruce's men had miscalculated: there were at least forty-five enemy in this village, not twenty-five. I said to Bruce, "Ask Saga if they have any guards posted. If so, where are they?"

As Bruce and Saga conferred, Saga began to laugh. He dropped onto the ground and raised one leg to cross over the other in a carefree manner. Then he imitated a Japanese smoking a cigarette, casually removing it from his lips, and moving his hand as if to waft away the smoke. He finally got up; we were all laughing. Evidently they felt so secure their guards were not alert.

Units supposedly far from danger and not bothered become careless. Discipline becomes lax. Never lower your guard! Trouble comes when you least expect it!

Finally, Bruce, Constable Saga, and I cautiously approached the river, each holding up a giant fern in front of our face, with two leaves plucked to allow for viewing. There, on a protruding rock in the center of the stream, was a Japanese soldier sunning himself. He was stark naked, about thirty-five feet from us. Occasionally he eyed our side of the river suspiciously. I photographed him with the Signal Corps camera I carried, also the many nipa huts 100 to 150 feet away, just across the river.

We backed off after I located a position for the 60mm mortar on our side of the river. At 7 A.M. the next day the mortar crew was to open direct fire on the huts, firing as many of the eighteen rounds as possible. I left two men with grease guns (submachine gun .45 caliber, MA1) to cover them. They were not to move into position until our jump-off time in the morning.

At 6:30 A.M., under a dark overcast, we crossed the river below the Japanese, easing up the trail to the edge of the village. I wished for our entire company after finding more Japanese than we had anticipated. I knew a tight run through their camp would wipe them all out, since they were all sleeping.

After the men spread out, the first mortar shell whizzed through the trees above us—the second was also high. They failed to explode. Yelling Japanese were rousted from their beds. The remaining mortar shells were on target, destroying one nipa hut after another. Our men were all shooting. Japanese ran everywhere attempting to escape; six ran past me so fast I could see nothing but their bobbing heads. They ran smack into Wells, who was covering the escape trail with his BAR. As I knelt in firing position, a Japanese I hadn't seen ran straight at me, jumping over me as he headed west. One of Bruce's men shot him as he passed. When all the excitement was over I checked him; he couldn't have been more than twelve or thirteen years of age.

Bruce and I were about twenty feet apart when a smoking

Japanese grenade sailed through the air, landing exactly between us. I covered my head and neck with my arms as best I could, as did Bruce. It went off, neither of us getting a scratch.

I knew the exact spot from where the grenade was thrown; releasing a Mills bomb handle, I held it to the count of three before tossing it that twenty-five feet. Then I followed with the second. One of the police boys ran to the spot, then held up four fingers. He turned to me, grinning. Per our count so far, we had fourteen enemy down and no one wounded. It was time to pull out. Carrying a wounded man nearly thirty miles in mountainous jungle was something I didn't want to worry about.

Taking another escape route up a finger ridge just outside the village, we ran straight into a heavy machine gun. The enemy were just in the process of turning it around to fire downhill. It seemed they didn't want to be caught again by Americans descending into their camp from above, hence the safeguard.

Below the camp we took to the water—fast! I was the last man to cross, but then saw a man drifting by, underwater. He had lost his footing in the fast water and his BAR was dragging him down by the neck. The water was so swift, chest deep, that I was lucky to snag the sling of his gun as he went by. Poor Wells was drowning, the sling tight around his neck. With men holding to one another, we got him out, but he was almost totally done in. Finally coming to, he coughed up copious amounts of water after we put him on the sloping bank, head down, facing downhill.

We got away clean. I recommended Bruce Watterson for a Silver Star and Constable Saga for a Bronze Star. Unfortunately, division command saw it in a different light, giving each a Bronze Star.

Lieutenant Milt Shedd, with his reconnaissance platoon, spotted many Japanese located in an unidentified village downstream. Visual contact was made while reinforcements in the form of Company H were sent for. Milt said, "While I watched the Japanese swimming, I wrote a letter to my wife."

This is Lieutenant Shedd's version of his attack:

I called for reinforcements as my group was too small to take on such a large group of Japanese. We attacked at daylight; each man knew exactly what he was to do; everything ran smoothly. We caught them by surprise and moved in on them before they could get to their weapons. We captured and destroyed machine guns, mortars, rifles, carbines, pistols, quantities of food, ammunition and clothing. The radios were the most valuable items.

We ran across this bunch just in time. They were packed up ready to move. I found their order from their Regimental C.O. I saw it translated; it was an order to die. It directed that every man in the entire group must die in order to abolish the disgrace incurred when this group had 14 men killed and then retreated (an unforgivable sin in the Japanese Army) when many of the men were too sick to fight. The former C.O. had written a message stating that he did not want the men to disgrace themselves further, so he committed suicide in order to bolster their morale. (His own words.) The Regimental C.O. directed that every man would assault even though if naked.

I held these documents in my hands. I took them from a dead officer's body.*

Later Milt Shedd commented on his move up to regimental headquarters after being named reconnaissance officer:

Tonight we had steaks and french fries—a good meal. I also had steaks for lunch. We have had more fresh meat lately than is enjoyable. I like my new job very much. The work is better than what I did as a platoon leader, however, I liked the officers of Company E and miss them.

---

*Author's note: This seems to substantiate my thought that this was part of the same group of enemy we hit, as we had killed fourteen.

The officers that I am around now are not here because they are good men—good soldiers or efficient workers—but rather because they are smoothies and backslappers.

I subordinate myself to them and inflate their egos, so I get along fine. *But,* I don't respect all the people I come in contact with. Being a man quick to notice discrepancies, *I have much unpleasant food for thought.**

Returning to X block we spent the night. In the early morning I told the patrol to take their time getting back to the perimeter, but Bruce and I set a grueling pace, arriving at our rear area by 3 P.M.

---

*Author's note: This surplus of steaks never reached down to our battalion or company, showing that the gravy train stopped at the top, with the non-combatants. The staff naturally kept the best for themselves.

CHAPTER 19

That evening, First Sergeant Joel Fedje informed me that we had been issued ten cans of beer per man. He wanted to know how many he should release to the men after retreat. Knowing what they had been through, without having a man wounded, I said, "Give it all to them, they deserve it!"

I hadn't given a thought to those men who didn't drink; they either sold their beer or gave it away. As the result, some of the company got mighty rowdy. Noncoms did their best to keep down the noise, but it was like trying to stop a runaway train. I was called on the carpet and given hell by the battalion commander. He said I should have known better. I shrugged it off, knowing the tension the men had been under. They were entitled to let off steam.

I was anxious to return the Signal Corps camera and film they had given me. I had been promised a copy of each photo for taking the camera along. When Pete Sherar returned the camera to the Signal Corps, their captain thanked him, but said, "I'm sorry, I can't give you copies—it's prohibited."

I had been double-crossed! That captain had had no intention of giving me copies of the combat photos.

Much later, when we were finally to leave the island, Sherar approached me. "Do you want to get even with that SOB?"

"Your darned right! But how are we going to swing it?"

"I'll tell him you're going on another patrol, willing to take more pictures of Japanese."

It worked. We used the camera and three rolls of film to

take pictures of the company. We also took the camera to the Philippines, where it mysteriously disappeared.

One of our own men, Corporal Tom Attardo, was a professional photographer in civilian life. He managed to take an exceptional picture of Mount Bagana, the active volcano to our north. He sold copies, and had them delivered in the States, for $5 each. His letters were voluminous, consisting of names and addresses of those to whom he had sold a picture. On our fifth war bond drive he won a $100 war bond for purchasing the most war bonds. Such ingenuity received an ample reward!

Somehow, somewhere, we had picked up a Big Twin Johnson outboard motor. Paul Clemens also liberated a brand-new four-cylinder Evinrude from the Navy. We soon located an engineer assault boat with a capacity of ten men. This opened the way to deep-sea fishing.

On Guadalcanal, mullet schooled close to shore, easy to get with explosives. On Bougainville, the giant, rolling surf precluded that. Paul got the idea of tying together ten camouflage nets, making a hundred-foot-long seine with 105mm nose plugs for weight on the bottom edge, and flotation bladders attached to the upper edge. With a hundred-foot rope on each end, our boat hauled it straight out into the ocean, turning back in a U-shaped sweep; coming close to shore they tossed the rope to a crew there. When the net was retrieved it held many kingfish. Sometimes it was a slow process due to rough surf, but it often fed the entire company.

The tide was high at times with a strong undertow. I saw a man swept out to sea, finally disappearing. Even with the risk, men body-surfed, some using mattress covers as surfboards.

Pete Sherar, through his Seabee connections, got several of us a Sunday fishing trip on a Higgins boat. Not many fish were caught, but countless bottles of beer were consumed.

The entire division participated in the fifth war bond drive. Easy raised $36,000, which I was antsy to put in the finance officer's coffers. The reason: During the war bond drive an officer from the First Battalion had collected cash and had left it in his tent. It was stolen and never recovered. He was forced to repay that money.

A good friend of mine, Colonel Mathewson, an Australian with the 132nd Infantry, invited me to accompany him to watch a tank attack in the jungle, near the ocean. I was to meet him at 8 A.M. the following morning.

Previously, I had called the finance officer to get an appointment. His return call came early that same morning: "Bring in your war bond money."

At the finance office they counted, counted, and recounted the huge pile of one-, five-, ten-, and twenty-dollar bills, each time getting a different total. I was anxious to get away, but couldn't. At 11 A.M. a message rippled through division headquarters: Colonel Mathewson, the executive officer of the 132nd Infantry, and two or three others had been killed by a Nambu machine gun the tanks had bypassed. I had lucked out again!

While waiting impatiently at division headquarters I saw a bulletin board near the G-1 tent. It read: *Colonel No-Good and General Nuisance, are each awarded the Silver Star Medal for outstanding bravery, risking their lives along the front lines.* (After the fighting on hill 260 and the attack on the 37th Division many months earlier, there wasn't a Japanese near any of our frontlines.)

You never saw these general orders posted at our regimental or battalion headquarters, only on the division bulletin board outside the G-1 tent. The commanding general of a division was empowered to award the Silver Star for bravery, but also cheapen this coveted medal by passing it out freely to the high brass. I saw it happen again and again. GIs worked under deplorable conditions, risking life and limb, while graduates of the great school along the Hudson padded their fruitcake chests.

I was also late for the battalion meeting, and was panned by the colonel. He asked me the reason. I said, "I delivered thirty-six thousand dollars to the finance office and they mulled over it for three hours."

He persisted, "Why did it take them so long?"

What I had seen on the bulletin board still rankled me. I replied, "The officer who counted the money must have been a West Pointer." So I buried myself a little deeper.

One evening, just at dusk, I observed something huge crawling toward a bulldozed pile of trees. Engineers had cleared much of the area between our company and the AA unit for a ball diamond. It was into this extensive pile of trees the creature tunneled. It was not a crocodile or alligator, but it was just as large. Its tail was six to eight feet long; dark-colored, it looked to have a smooth skin, not like the bumpy back of a croc or gator. I went over to where it had crawled under the trees and saw large claw prints. It had to be a giant monitor lizard, perhaps what they called a Komodo dragon. However, I wasn't aware that any Komodos existed on Bougainville; weren't they in the Indonesia area?

Another prevalent animal was the kinkajou, a species of the raccoon family, normally native to South America. About the size of a cat, it had fairly short, firm hair, and was a great climber, eating fruit and blossoms. During periods of tension at night, its rustling high in the overhanging trees caused apprehension among the men.

As we were preparing for the invasion of the Philippines, the Australian Home Guard was brought to Bougainville to relieve us. It seems that country had two armies: the volunteers who fought overseas, such as at Anzio, and the volunteers who were not to be shipped out of the country. These Home Guard troops were not happy about being shipped to Bougainville; in fact, they were mighty grim about it.

We Easy officers were invited to visit an Australian unit after a brief acquaintance. By midnight we were all home again, but with three Aussies who promptly decided to sleep on our floor. When I woke up on Saturday morning to take reveille formation, the Aussies were still sleeping.

After our formation, while awaiting breakfast, I heard a

shot fired just past the mess tent. Crossing the road I met a man midway along the company street. He was holding his bleeding arm. I said, "Get to the battalion surgeon."

Backtracking, I found that a medic attached to our company had fired the shot. After the inspection he had placed a loaded clip in his carbine, and without thinking, slid the bolt home. (It had been open for inspection.) Holding his carbine at hip level, he'd stupidly pulled the trigger. At the time it seemed an accident without serious consequences.

Minutes later I heard yelling farther up the company street, on the opposite side. Upon checking, I found that an Easy man who had just returned from the hospital (he had prior wounds) was dead. The bullet had passed to the opposite side of the company street from where it was fired, passed through a man's arm, then struck a glancing blow on a fragile orange crate used to hold clothing. A shallow groove was cut in the thin board, the bullet striking it at a slight angle. It ricocheted from this springy board, crossed back to the other side of the street, entering the second man's temple.

I sent the medic to battalion, where he was moved farther on. I constantly stressed gun safety, but sometimes you are powerless to control the whims of men. In our entire year on Bougainville, we lost only two men, but we killed well over eighty-five enemy while on patrol. We shouldn't have lost either of those two men. Stupid things did happen!

When a man was wounded, another stepped into his place. We recovered every man we lost, making sure they were turned over to Graves Registration. Our wounded received the best care possible, even under pressing circumstances.

Lieutenant Charles Ross organized a tracking school that I unfortunately missed. I found it received rave reviews. He had obtained his instructors from the Third Fiji Battalion.

At one point, I was told, a man was asked to touch leaves on a vine. A Fijian was then asked to detect which one the man had touched. He picked the right vine by smelling each. It brought to mind the ANGAU police boys showing me the faint blood trail high on the leaves while patrolling on the East-West Trail, and of their pointing out the deep imprints of feet, indicating two Japanese carrying one of their own. Basics of tracking should be mandatory, if knowledgeable men can be found for teachers.

The talent among the men in Easy was amazing. We had miners, carpenters who could build anything of wood, plumbers, cowboys, mechanics, electricians, men of nearly every trade, even a first-class barber.

One man, Private Blackwell, took over the winches on a ship when the ship's crew refused overtime hours. He made the regular merchant marine crane operator look like an amateur.

It is said that it is lonesome at the top. Well, I wasn't very far up, and I admit, it *was* lonesome at times. Fortunately my wife sent me reading material, books which I read many times.

There are other sayings: Familiarity breeds contempt; monkey see, monkey do; etc. To a certain extent, these sayings are true. Respect must be earned; it doesn't come with Army rank. Yet, 75 percent of the high-ranking officers I met didn't realize their failings. They thought they had been anointed by the great school they had attended. I found the most capable and humane officers were of civilian status, or had come up through the ranks.

Yet someone up at regimental must have liked me; word came down that I was to get a Silver Star cluster for a patrol on the Tangarunga River, wherever that was. Apparently they had maps of Bougainville at division headquarters, but they weren't distributed to those who should have had them.

CHAPTER 20

Late in December of 1944, a short, stocky, businesslike captain appeared at Easy Company; under his arm he carried a bulging briefcase. He held out his hand to me as he introduced himself.

"I'm Mark Fahres.* I'm here to teach you how to combat-load a ship, a ship that will be joining the Southern Philippines Task Force. You probably know that Kruger's Sixth Army landed on the east coast of Leyte on October twentieth. The Americal Division will be needed on the cleanup operation there."

I was flabbergasted. "I don't know anything about loading a ship. How did this come about? Who sicced you on to me? To whom am I indebted for this great honor?"

He began to laugh; it was plain he was a jovial man you couldn't dislike.

"Your battalion boss picked you. I don't know the circumstances, but you're it! It really isn't too difficult. Your battalion will be aboard a liberty ship named the *Lew Wallace*. You've probably heard that name before."

"I know he was a Union general during the Civil War and wrote *Ben Hur* after his retirement. He was also appointed governor of New Mexico, where all that feuding occurred."

"That's the man! The ship named after him has five cargo holds, and this booklet [he produced a large folder of sheets]

---

*It's a small world, since I later met Mark Fahres at Command and General Staff College, Leavenworth, Kansas, in 1948, when I attended the G-3 training course. We were roommates with five other officers, all good friends.)

is called a 'ship's characteristic pamphlet.' " He went on to explain what each hold would carry, the many decks in each hold, and the size of each hold and deck. He said, "It's easy; you have so many vehicles in your battalion. Make paper cutouts, an eighth inch to the foot for every vehicle, then place them over these same-scale drawings of each hold and deck. You'll know just where to place each—what fits where. But be sure to spot equipment in the order you want it unloaded. Dunnage can be stacked between or on the vehicles. Of course, your combat loads of ammo will be on the vehicles, plus your heavier weapons."

Sure enough, he set me up to the point that when the convoy of ships arrived, we loaded the ship quickly, almost painlessly. The only catch was the reconnaissance outfit. Someone at division had forgotten about their tanks. As we had one of the few winches capable of lifting them, a forty-five-ton winch over our number-two hatch, the tanks were deck-loaded on our ship. The skipper and the ship's officers weren't happy about this heavy deck load, but were forced to accept the decision from above.

I hoped the trip would go well, but was a bit skeptical. We had Army troops, a merchant marine crew, a Navy gun crew, and a pickup lot of ship's officers. The latter looked mighty sloppy, and later proved so.

We were scheduled to enter Hollandia Harbor in New Guinea a few days later, at 4 A.M. Seven A.M. found us blithely steaming up the coast, far past our turn-in to Hollandia. I was told the navigation officer had overslept. As most men were sleeping topside (on deck) I awoke to hear shouting along the port side. Suddenly a tremendous explosion occurred just in front of the bow of the ship. We were deluged with seawater from the blast. Several men swore they saw the torpedo as it came from a rear angle on the port side of the ship. Whether it actually struck the ship, glanced off, and discharged, or had some magnetic type of detonator, is a moot point, but it did explode within a few yards of the bow.

Whoever was at the helm of the ship turned sharply to

starboard in a half circle before straightening out for our return to Hollandia. We entered a narrow inlet about 10:15 A.M. to find the huge harbor filled with hundreds of ships.

As we dropped anchor between a hospital ship and a troop transport carrying our Third Battalion, those men of the Third shouted across to us, "You should have been here last night. A sub tossed torpedoes into the harbor, hitting an ammunition ship—it blew up! Lots of fireworks!"

I wondered at the time how all of these ships would ever get turned around in the harbor, as apparently there were about five hundred involved in this southern fleet. Somehow, two days later, it was accomplished. For a few days the huge convoy had fair weather, then we entered the edge of a hurricane with exceptionally heavy seas. The *Lew Wallace* rolled badly, perhaps abetted by the deck load. Ship officers said it nearly overreached its safe maximum inclination. At its utmost slant, hesitating there for as long as thirty seconds, someone said, "She's going over next time!" The sea was so heavy we were all belowdecks sitting in hatchways.

We reached Leyte, the Philippines, near Dulag, just before dark on January 21, 1945. As the ship eased toward shore it suddenly ground to a halt, stuck tight in a bed of sand. Fortunately, near midnight, a bit more tide enabled the ship to reverse engines, back off, and anchor in deeper water until daybreak.

About 7 A.M., we began moving north to the Tacloban docks. As we began to pick up speed I noted a large yellow marker buoy. This warning was only about one hundred feet to the left front of our ship. I was standing on the number-two hatch and suddenly saw very shallow water ahead. The bow of the ship began to rise amid horrible crunching sounds. The ship came to a halt, bow almost out of the water, with the stern sunk almost to the rails.

That evening Japanese aircraft attacked our naval escort about eight miles east of us. The sky was instantly black with AA fire. A lone aircraft appeared out of the melee, headed straight for us. Our new battalion CO (my nemesis from

Company G), who was standing next to me, said, "Chuck, they can't sink us, we're already sunk!"

The aircraft pulled up just in time to clear our masts, going inland. It was Japanese.

For several evenings ocean-going tugs, LSTs, and other ships attempted to pull us off the reef; all failed. Finally a Navy salvage crew came out from shore with a barge. They placed it at the bow, lowering the ship's anchor on the port side, down to the barge. Towing it to the rear of the ship, the anchor was then lifted and dropped into deeper water. The same was done on the starboard side. By using the ship's anchor winches, the ship was pulled off the reef by its own power. I was told leaks in the bow plating were minimal.

We were on this reef for a total of twelve days before our battalion was loaded into small craft for the trip to shore. We had almost run out of food, but the cooks made bread from old weevily flour found in the ship's stores. We picked out the dark spots as we ate the slices.

In retrospect, I believe the Japanese submarine used its last torpedo on us, since we were an easy, cold-turkey shot. If they had more torpedoes they surely would have sunk us. Risking losing the ship, and the lives of several hundred men to drowning, by the incompetence of the *Lew Wallace* officers deserved nothing less than severe punishment to those guilty. But we knew it would all be covered up as usual.

CHAPTER 21

Finally onshore, we bivouacked inland a short distance to await the unloading of our vehicles. As in prior instances, maps were at a premium. Those issued to us looked more like cartoons. Our destination was to be the town of Valencia. Traveling west through Dagami, up the Leyte Valley toward Carigara, we passed a small fighter strip with a few parked P40 aircraft—there seemed to be little action at this field. Reaching Carigara we found the road that ran along the beach badly washed out by wave action for nearly ten miles. Engineers had built plank bridges here and there to cover gaps, but the road required constant repair due to wind and tides.

Entering mountainous country we witnessed the devastation caused by the Japanese. American tanks lay along the road, burned out or destroyed by direct fire from Japanese field guns. Each sharp turn concealed an enemy cannon, still in place, destroyed by the 1st Cavalry and 24th Infantry divisions. We had been warned that a few Japanese sore losers often shot at the trucks from ambush, but we traveled without incident.

Reaching Valencia at noon, each company organized its bivouac area. Previously made latrine forms were nailed together and a low latrine tarp was erected for modesty.

By 4 P.M. we were fully settled, but before I reported to battalion headquarters, I was approached by one of the men.

"Captain, I can't use the latrine—you should see what's going on over there." I accompanied him to the latrine to find at least twenty-five Filipino women laughing and gesturing at the endowments of some of the men, who seemed not a bit bashful. In fact, a few were braggarts, showing off! It was apparent these women had associated with troops before, as most were evidently prostitutes. I was forced to place a temporary guard to put the run to them.

To our west were plenty of enemy, some units disorganized, but many groups were headed up the Ormoc Valley to join General Suzuki in a last defensive position in the mountains near Abijao.

The next few days were spent on short patrols. One of Easy's platoons captured a Japanese who turned out to be from China. He claimed to be Chinese, having been captured there, and forced into the Japanese Army as a truck driver. It brought to mind a story I had heard: about a year earlier, John Gossett had asked a naval officer how you could tell the difference between a Japanese and a Filipino. The answer John got: "Line them up and slap their faces. The ones who slap you back are Filipinos."

After getting our equipment back in shape I was called to battalion headquarters and given a crude map of the road to Ormoc. I was instructed to load up my company the next morning and clear the road of Japanese.

We loaded up in several two-and-a-half-ton trucks, moving north of Valencia to intersect the west road. We hadn't gone far, perhaps five to six miles, climbing a mountain ridge, when I heard machine-gun fire ahead. Stopping on a slight grade, I walked to the top of the hill to find several guerrillas firing down at two clumps of brush located amid rice paddies. Directly across and parallel to our ridge was another a mile away, but between the two, all was rice paddies and water. Below our ridge, to the right, lay a small village with a few huts.

I noted the light machine gun they were firing was rusty; they were having problems with it. This was true of most weapons the guerrillas had. No one had ever taught them how to care for them. They had been smuggled in by submarine and given freely. Why bother to clean and oil them?

"What are you men firing at?" I was curious.

One man spoke up. "Some Japanese came into our village last night and took a young girl. They are using her in one of those patches of brush."

Unfortunately, there was little discipline among the Japanese troops when it came to women. The officers were even worse. Later I was to find captured white women carrying the results of rape in their arms. No woman was safe from the Japanese; they took what they wanted, when they wanted, or they killed you.

I walked back to the edge of the road, beckoning to my jeep driver to bring up his vehicle. There was no point in asking the guerrillas what they were going to do. Their machine gun had finally stopped on a ruptured cartridge. They were on their last few rounds in the gun belt.

By this time, Shorty Breding, my driver, had the jeep on the edge of the hill overlooking the rice paddies. The vehicle had a .50-caliber machine gun mounted on a pedestal.

I weighed the pros and cons, finally deciding on dropping a 60mm mortar shell in the larger clump of bush. I did value the life of the girl, but if she was flat on her back she should be reasonably safe. "Shorty, go back and have the Fourth Platoon bring up a sixty-millimeter mortar with a few rounds. Then load up that fifty-caliber."

Our mortarmen were good; the first round landed smack in the center of the largest clump, tossing a spray of water in all directions. A second later enemy soldiers exited the brush in a panic, running out into the water-covered rice paddies. Between the rifle fire of the guerrillas and the .50-caliber machine gun, all were shot.

I called Valencia to report our brief stop, and was told to return to base. No reason was given for this abrupt change in plan. The problem of the girl was left to the guerrillas.

The next day I was told to send out a platoon patrol to the west. Lieutenant Charles Ross took Second Platoon with plenty of rations. He reported back late that afternoon about 5 P.M., saying he had killed approximately forty-five enemy without loss to his men. (His further total after completion of his patrol was much, much more. He was recommended for a Silver Star; it was awarded.)

Because of his ratio that first day, I was further ordered to send out my First and Third platoons for the same patrol duties. On the third day I was told to take the remainder of my company, headquarters personnel, supply and kitchen help, to provide a fourth group for another patrol. I got two light machine guns from Company H for additional support.

Initially, Charles Ross's platoon had run into two Japanese machine guns on their move toward Ormoc. His comments follow:

These two machine guns were located on the side of a mountain. The platoon had no artillery or mortar support and no radio contact. A young Filipino, Victorio Maget (we called him Vicky), volunteered to fight with my platoon; he took over as lead scout. I was the number-two man. Near the foot of the mountain I stopped the patrol and looked in the window of a one-room shack, but saw nobody inside. I moved off a bit. Vicky entered the shack, then fired two shots, killing two Japanese officers. He came out carrying their Samurai swords. Passing the swords to the rear, he continued to lead the way.

The mountain was steep, covered with heavy vegetation. As we moved single file up a dry stream bed we got into a fire-fight, the enemy firing from behind huge boulders in the stream bed. I removed a pistol from a Japanese officer we shot. I was concerned that the noise from the fire-fight would alert the enemy we were approaching. Our plan was to circle wide around the machine-guns and attack from the rear. As the platoon came within a hundred or so yards of the gun positions, Vicky was still lead scout. I was about five or six yards behind him. Just as Vicky reached the point where the trail made a 90-degree turn, a single shot rang out and Vicky fell forward. Immediately an enemy soldier approached him. I fired eight rounds into him as fast as I could pull the trigger on my M1. Vicky died almost instantly. Sergeant Jeffrey came to me to ask about moving out. I nodded. Jeffrey then led out as scout. As we set up a skirmish line and moved up the mountain we found the enemy had retreated. Jeffrey didn't ask me if he could be point man, he just took over the job. He had courage.

CHAPTER 22

Minutes before my composite group left Valencia, I received a radio call from Mac, the battalion commander. He said, "Don't bring in any more prisoners; we have no place for them."

I knew this was against the Geneva Convention; this was a surprise! I asked, "Will you put that in writing for me?"

He was actually laughing on the radio. "Hell no! Just do it!"

We proceeded past Mount Magueng, which we had nick-named Chalk Mountain (the side to the east had a huge white scar). Climbing around to the rear, we were about to bed down for the night when we heard a rifle shot about one hundred yards ahead of us. At first I thought we had been spotted, then I heard a chicken squawking, followed by loud laughter. We were next to a group of Japanese, perhaps twenty to twenty-five, who were gathered near a house raised on wood piling, just across a small, dry wash from us.

We sized up the situation at dawn. Just below us, I watched two Japanese enter another house in the bottom of the wash. Sergeant Jim Cecil was with me. I said, "I'll set up a base of fire for the house across the gully, but I'm going to get one of those two Japanese in the bottom. Are you game for the other?"

He grinned. "I'll take one of them."

When the shooting started we ran down into the gully just as the two enemy split from the house. My Japanese took to the bush; I ran him down. Jim's was too fast, but while climbing up the far hill someone got him. The enemy on the far side of the gully had defensive holes dug beneath the raised house, delaying us for a few minutes. I could see why Lieutenant Charles Ross was racking up that body count; we had nearly twenty-five enemy already. We pressed on, seeing Japanese everywhere, flushing many out at easy rifle range. Others were too far away, but we persisted, getting them.

Traveling north-northwest, I knew we would eventually meet up with the rest of Easy. Passing through a deserted village, we ran into a hornets' nest. One of our men was struck a glancing blow on his forehead by a bullet; it made a half-cup-shaped indentation above his forehead. He was instantly unconscious. A medic moved in to care for him. I found a man had abandoned his forward post, refusing to go on. He said, "I'm not leaving my buddy! I'm going to care for him."

My first sergeant was beside me when I stuck my rifle muzzle into his stomach. I told him I would count to three, then I would blow him away if he didn't get back to his squad. At two count, he left. Sergeant Fedje looked at me curiously. "Would you really have done it?"

The man had caused trouble before—I knew him well.

"I had no choice. If I let him get away with it, the company wouldn't be worth a damn!"

Fedje said no more.

By noon we climbed a hill to find a house with several sick Japanese. As I walked to the door, one of my men behind me cut loose with a BAR, shooting from the hip. He barely missed cutting me in half. I found swear words I hardly ever used; it was the first time I ever swore directly at a soldier.

Stopping on a hill to rest, we had a view of perhaps two and a half miles in nearly every direction. There, across a river, a bit over one thousand yards away, was a Japanese peeling a coconut with a machete. He was so small, so far away.

My scope rifle was zeroed for three hundred yards, but a bullet at one thousand yards drops about sixteen feet. (I had shot on the Camp Perry range many times at one thousand yards.) Lazily I put the gun across my knees, judging the drop, not actually intending to shoot. Someone said disgustedly, "Hell, you're not going to shoot, are you? It's just a waste!"

His remark burned me, so I shot. Nearly two seconds later the Japanese dropped. What none of us knew was that there were about thirty more enemy around him in defilade that we couldn't see. They panicked, running as a close-knit group up a far hill. Everyone cut loose then, aiming high. Amazingly, they knocked down one more of the enemy. That's musketry fire for you—concentrating fire on one point— effective!

We bivouacked for the night, pushing on the next morning, carrying our wounded man. Climbing to the top of a ridge, Breding and I had a cigarette while the patrol rested. About one hundred yards across from us was a sheer cliff, paralleling our ridge. The valley to our left and right was narrow with short grass. Far to the right we heard a Nambu machine gun firing (a far different sound from our .30 caliber). Eventually, I saw a single file of men headed toward us, perhaps eight hundred yards away.

Breding said, "That must be Peterson's squad; we must have caught up with some of our outfit."

I looked through the scope. "Like heck it is! There are ten Japanese going to be just below us within minutes. When they pass by us, I'll take the front end, you start at the rear."

I let the lead Japanese pass me about thirty yards, then cut lose. These Japanese weren't dummies; they were experienced, spaced about fifteen yards apart. When the first man was down, the second turned to face me; the third hit the deck, as did the fourth. There was no place to hide. To my right, below, a Japanese grenade went off. I figured the man committed suicide. As the first shot was fired, my men below me boiled over the hill. It was all over in seconds.

By noon we approached the Ormoc road, just in time to meet Lieutenant Colonel Gee, who had come along in an armored car. He said, "I'll take your man to Ormoc; there is supposed to be a field hospital setting up there. We'll have to tie the litter on the back of the vehicle, for there's no room inside." (We found later that there were two surgeons in Ormoc, but their hospital equipment had not arrived. Using razor blades for scalpels, they worked on our man. He lived.)

Just past the Ormoc road we met the remainder of Easy and bivouacked together for the night. When morning came I noticed a tall dead tree loaded with monkeys on the top branches. Did they do this for safety, or did misery love company? Many men in rear areas bought monkeys from the natives. They might look and act cute, but they couldn't be housebroken.

That morning one of my platoons got in a firefight on a hill. (Although a company, we split up and spread out for small, individual operations.) They lost a man. Some minutes later one of our L4 Cubs flew over. The pilot dropped a red smoke grenade on top of the hill, indicating dug-in Japanese. We already knew that!

Up to this period of two to three days of travel across country, our score for the entire company totaled 182 enemy killed with a loss of two men and one man wounded.

I received a radio call from a company near Ormoc. They said, "Chuck, you should see all the decorative pompoms sticking out of the ground over here—the kind of tassels you wear on your winter caps in Dakota."

I asked, "What about them?"

"You're supposed to pull them out of the ground. Trouble is, they're tied to a stick grenade. We dug up a couple to check. Just thought you should know."

We found enemy dying of disease and starvation, so helped them along. As I lowered myself through bushes to a riverbed, a man behind me tapped me on the shoulder. He pointed. Across the wash was a Japanese sound asleep, his body covered with a piece of canvas. I looked down at him as he softly snored, totally unconscious of the noise a shot makes. Immediately, his group, who were nearby, hit the jungle, en masse. We heard them scramble.

Climbing another ridge we saw Company G. They were

assaulting a hill on a ridge far to our left. We could see the Japanese standing upright to toss grenades down upon Company G's men.

I called their CO, telling him the circumstances. I told him to warn his men that we would provide overhead fire to pin down the Japanese for his attack.

One of our bipod machine guns opened up at about fifteen hundred yards across to the target, pinning down the enemy. The Company G men had been warned that we were firing; they paid no attention to the snapping bullets. At the last moment we ceased firing, they took the hill. Someone called on the radio, thanking me.

An hour later we ran into another hot potato. Johnny Divers, a Company H machine-gunner, an experienced man, decided to take the point of one of our platoons. There was a single shot fired to my right, above Fedje and me. We tried to penetrate the bush toward the shot, but at that instant someone at the head of our patrol began firing steadily. We hurried to Malcolm Walsh to find he had killed nearly twenty Japanese soldiers who thought they were surrounded in a box canyon. One enemy had laid back on a huge boulder and committed suicide with a grenade. Walsh was not excited, the coolest man I ever saw. I made sure he got a medal for his exceptional courage.

We went in the back way for Divers, to find him dead. A Japanese had searched him, as I knew he wore a jade stone on a chain around his neck—it was gone. A tremendous boulder stood about one hundred feet to the east of us. Someone thought he saw a quick movement behind it. Edging around each side of the giant rock, the men got another enemy soldier.

Sergeant Fedje went back to check the Japanese that Walsh had shot, to find another Japanese robbing their bodies. He shot the man. Fedje recovered some excellent maps, all indicating a defensive position the enemy was preparing up north, the direction we were headed. Complete instructions were included on the maps, so simple that even we could fathom them.

We climbed farther up the mountain and reached a narrow path curving around a steep grassy hill on our right. The left side of the six-foot-wide trail ended in a sheer drop of at least three hundred feet. I was the third man in the patrol, suddenly aware of a noise above me. A Japanese soldier had spotted our patrol, and trapped, climbed above us. He was clinging to grass roots above, hoping for safety until our patrol passed by. It was my luck that he slid down onto me; the roots he was holding had pulled loose. We both had our rifles on our shoulders. As I grasped at his chest with my left hand, he hit me in the face with his fist, knocking off my glasses. I dared not step back, and no one could help me. My runner, Cagle, fourth man in line, was yelling, "Kill him! Kill him! Kill him!"

Lordy! I didn't have to be told! Fortunately I was able to thrust him back against the almost vertical bank and managed to retrieve my knife with my right hand. Believe me, a good knife should never be used to open ration cans, it dulls the edge. I felt a sudden relief; it had been close!

Things settled down and we got off the trail just around a long bend. In a valley ahead was a nipa hut. It had an open window and with cover fire I snuck ahead to toss in a grenade. My toss was lousy; the grenade missed the window and bounced back toward me. I turned back and hit the dirt. It proved that our U.S. hand grenades were nearly worthless; no one was even scratched. Inside the house I garnered a .25 Colt automatic, a Nambu 7.65 pistol, and best of all, a fine camera with three spare rolls of 120 film. I gave the guns away.

Before dark we bivouacked on a ridge overlooking the so-called town of Abijao, along the ocean beach. It was no town now, having only one house left. To our north, about eight hundred yards away, a bit above us in elevation, a Japanese stood upright. He was about to direct mortar fire upon us. His first round struck far to our left. In seconds one of our 60mm mortars hastily set up and dropped a round exactly on top of him. He had turned and was bent over to run when the shell exploded within a few feet of him. I marveled at the skill of our mortarmen, a perfect bull's-eye! There was no more mortar fire on us that evening.

About 11 P.M. we were subjected to repeated Nambu machine-gun fire. Bullets ricocheted everywhere; luckily no one was hit. That brought to mind another vital rule: Always move your position after dark when exposed in open country! When possible, we did this, sending out a scouting party just before dark to locate a safe bivouac. We lucked out this night.

The next morning I sent out Lieutenants Ross and Sherar with their platoons in different directions to scout around before we descended from the mountain down to Abijao. Lieutenant Pete Sherar successfully ambushed more Japanese while Lieutenant Charles Ross ran into trouble. Encountering a Japanese group, a rifle bullet hit one of the M1 clips in Ross's cartridge belt. As I remember, a few remaining bullets in the clip caught fire. Pieces of the slug penetrated his abdomen. His men carried him back to us. After recovering Sherar's patrol, we headed downhill. Charles was evacuated by boat at Abijao. I would sure miss him, he was tops! (He was evacuated to New Guinea, but returned to Easy about two months later.)

This is Charles Ross's story:

Our platoon moved single file because of the thick vegetation. I followed the lead scout with a BAR man just behind me. Suddenly we saw enemy on the trail about 30–40 yards ahead. Without stopping, the BAR gunner and I moved up to the lead scout and walking forward, began firing. I fired three clips of eight rounds each from my M1 before being shot in the hip and knocked down. My left leg was paralyzed and I could not get up or even crawl. In a few seconds my platoon medic, Tighe, was there examining my wound. My platoon sergeant, Jeffrey, knelt beside me, the enemy still firing steadily at us. My lead squad quickly set up a base of fire to cover us.

I told Jeffrey, "You're in command now."

He said, "We're pulling back."

Under the circumstances it was the proper thing to do as we were only to scout out a short distance. Jeffrey withdrew the platoon without any other casualties. As I was carried back bullets were cracking all around us. We arrived back at our rendezvous point on time.

CHAPTER 23

Down at the beach we found our Easy Company kitchen gear had been transported to Abijao by LCM, and was to feed the entire battalion as they arrived. That evening our regimental commander, Colonel Mahoney, and Captain Williams visited Abijao. Williams, a former company commander of the 164th Infantry, was to be rotated home and had come to say good-bye to us all. He and Colonel Mahoney slept in the house at the north edge of the camp.

At dawn I awoke to Nambu machine-gun fire from the north beach. Sergeant Fedje was already up; he hit the hole we had dug in the sand just a second after a bullet struck a kitchen range and then ricocheted exactly where he would have dropped.

I kidded him. "Darn good thing you were slow or you would have had it!" I dug the bullet out of the sand, then dropped it. It was hot!

Sadly enough, the Japanese had shot up the house, killing Williams. No one else was even scratched.

After eating a noon meal at the Easy kitchen, we drew rations and replenished our ammunition, moving a short distance farther north. From there we climbed east, up to the first mountain ridge to set up a defensive zone to protect Abijao from further shooting from the north.

While digging in, I observed several enemy enter a clearing far above and south of Abijao. I reported it as an artillery target, but was informed we had no artillery as yet. Evidently Company H mortars were not available. Nothing was done about this group of at least forty to fifty Japanese; they stopped to rest high above Abijao, only a mile and a half away.

On our south flank a narrow ravine led down to the ocean. It was the gully the Japanese had used when they shot up the camp that morning. We dug firing holes to plug the trail and around our company perimeter.

It had just turned dark when Lieutenant Roush was bitten by a poisonous centipede. He was given morphine to reduce the pain as the terrain was too rough to move him down to Abijao after dark.

About midnight I heard a BAR firing down in the ravine. There were two or three grenades thrown. All was quiet, so two of us checked; we found our BAR man dead. He had opened fire with his weapon instead of throwing a grenade as the Japanese patrol came down the ravine. They were evidently going to repeat their performance of that past morning. One Japanese was lucky; his grenade had landed into our man's dug position. From then on we booby-trapped all approaches.

Our battalion commander, Mac, showed up the next morning, telling me to send out a patrol higher up the mountain to the east. Each hill in this area was covered with trees and brush; the small, narrow valleys had short grass. We were in the midst of General Suzuki's gathering area of several thousand Japanese.

We got into a hot argument. I told him it was stupid to even think of sending out a small patrol where every hill was loaded with Japanese with weapons covering the draws. I told him, "We'll lose men without gaining a thing."

Mac was adamant. "Mahoney, the regimental commander, has ordered me to patrol that area; you are damn well going to do it!"

I had bad feelings about this. Japanese were more than plentiful; they had their backs against the wall—and this was their selected rendezvous area!

It was Lieutenant Pete Sherar's turn for the patrol with Third Platoon. I advised him, "Don't go a darn bit farther than you have to. I'm not telling you to dog it; just play it safe. Abijao is inside the Japanese defensive boundary shown on those maps we captured."

He nodded. "I'll try to stay under cover, but there are open spots. We'll give it a shot."

Twice that afternoon we heard heavy firing; finally the patrol returned, just as we were preparing to go to their aid. Sherar had caught a machine-gun burst in his knee; his platoon sergeant was shot through the hip; at least five or more men suffered wounds from the rifle and Nambu fire. One man approached me, saying, "Look, Captain! I'm the luckiest man in the world! I've been shot through both ears. One on the way out on the patrol, the other while returning."

True! A bullet had grazed his right cheek from his eye back through his ear. The opposite ear had a clean hole just above the lobe.

I was told later that Sherar refused all medical aid until each of his men was cared for—another exceptional officer I was mighty sorry to lose! He was moved to the States.

I made sure Mac was informed about this stupid patrol he had insisted upon. He turned away, giving me a scornful look.

Two days later we went downhill to the beach, moving about two miles north before again climbing into the mountains. One of our companies had been attempting to take a major hill that overlooked an internal valley of about four square miles. They had not succeeded.

I had lost my executive officer (Mork) earlier and, after also losing Ross, Roush, and Sherar, was now down to Clemens. I was glad to get a replacement officer to help fill our ranks, Lieutenant Baranowski. Luckily, we finally had supporting mortar fire, also 105mm backup from the 245th Field Artillery.

Lieutenant Clemens suggested, "Charley, I believe we can take that hill after dark by shelling it with our eighty-one-millimeter mortars."

"You think they'll back off the hill, then come back up after the firing?"

He grinned. "Wouldn't you?"

I would, and he would. When daylight came his platoon was dug well into the holes created by the delay mortar shells we had dropped. He had a warm reception for the Japanese coming back up the hill at first light. I moved the balance of the company up and we began improving the mortar holes.

There was another, lower hill two hundred yards east of us, another three hundred yards west of us, and one straight ahead, all occupied by Japanese. From our advantageous height, we could see Japanese everywhere, singles and groups. After all, there were thousands of enemy in these few square miles of the Abijao area. Our 245th Field Artillery observer had a field day, as did our 81mm mortar fire director.

Our hill was critical. The enemy had to retake it—they were being slaughtered by our artillery and mortars. Just at dusk we received machine-gun fire from both sides and the front. Below the nose of our hill a large group of enemy attacked; we held. They hit us three times that night, causing us severe losses.

When daylight came I had six men dead and a score wounded. We handed out plenty of punishment too. What we would have given for parachute flares that night!

Sergeant Fedje and I occupied a mortar-created hole about twenty feet from the north edge of the hill. The heaviest attack occurred at the east nose. One of the artillerymen was plastered with grenade fragments and crawled to our hole. A second man, Barnes, arrived, saying, "I can't feel my leg."

I ran my hand down his left leg to find heavy damage to his calf. Farther down, his ankle was gone, the two straps of his boot still holding his foot in place. I put my belt just below his knee for a tourniquet, knowing he had already lost a lot of blood. As Joel began to unwrap a unit of plasma, I shot Barnes with a half tube of morphine.

The plasma kits were complicated, especially when working in total darkness. There was a blood plasma unit, plus a can of distilled water and hoses—the liquids had to be mixed. Covering up the best we could with ponchos, using a Zippo for light, we finally got a unit prepared. All this time there was heavy firing and grenades were exploding.

At that instant a man panicked, breaking from the north edge of the hill, running across the perimeter. Someone shot him. A call came from a medic: "Anyone got a unit of plasma?"

Our man with the damaged leg said, "Give it to him. You can fix one for me in the morning."

A small diversion came from the north. I heard a grenade land a few feet from me. I ducked my head, but didn't pull in my arms; several pieces of rock penetrated the skin of my forearms. I had stupidly left my sleeves rolled up. I dug the pieces out when daylight came—no sweat.

With the dawn came the quiet. We mixed another unit of blood, but I was unable to locate a vein in either of our wounded man's arms—he had lost so much blood. I did what I had been told: inserted the long needle into his buttocks, a slow process to move plasma.

At that moment a Piper L4 flew very near us. The pilot or passenger was firing a Colt .45 down between our hill and the adjoining one to our left. The pilot raised us on our artillery forward observer's radio. "There is a large group of Japanese just below your hill. They're running east now."

A carrying party took away our casualties and wounded, while our artillery and mortars resumed punishing the Japanese. I realized this was no cinch. They were hurting; they were desperate to retake this hill.

That afternoon the Second Battalion Reconnaissance Unit, under Lieutenant Buie, attempted to take the hill to our south. One Japanese came charging around the hill toward Buie, who was crouched in low brush. His Arisaki rifle with bayonet seemed much too long for him; his shrill voice came clearly: *"Banzai! Banzai!"* He was mowed down by men from our hill.

Buie was engaged in a hand grenade duel with Japanese just ahead of him. Unfortunately, a Japanese grenade fragment entered his eye. He was forced to pull back.

Twice that day we watched the enemy carrying mortar shells across country from the north, delivering them behind the hill just to our front. They hit us twice again that night; we held, with fewer losses.

When daylight came I heard a deep *thunk!* I knew it was their mortar firing. The first shell went over, exploding just to our rear. Knowing the havoc a mortar could create, I ran over the forward slope of the hill, well past our perimeter line, to locate the mortar by sound. The next round landed in the rocks, twenty-five feet in front of me; thankfully it was a dud. Rock particles spewed from it. Turning, I ran back into the perimeter, to get whacked in the rear; it was like being hit by a heavy plank. I had passed those pull-type igniters out too freely, without warning the men to pull in their booby traps at daybreak. The grenade had exploded three feet from my rear end.

As I lay flat on my stomach, momentarily stunned, two men lifted my jacket, then slid down my pants. They were grinning. "Geez, Cap! You're a lucky one!"

Those first two nights we threw at least three hundred–plus grenades. Many just popped, breaking in half. We knew the contractors who had made them had cheated. Most had only a teaspoon of EC blank powder inside. It was reported many times, but nothing was done. Give me a Mills or Japanese grenade any day!

Evidently, two mortar rounds were all they had that were serviceable, and the one had failed to detonate. We lucked out again; no more rounds were fired.

Since Lieutenant Paul Clemens had been through much in Bougainville while with Easy Company, I had the utmost confidence in him. Both of us were of the same opinion: we had too many men on this hill. If the Japanese acquired more mortar shells we might have to evacuate. Our losses indicated it was time we took the hill to the north and eliminated that aggravation. I was sick and tired of enemy there taking shots at us every time we popped up a head. But even with heavy covering fire from our hill, we knew the attack might be costly; the enemy were well dug in.

We discussed it. "Paul, we're okay here; both of these new officers [we had gotten another] know their stuff. They've coped with all the hell of the past two nights. I doubt the Japanese will hit this hill again tonight, but they'll sure try to retake that north one if we grab it. All the approaches to it are gradual, much easier for the Japanese."

He said, "I'll take my platoon up on the west side. You'll be able to see us all the way to give covering fire. Can you have the mortarmen from Company H register just beyond, on the back slope, so I can call them if necessary?"

About noon the First Platoon passed down the back side of our hill and crossed the ravine to begin their climb up to the Japanese. We began a massive covering fire as they neared the crest. The din of our firing ruled out any sounds of shooting by Clemens's men. As they topped the hill I watched the men scatter, knowing they were firing and being fired upon. I watched one of our men drop, then the men who were now spread over the entire hill disappeared into existing cover. No Japanese escaped, all were killed.

Paul called on the 300 radio: "We cleaned it up, but lost a man. They were deeply dug in, and had rocks piled around their positions. I'm going to set up a defense mainly toward the north and east."

I spoke with our new officers. "I'm going over to spend the night with First Platoon later this afternoon. You've got plenty of men to hold this hill. I doubt they'll hit you tonight, they've been burned plenty. But I'm sure they'll hit the other hill, since they'll know Clemens has few men. [Our company was now down to less than one-half strength.] If the worst comes, I can direct mortar fire from Company H myself. If you see our machine guns fire, it means they are pressing us hard. I want you to follow the tracer fire from our gun muzzles, then spray as close as you dare in front of them. Understood?"

These were replacement officers; I knew nothing of their previous experience, but they were gutsy and capable. I noted them checking their men, cajoling them to improve their positions to avoid thrown grenades, yet there was no bullying. I also knew the men in their platoons; there was no give in them.

With disgust I noted piles of worthless grenades lying about. The men had poured the EC blank powder from two grenades into one, discarding the empties. At least with a double charge of powder they wouldn't just break in half. Our front area to the east was littered with large chunks of grenades. Good grenades probably would have broken the Japanese attacks sooner, saving us many men killed and wounded.

We were grateful to the carrying party who had come up to help with our casualties. They brought food, water, ammo, and many more cases of those almost worthless grenades.

CHAPTER 24

I moved to Clemens's hill shortly before dark. We set pull-type igniters on the east side of the hill, along a main trail that led up from a ravine.

At dark our other hill was hit briefly, but that attack was quickly beaten off. When the attack on our hill came, it was just close rifle fire; no grenades came in. (At this time the enemy must have been short of grenades, for many had been used on the attacks of the prior nights.) It was obvious the enemy had crawled up within a few feet of our positions before firing. Even our grenade throwing failed to discourage them.

They had a distinct advantage as there was a hair of light in the sky—we became outlined if we moved. I called the Company H mortars in close, but even that failed to dislodge these determined Japanese. Finally I brought them in so close the exploding shells flashed in the darkness; they struck close enough that the shrapnel flew everywhere.

We had to keep still; the human eye is good at detecting movement.

After nearly two hours I'd had enough. I told our machine-gunners to open fire. Those guns from our high hill sprayed down around us, just to our front. The covering fire made all the difference.

We heard one of our booby traps go off on the trail leading down the hill, then the shout of a Japanese. He was evidently giving a command, calling off his men—all firing ceased. Still, we had lost another man and had several wounded. A fixed location is always vulnerable.

The following afternoon the men wanted to know how close our mortar shells were to us, so I asked Company H for a smoke round. It landed just fifteen feet from our line. The men just shook their heads, shocked.

The accuracy of the sustained fire from Company H was fantastic, all done in total darkness. Kingston had trained them well; he was an exceptional officer.

Competence in combat comes primarily from training and experience. But personal experience is the great teacher. You can learn so much from books, but a practical application of that knowledge is absolutely essential.

I realized that we men, even with our two years of combat experience, still had lots to learn. We had scored highly in deep jungle fighting, but this mountainous terrain and sometimes semiopen hills brought problems we had never anticipated. Mortar and artillery fire seemed the answer. Close-in aircraft support would have been useful, but we had none.

Toward evening a carrying party came up with supplies. They were Filipinos accompanied by a few infantrymen for protection. These natives gathered together like a clan, difficult to disperse. I warned as they were gathering immediately behind me, farther up the ridge, "Get those men spread out, they're going to draw fire!"

I had another problem. One of our 300 radios would receive but not transmit. The other would only transmit. I had removed the covers from each radio (prior advice by the communications men) to look for those peanut tubes that weren't lighting up. (Each radio had at least twelve to sixteen small radio tubes about five-eighths of an inch by two and a half inches long.)

The incessant talk behind me forced me to lean forward amid the boulders to blanket out their conversations. At that moment the ration box in front of me disappeared amid the snapping bullets of a Nambu. The gun was firing from the east hill, about four hundred yards away. One of my men behind me, Sergeant Peterson, who had been lying on his stomach, caught a bullet through both cheeks of his buttocks.

My timing had been perfect; one bullet had pierced my

cap in the center top as I leaned forward to blanket out the noise. If those men hadn't been so loud, I would have bought some real estate.

Wiggling the radio tubes in their sockets did the job. Both were again working. Moisture must have corroded the contacts a bit. We resumed firing that evening, for we could see the smoke of many fires a mile or more to the north.

Shortly before dark I received a message to bring the company back off the hill. We were to be relieved by a unit yet unnamed. As no unit was present to take over immediately, I knew the Japanese would move back the instant we left. What a waste of lives—poor planning, no coordination.

I sent men to locate a safe place for a night bivouac. They returned at dark, so we slipped off down the mountain to a level spot in dense jungle. We set up a tight perimeter for the night with fewer than normal guards. When morning came, we moved farther to the north, to again climb back up into the mountains.

CHAPTER 25

This new climb was up a semibare ridge with a bald spot at the top; beyond that were even higher mountain ridges. Support units of our Second Battalion were moving in behind us, locating along the coast.

We reached the bald spot at the peak of this lower mountain by 1 P.M. The remainder of Easy was strewn back down the ridge for perhaps four hundred yards.

To our left front, just below us, was a nipa hut with enemy activity. With about six to eight men, I dropped down the ridge to a gully that approached the hut. The lead man turned to me, signaling silently that a Japanese was just ahead. I crawled up beside him, hidden by the base of a tree. As I slowly peeked around the trunk, the Japanese soldier did the same, peeking toward me from another tree only thirty feet away. I froze in shock, then realized he didn't see me; he was looking up at the bald spot on the hill. We were below him, bunched, suckers for a single Japanese grenade. I moved my head back so slowly he didn't notice, at the same time motioning for us to get the hell out of there. We would take care of him with mortar fire after regaining our hill.

Because our 60mm mortars were not set up, I called downhill and contacted Captain John Landeck. He told me Company G mortars were ready to fire. I told him the problem, asking if he could see us on the bald spot.

"Sure, I see you. Tell me what you want."

"We look to be about nine hundred yards from you. Set a mortar to fire thirteen hundred yards for one shot. I'll bring it in from there."

Only three of us were on the peak: a sergeant from Company H, Lieutenant Clemens, and myself. Minutes passed. Finally the mortar popped, then seconds later we realized the shell was coming down on top of us. The three of us lay tight, side by side, Paul in the middle, sandwiched by the H man on one side and me on the other. I heard the hiss of the descending round, but never heard the explosion.

I woke up some distance down the hill. Later, a man told me I flew through the air like a rag doll. It couldn't have been more than a few seconds before I regained consciousness. I lay on my stomach, facing up the hill. I could see no men, but a liquid was shooting in an arc across about a four-foot span. As I watched the pulses, the arc became shorter and shorter. I finally realized it was blood pumping from a large severed artery.

I felt no pain, but my legs refused to work. Crawling with my hands and elbows upward about fifty feet, I found our artillery forward observer valiantly trying to stem the flow of blood from the Company H man's torso. Paul Clemens lay on his back, his jacket front gone; several chunks of material were embedded in his chest. Almost in a dream, I began to pick pieces of stone and shrapnel out of his flesh. I remember saying, "Poor Paul is dead! Poor Paul is dead!"

After a moment of dry heaves, I got John Landeck on the radio and told him what had happened. He had witnessed the shell striking us and had been checking. The Company G mortarman was to have set the mortar at 67 degrees. Instead, he had mistakenly set it for 76 degrees, causing a three-hundred-yard short. This error should not have happened. A repeat order should always be given when firing a mortar. The mortar gunner should have called back the setting after he made it.

Within minutes my legs mysteriously began to work again. I had feared a spinal injury from the shell, but the men checked me and found no blood, only bad scrapes and bruises. It wasn't until 1954 that my body finally rejected a piece of cast iron from my rear. All those years I thought it just a big sebaceous cyst.

By the time we had things straightened out and the casualties removed, a man came up to me from below.

He said, "Captain, down to our right, about three hundred yards back, we saw Japanese—they disappeared. We figure they have a cave there."

Third Platoon of Easy were already involved; some men had descended partway down the hill and discovered the cave; they were covering the entrance from two sides. Before I arrived, they had thrown an HC smoke grenade inside, then followed it with hand grenades.

Two aggressive men had crawled inside to inspect the damage. The Japanese, still alive, tossed a grenade, wounding both men. One was a young Jewish boy (Ehrmen) whose parents had been lucky enough to ship him from Germany in 1939. I believe they died in a concentration camp. He was clutching a Japanese officer's saber when he crawled out, not parting with it as he was loaded onto a litter. He was fearless, a bit over five feet, no doubt the smallest and lightest man in the company. The officer wounded with him was one of our recent field replacements.

I called downhill for explosives and a flashlight, finally getting four bangalore torpedoes and a single detonating cap with fuse. The medics sent up a three-cell flashlight, the batteries of which were nearly shot.

Sergeant Joel Fedje and I slipped down under covering fire to drop two of the bangalores into the cave entrance. We took cover about seventy feet up the hill—nothing happened; the darn thing failed to explode. That left us in a quandary, for we had no detonator cap for the last two torpedoes. (Since this was rock country I had not carried my usual block of TNT with detonator.) I suddenly remembered the bangalores were filled with Amytal, not TNT, requiring only a number-six detonator cap. Removing the top of a white phosphorous grenade, I cut off the cap with my knife and bit it to a fuse. The two of us again made our way down to drop the two explosive tubes on top of the first pair. Scurrying up the hill I said to Joel, "We'd better get further away this time. If it goes off, there will be one hell of a bang!"

The explosion was massive. Descending to the cave, I took the flashlight to crawl inside. There was still so much smoke that I could see nothing, just feel bodies as I crawled over them. Back in the recesses I heard a man breathing heavily, as if he had asthma. I froze, then backed out, knowing there were Japanese still alive.

We booby-trapped the outside of the cave before dark and were rewarded at about 11 P.M. when we heard the grenade explode.

In the morning I again crawled into the cave; it was now clear of smoke. There, up high, behind a massive rock, a Japanese held a pistol pointed straight at me, his hands resting on the boulder. It didn't seem right that he was alive, as there were dead enemy everywhere. I moved the flashlight to the side, realizing his gun didn't follow the light. Evidently the concussion had killed him. He was locked with both hands on the pistol, prepared to fire at anyone entering the cave.

There were fourteen bodies in the main part of the cave, nearly all officers, but I didn't check recesses that led deeper. Evidently the cave had been used as some sort of command post. I gathered up two sabers and the pistol and went outside. It was then I realized I was loaded with the biggest, largest cooties that ever existed. (They could have been bed bugs.) I shed my clothes and shook them out vigorously. Those Japanese inside were infested!

I almost forgot to mention the huge brass bed in the cave. They were in great demand after the war. I often wondered how and where they'd got it.

That evening a few of us climbed down from the cave to the ravine below. At the bottom were boulders the size of automobiles. It was dusk, and just as we were going to climb back up the ridge, someone said, "Look up there!"

To the east, about 250 yards away, was another ridge, much higher above us; it ran across our front. It was razor-backed with almost vertical sides. An aircraft had evidently dropped a bomb on it some days ago; the cleft from the bomb was about forty-five feet wide and ten feet deep. A column of Japanese were attempting to negotiate this cleft, one by one.

Two of us had scope rifles, only three-power Weavers, but it brought them within 250 feet of us. Although it was near dark, they were illuminated in the fading light. When I emptied one clip, the other M1 began to fire. It was a soldier's dream; they just kept coming and coming, clambering down into the cleft, running across and attempting to climb back up to the trail.

I wondered at the stupidity of the Japanese. Why did they persist, why not wait a few minutes for complete darkness? It was beyond belief. There had to be someone pushing them—Army troops, no doubt. We each emptied about four clips (sixty-four rounds) before it became too dark to see—it was dirty work, but necessary. Judas! There were sure a lot of Japanese around us!

CHAPTER 26

The next evening we were still high in the mountains overlooking the ocean. That evening we were treated to a show between a PT boat and a persistent Japanese aircraft. The Japanese had been sneaking across from this northern tip of Leyte to Cebu Island, only a few miles to our west. PT boats were endeavoring to stop this traffic, while Japanese aircraft were trying to eliminate them.

This particular PT boat had a 40mm gun aft, tracking the Japanese pilot as he circled to drop his bomb. He was cautious, as the PT boat anticipated his every move, always keeping the stern gun available. After a long period of cat-and-mouse, the pilot evidently thought enough was enough. He dove at the PT boat and released his only bomb. It was a standoff, since both the bomb and the 40mm gun missed their targets. The Japanese pilot scooted for home.

When darkness fell we became aware of signal lights flashing from the island of Cebu to the enemy in our vicinity. They blinked intermittently, probably indicating small boats and *bancas* (native canoes) available for travel that night.

One evening while on the move we contacted Clayton Kingston's group. They had taken a prisoner. I approached the man, who wore no insignia. He was elderly and thin, wearing a noose around his neck for control. His lack of insignia caught my attention; he didn't look like a common soldier, more like a high-ranking officer. I handed him a Camel cigarette and took one myself. Before I could offer him a light, he held the cigarette up to the twilight to examine it. He smiled and said, "It's a Camel! I used to smoke Luckys before the war."

I lit his smoke, amused. He was no common enlisted man. He spoke perfect English with no foreign accent. I would have conversed with him further, but Kingston's men were moving out.

A final fight was in the making on a ridge near the ocean. We became embroiled in another three-day ordeal, losing more men. At this point I was surprised to receive nine replacements at noon on the second day. Just as they arrived, one of my men was being carried out. I pointed to him. "Don't stick your heads up looking for Japanese; look from concealment, not from the top of a rock. That man became careless!"

One of the new replacements, Bill Kiker, later wrote to me:

From the 4th Replacement Depot in Tacloban, Leyte-Philippine Islands, a bunch of scared, green young infantry replacements boarded a barge on the other side of the island for a much shorter ride to an encampment on the beach behind which rose mountain after mountain. We arrived at 2nd Battalion headquarters of the 164th Regiment to which all had just been assigned. The 164th Infantry Regiment was part of the Americal Division. Those of us in basic training in Camp Roberts, California, knew the Americal to be one of the premier infantry divisions in the South Pacific. We had been told that Americal units were involved in *mopping up* operations in this area (Ormoc, Palompon, Abijao). The time was early 1945.

The next morning with a couple of noncoms and a carrying party we set out for our individual assignments. Several of us were to go to Company E, and others to companies along the way. In the afternoon the going became very hard, all of us covered with sweat, the temperature nearly 110 degrees.

One of our group was very heavy and having a difficult time climbing the hills. After falling several times, he declared he could go no farther, and for us to leave him there. The non-com leading us came back to talk to him. He told him that if we left him, that he would not survive the night. He began to whimper and cry. Private Kingery and I decided that we would see that he got to his assigned unit. I took his M1 rifle and bandolier of ammo, and Kingery took his web belt and pack. We got him standing up and with each of us on either side, got him back on the trail.

About a half mile further we handed him off to the 1st Sergeant of the unit that he was assigned to. Others in our column made it to their units, and finally it was just the balance left that was assigned to Company E. Their command post was on a hill presided over by a 1st sergeant, giving someone hell about using Filipino carrying parties to carry their packs to the hill at the front, and to where I finally ended up.

A short time later the C.O. of Company E, Captain Walker, arrived and began to brief us. The first thing that I recall him saying was that if any of us were wounded, every effort would be made to get to us. He told us one of his NCOs had just been wounded. Moments later, he was informed that the man had died.

When we finally made it to the next hill where the rest of Company E was dug in, it was just before dusk. Since there was not time for me to dig in, I was placed in a slit trench with a BAR man and another rifleman. I was told that we were covering the *flank-side* of the hill. About that time the Japanese launched an attack on the forward slope of the hill. The attack was repulsed, but there were casualties. I continued to observe the bottom of the side of the hill where we were located after the attack. The two guys with me correctly guessed that I was a *green,* scared replacement and not likely to fall asleep on guard. Soon they were totally out. There was still some light and a moon when I noticed three figures moving along the bottom of the hill. I decided to go ahead and open fire. I took a sight picture on the lead figure. They were about 40 or 50 yards from our position (lead the figure just a tiny bit) when I opened fire. I then fast-fired the clip at the other two figures who had hit the ground. I could have possibly hit the lead man, because I saw him kind of tumble. I saw no movement after that.

The firing woke up the BAR man and the other guy. A non-com slid down on our position and asked what we were shooting at. He told us to stay alert as there could be an attack on our side of the hill. He then told the BAR man to lay down some fire all along the bottom of the hill if there was movement.

The next morning I watched as three or four dead were being wrapped in their shelter halves to be taken down to battalion by the carrying party that was being assembled.

That was my first night-day in combat. I was still scared, but no longer green.

Near dark the third night, I received a call from the regimental commander, Colonel Mahoney.

"Can you hold that hill another night?"

I said, "It's dark now, too late to pack out. There's only one problem; I'm the only officer left. I have sergeants running all four platoons."

"Give me two names. They'll be second lieutenants in the morning."

I looked at my top choice, First Sergeant Joel Fedje. He had heard the conversation on the radio. He shook his head. "I have enough trouble taking care of the men; I don't want to be an officer."

I had several excellent men in mind, but the first two names that came to me were Gordon Lindvig and Claire Tongen. I named them. At 7 A.M. the next morning I was informed they were indeed officers.

CHAPTER 27

We were ordered off the hill to move back to Abijao for transport by water to Ormoc. On the way one of my noncoms was unable to rise after a short rest on the trail. Nathan Somberg, our battalion surgeon, who was nearby, administered a unit of plasma to him. It was like a miracle; the man got up and made it to the boats.

LCVPs transported us to the Ormoc pier, a cement structure that extended about four hundred yards out into the ocean. The concrete deck had massive bomb holes we had to carefully skirt.

Our first stop was at a level area where the road came into town from the east. Here, our remaining sixty-four men of the original 187 of Easy Company received a number of replacements. Many were our wounded just released from the hospital; others were men who had transferred to other units. They had one thing in common: all held infantrymen qualifications. We also picked up two more replacement officers, both of whom were well qualified.

While tenting in this area Filipino women came through camp to pick up laundry. It was delivered the very next day, clean and spotless. One of the girls was beautiful, but seemingly bashful. The men looked forward to seeing her each morning.

Two of our men came to me with disturbing news. They had checked with the temporary hospital in Ormoc, also at Graves Registration. They'd found no record of their buddy Paul Barnes being at either. A day later they again came to me. They had found him buried in the Filipino cemetery; he had died and his body had been left on the Ormoc pier. Graves Registration had not picked him up, so some kind Filipinos had moved him to their cemetery for burial. They had hung one of his dog tags on a homemade cross. I wasn't happy with our burial facilities and told Graves Registration so. They just shrugged their shoulders, but Barnes was moved.

Our next stop was at an abandoned former Filipino Army barrack much in need of repair from strafing and shell damage. Here, we worked over our equipment, readying it for our future move to Cebu Island.

In the city proper, the main street had been cleared as a landing strip to be used by light aircraft such as Stinsons and Pipers. To one side of the street there was an iron-barred, open cage holding Japanese collaborators. All females had shorn heads; they sat in the center of the twenty-by-thirty-foot open cell attempting to avoid urinating by the spectators, who mocked them from the outside edges of the enclosure. Two Filipino guerrillas seemed to be in charge; they did nothing to discourage the shenanigans. It was an abhorrent and degrading spectacle, people acting like animals. Still, knowing the atrocities the Japanese had heaped upon these people, I hardened myself to the excesses.

Since we would be in Ormoc a few more days I decided to visit our wounded across the island at the Tacloban hospital. Leaving early the next morning my driver, Breding, and I found the roads dusty, with heavy traffic. We arrived at the hospital about 3 P.M., to find a tent encampment, certainly not the best. (We were lucky that day, for a truck convoy carrying supplies to Ormoc was ambushed by Japanese. Only one driver survived.)

I found Pete Sherar first; he was in a tent ward with several of our wounded from Easy. As soon as he saw me he called, "Hand me that Japanese saber under my bed. I want to cut down these damned ropes holding up my leg." He was in traction, grinning as usual, so I knew he was kidding.

He confided, "My platoon sergeant, Christianson, died

yesterday morning. He developed peritonitis; the bullet through his hip was responsible. He was in a cast and the pressure on his stomach was too much. He begged me to tear out some of the plaster cast to allow expansion. I did that." Pete looked grim. "Would you believe the doctors and nurses held a dance night before last, leaving only one nurse on duty? She was too afraid to remove part of the cast to relieve Chris, so I took it upon myself. These hospital people should be shot. A dance is more important than all of these wounded men!"

Breding and I visited with several of our wounded, some of whom would be going back to duty—others, more seriously wounded, would be returned stateside.

I spoke with a soldier who told me of a transient camp located a few miles to the south, near Dulag. Since dusk was rapidly approaching, we drove there. We found ourselves next to a camp for women who had been released from Japanese prison encampments. Most were carrying and tending to their half-Japanese children; some of the women even had two. They were tough; they had to have been to stay alive.

Early the next morning we left for our return to Ormoc, to hear the 182nd Infantry had made an assault landing at Cebu City, on the island of Cebu. That island was in sight to our west. They had run into a wild fight, with mines in the water and a well-organized defense. Still, they had taken the city of eighty thousand inhabitants.

A patrol torpedo boat group arrived in Ormoc and we struck up a trade. A Japanese officer's saber gained us a hundred-pound sack of sugar. Sugar had been in short supply, but the Navy (as usual) seemed to have plenty.

Incidentally, those swords sold readily to naval personnel for $100 or more at the time. Many men scored cash sales. Fortunately, we had a few spares for trading at the Easy supply room.

I found Lieutenant Milt Shedd had an exciting experience with the PT boats worth relating. Following is his experience as a crewman:

On March 25, 1945 I received permission to accompany two PT boats at Ormoc on an attack on Japanese shipping at the Island of Cebu. We departed at 17:00 with the expectation of returning the next morning at 08:00.

We were to create a diversionary attack on two coastal vessels in coordination with A20 bombers who were to destroy the Japanese ships. Shortly after dawn we roared in, creating big rooster tails toward the vessels while the bombers began strafing and skip bombing. One of our aircraft began smoking and crashed in the vicinity of Mactan Island.

Turning both boat sterns to the shore we took five enemy barges under fire as the two coastal freighters began to burn. The five barges burst into flames as we poured 40mm and machine-gun fire into them; we laid hove-to in the water meanwhile. Unfortunately we were in shoal water with large coral heads, the recoil of our 40mm gun constantly driving us further into the coral. Attempting to get out, we found ourselves firmly aground.

Our companion boat pulled up on the other side of the reef and attempted to pull us clear, but plainly it was impossible. They would have to come inside the reef to assist us. Meanwhile as we were only 600 yards from shore the Japanese began to riddle us with rifle and machine-gun fire. Several of our crew were wounded as we continued to defend ourselves with the 40mm and machine-guns. A headquarters supply sergeant from the 164th who had accompanied me, took over as gun loader on the 40mm because of the wounded. He was inexperienced at the gun, losing a thumb.

Three P-61 night fighters arrived to strafe the shore facilities, easing things somewhat until they ran out of ammunition. Firing our last 40mm rounds we found we had over 100 Japanese bullet holes in our craft and many wounded. In the event we had to abandon the boat we were prepared to swim beyond the reef to the other PT boat.

Finally the other PT boat, realizing our peril, came inside the reef and managed to pull us off. We ended up with

50% of the men wounded and two killed. We were under constant fire for over an hour, a sitting duck.

Our propellers were badly damaged by the coral and we could only make five knots speed, but the skipper, although wounded, determined to rescue the downed aircraft crew if possible. We slowly cruised up to Mactan Island to the wreck and saw a young Filipino boy swimming out to us. He spoke English and told us there were no survivors in the aircraft, and that the beach back of the mangroves was loaded with enemy. By this time it was somewhat after the noon hour.

We began the long cruise back to Ormoc, but because of our very slow speed arrived there the next day at daybreak.

Milt's remarked about the guerrillas:

We can't hope to kill all the enemy. Our objective is to disorganize them and scatter them into the hills where they have no supplies stored; they will cease to be any sort of menace, as the guerrillas can take care of them—that is, if the ratio is 25 guerrillas to each enemy and the enemy are unarmed and in groups of not over two or three. In general the guerrillas are not even an excuse for fighting men. In some instances they have helped, but the propaganda one hears concerning their prowess is nauseating to a man that has worked with them, and I have worked with them.

After a few days' rest at Ormoc, we loaded our equipment onto LSTs, making the brief trip across to Cebu City. Here we bivouacked along the main highway, south of the town.

The next four days were spent writing seventeen letters of condolence to the families of Easy men who had been killed on Leyte. This was the hardest task I had ever undertaken. I was familiar with the men's names, but knew little of their hopes and aspirations, little or nothing of their families.

I consulted with their friends in the platoon, gaining considerable knowledge and understanding. Thankfully, regimental headquarters did the final typing, correcting my composition.

Even with our replacements, the company was nowhere near full strength. Our only consolation: we had eliminated over 360 enemy on Leyte. We knew there were many more from our mortar and artillery fire.

CHAPTER 28

The next day we loaded into trucks, moving south a few miles to the cement plant below Cebu City. Here we unloaded to begin a trek around to the rear of the city.

Three natives met us, traveling in the opposite direction. I began to laugh as I recognized my old company commander.

"John, what in heck are you doing dressed in those Filipino clothes? Where have you been?"

Gossett had a wry grin. "I've been a spy traveling with these two guides. I'll sure be glad to shed these itchy, grubby clothes."

The thin Gossett, with his deep, dark tan, did look like a Filipino. And borrowed clothing, crudely woven from flax straw, was indeed itchy.

"What did you find?"

"Chuck, the Japanese are up on the mountain ridge behind the city. They are dug in with mutually defensive positions. You'll have a tough climb and a tougher fight, since they can see you all the way. It won't be easy to dig them out; I suspect it will also be costly."

We continued up the valley, headed north now, all the while watching the ridge to our right. Twice I saw Japanese standing on peaks, peering down at us, the range about two thousand yards. I was surprised we didn't receive mortar fire from them.

When we finally stopped we were assigned positions for the uphill assault. Meanwhile, a 105mm self-propelled gun took the hill in Company G's sector under fire. Enemy could be seen moving around on the crest. Few shells exploded;

most ricocheted off the top of the hill. We received a message that the Japanese were shelling the airfield at Cebu City; the airport was closed. Hells bells! It was discovered that our own self-propelled gun was responsible!

For the immediate attack upon the hill, Company F was on the left flank, Easy in the center, with Company G on the right. We later found the section of ridge assigned to Easy had no Japanese defenders, but every inch was covered by frontal and flanking fire from a distance.

I had Gordon Lindvig, one of our two direct-appointment officers, place his 60mm mortars on a level spot, in defilade, partway up the ridge. A sound-powered-telephone line was laid as we advanced. As we reached our objective we came under heavy rifle fire from, of all places, the high hill in front of Company G. The crest of this hill was perhaps one hundred feet higher than our position, and was littered with hundreds of round stones, almost the exact size of a military helmet. I judged the range to the top of this hill to be about three hundred yards. Evidently the Japanese had a scope-equipped rifle, or else someone up there was a crack shot. They were that good, for in a matter of minutes several of my men were wounded or killed.

I ran to the man holding the spool of wire that led back to our mortars. Hooking up the sound-powered phone he carried, I called for mortar fire on the top of the hill to Company G's front. At that moment someone shouted, "Blackwell's been hit!"

Handing the phone to Lindvig, our new lieutenant, I said, "Get the mortars firing on that hill or we're going to lose a lot of men!"

Running the forty or fifty feet to Private Blackwell, I dropped to his side and noted blood coming from his left ankle. That shouldn't have stopped him, so I rolled his head to the side. He was dead.

Rising, I ran back to Lindvig. At that instant a bullet struck him in the chest. He held out his left wrist to me as I supported him. He said, "Take my watch, I won't need it anymore." He was gone. He had taken a bullet meant for me.

Our mortar shells crashed down on that pile of boulders at that instant, stopping further rifle fire from the hill. By keeping up a steady mortar barrage we were able to dig in, to some extent. Because we were on the peak of the ridge, we dug into the back slope, under the top edge.

An hour or so later, I received a call from the battalion commander, Mac. He said, "Chuck, have you room for me up there? I'm coming up to join you."

I said, "Sure, but bring a pick mattock. I've started a hole in the shale, but it needs a lot more work."

I was to find out later that he had been admonished by the regimental commander, ordered to get the hell up where the men were fighting. Since we had to work closely together now, I mentally declared a truce.

When he arrived, I put him to work; he didn't complain as we took turns tunneling into the top edge of the shale rock, making a final hole about eight feet deep into the ridge.

There was a clump of grass growing about three feet high just above my position; I added to it each night, using brush and small branches, being careful not to overdo it.

Mac had brought up a spotting scope that was worth its weight in gold. While on Bougainville I had written the adjutant general of North Dakota, begging him to send us the spotting scopes owned by the National Guard. They were used yearly at the Camp Perry matches held in Ohio. I'd shot on the National Guard team in 1940, so I knew of the scopes. At that time the National Guard had at least a dozen on hand.

With a nasty war going on, that adjutant general wrote me a surly letter, saying, *The spotting scopes are the property of the State of North Dakota. They will not be sent to the 164th Infantry.*

I wanted to find that stupid ass after the war, but the years healed my temper.

That first evening the Japanese dropped a few mortar rounds on us, probably to register. Early the next morning I received a call to send down a man to guide five replacements up to our company. They had reached the halfway point on their return, when the Japanese lobbed mortar shells over our ridge. I watched the impacts down below; one shell landed perfectly upon the six climbing men. Stupidly, they were bunched up. All were killed or seriously wounded. There was no doubt in my mind: a Japanese soldier on that high hill in front of Company G was directing the fire.

Shortly after 2 P.M. the next afternoon, Company G made an assault upon the high ridge without asking for our support. We could have helped immensely, and did to a certain extent, but it caught us by surprise. I watched Company G men get very near the top of the hill, then stopped by Japanese rising up to throw grenades down upon them. If we had been warned, we could have cut down those enemy soldiers with machine-gun fire. Someone had screwed up— there'd been no coordination. Company G men could have taken that hill and saved us all a lot of grief!

When darkness fell that night we were subjected to a severe mortar shelling. One mortar shell landed directly over my hole. Mac and I were protected by three feet of solid shale, but the explosion stunned us both. I got a call from Company F, requesting medical men. Their command post had been hit hard, with several men killed or wounded, not having dug in as securely as we. Their captain, John Landeck, was killed in this mortar barrage. It lasted for about ten minutes; I guessed perhaps one hundred or more rounds came in. We spent the rest of the night solving our problems; a Lieutenant Campbell was now running Company F.

I managed to get a .50-caliber machine gun sent up with a panoramic sight. Concealing it in the grass I sighted it about fifteen hundred yards to the right front, where I had seen Japanese moving between positions. That evening we began receiving grenade launcher shells (nothing like the 81mm or 90mm Japanese shells). Sighting through the panoramic, we saw two Japanese. It was obvious one was teaching the other how to fire the grenade launcher. They were in the open, but at a long range. A brief burst from the .50-caliber machine gun changed their minds, both disappeared.

Early the next morning, Mac, who was looking through the spotting scope, said, "Hey, look at this!"

I peeked into the telescope to see a pair of Japanese eyes about fifty feet away. He had on a helmet that blended perfectly with the adjoining rocks. I marked his position carefully, looking through my 3-power Weaver scope. He was so small in the glass, I would be lucky to get him. I said, "He's in the shadows now. Let's hope that when the sun swings west this afternoon, he'll still be watching from the same spot."

We waited until about 3 P.M., when the sun was in his eyes. Mac spotted him again. "He's there, in the same hole. Think you can get him?"

This time I could see his helmet but not his eyes. Sighting just below the edge of the steel rim, I fired. Lifting my eyes quickly I saw his helmet tumbling backward up the hill. Mac said, "I think you got him in the forehead. The bullet must have gone through his head, catching his helmet at the rear edge."

We studied the hill for the rest of the day, but saw no other Japanese faces.

It was about noon the next day when one of my noncoms approached me. "I'm sorry, sir, but I'm dripping!"

Mentally counting back to the time of his infection, I said, "It had to be in Ormoc; who was it?"

"Remember that cute laundry girl?"

I certainly did! It was the beauty! "Who else got to her?"

He named two men.

"Get them!"

After speaking with them, one man admitted that he too had the clap. The other man was smarter; he had used a condom. I was disgusted and said, "I'm mighty disappointed with both of you. I thought you knew more than that! Get down the hill for your shots, then get back as soon as they turn you loose!"

Due to the lack of medical facilities and supplies during

the Japanese occupation, gonorrhea was almost a sure thing among the prostitutes.

That afternoon we were treated to a show; aircraft bombed the positions just across the valley, on the city-side ridge. The shock waves were spectacular; the air compression from the explosions looked like growing waves of water. We were unable to see any discernible results.

Late that afternoon we were subjected to white phosphorous mortar shells that set the grasses and brush on the back slope of our ridge on fire. There was no danger, but we mulled over the portent of this change. We finally decided the Japanese were pulling out, using the smoke for cover. There was only one way for them to go; north, up the intermediate valley between the two ridges. I didn't think they would get far; surely the other regiments would have the routes blocked.

How they escaped was never explained to us, another cover-up by Americal Division headquarters. The Japanese were supposedly surrounded.

CHAPTER 29

Word came the next morning that indeed, the enemy had decamped, and that we were to push across the ridges down to Cebu City.

After our initial attack upon the mountain, aided by our 60mm mortars, our 81mm mortars had taken charge of firing on the local ridge. I had moved our 60mm's up to the ridge to fire on the opposite ridge overlooking the city.

Mac left, accompanied by a few men from battalion headquarters and a Filipino carrier group. The rest of the battalion followed at intervals.

I was interested in the Japanese positions straight across from us, so took a shortcut to them. To my surprise the Japanese had tunneled as much as one hundred feet or more through solid rock, all below the back slope of their ridge, concealing small holes in the hillside facing us—certainly exhaustive work. These concealed holes provided covering and enfilade fire on our positions. We also found literally hundreds of rounds of mortar ammunition; why hadn't they used it?

Working east we found a printing press with plates, hastily abandoned, also cases and cases of printed peso bills—occupation money. Everyone grabbed a souvenir handful of this worthless paper.

Finally, below us, we spotted the highway leading up to the ridge on the city side. Here we found a multitude of man-made storage caves cut into solid rock; some even had electric lights. Inside were stored goods from the department stores of the city, all materials looted by the Japanese. Each cave held different items, hardware in some, clothing in others, as well as fuel, and about anything your heart desired. Everything was new, just as it had been taken from the downtown stores.

It took only minutes for the men to find new wheelbarrows in which to carry two electrical generators, expensive surveying equipment, and other supplies we could use. Some men garnered crated, upright Singer sewing machines to be traded to the Filipino women for favors or money. (A woman with a sewing machine was self-made; she was in great demand as a seamstress.)

I allowed the men to prowl the caves for an hour or so, knowing the entire population of Cebu City would be onto this treasure trove within hours. (Before dark, hundreds of civilians were looting—the next afternoon most everything was gone.)

At the entrance of one cave I noted a wide board lying along the narrow entrance. It was one by twelve inches, about twelve feet long. It seemed unnecessary to me, out of place. Cautiously I raised the board on edge to find a tape-measure mine where I would have walked. I picked it up and unscrewed the cap, removing the small detonator. I hoped everyone would be careful; they had been warned, again and again! It made sense that the Japanese would booby-trap the caves.

Finally, after rounding up the company, we headed back down the mountain. At the bottom trucks picked us up, transporting us to our old bivouac area.

Thievery became a problem. The civilians had little or nothing. In one case a group of Filipino thieves were stealing barracks bags from our supply tents, which were poorly guarded. One of these men was caught in the act at night as he ran with a heavy bag. His mistake was running under a streetlight. His body lay for three days in the middle of the intersection. Vehicle traffic was heavy, but all carefully drove around the corpse. It was finally removed the third night.

I anticipated the problem of writing more letters to parents; fortunately regimental headquarters was not ready for this necessary paperwork. I received a general order awarding me a second cluster for my Silver Star. My Bronze Star had come after Guadalcanal.

Mac picked his new executive officer. Because of his animosity toward me, I wasn't at all surprised that it was not me. After a couple of days passed, I received an order to report at regimental headquarters. Here I saw a grim look on the face of the regimental commander. He ordered me to report to Mac as his executive officer. (He evidently had been informed of the situation, and Mac had got his butt chewed.)

Mac wasn't a bit civil to me when I reported at his command post. Looking at me as I walked in, he said grimly, "I guess we'll have to learn to get along together."

I replied, "The problem is yours; I've done my best."

I knew his hard-on related to the time he'd sent me to close the gap at Koli Point on Guadalcanal and was nearly relieved of his command. He wasn't the bravest man, but of necessity, we had to get along. I was agreeable, but wary.

After a few more days the battalion troops loaded aboard LCIs (landing craft infantry) for the assault landing at Dumaguette, Negros Island. While still miles away from Dumaguette, we saw the smoke of many fires. The Japanese were burning supplies and part of the town.

We landed six miles north of the town, the enemy airfield being two miles to our south. Luckily, the airfield had been worked over by our Air Force as the twelve to fifteen aircraft in the parking area had been reduced to junk. We were not bothered by enemy fighters.

At the point of our landing, a road ran inland about a half mile, ending abruptly, a dead end. In order to clear the beach, I temporarily moved the battalion vehicles onto this short road as they arrived at the beach. Mac took the battalion from the end of the road through jungle, cutting at a 45-degree angle to the southeast to intersect the road leading from Dumaguette inland to the mountains. A safety perimeter was established around our vehicles and supplies as we settled down to await further orders. Being battalion exec, I was stuck to handle any problems that arose.

About 11 P.M. a firefight erupted. The sound came from the direction the battalion had taken. I guessed the firing to be about six or seven miles away. Apprehensive, I called on the radio several times before finally getting an answer.

Mac sounded tired and disgusted. He said, "Charley, you won't believe what just happened. That damned recon group called me on the radio saying they were in Dumaguette and coming out the inland road to join us at our position. I had a battalion perimeter set astride the road with machine guns covering the road in each direction. I guess the men were tired and confused when I told them the recon group would be joining us after dark. They heard the approach of whining gears and assumed it to be the recon's armored car. Instead, two flatbed trucks loaded with Japanese troops casually drove into our perimeter, and a few seconds later drove out the opposite side. Not a shot was fired; the Japanese didn't even realize we were here!

"Two minutes later a long column of enemy, on foot, followed the trucks; our gunners were finally alert. It was their firing you heard. It's quieted down now, but I'm told that the road is littered with enemy bodies.

"At daylight I want you to leave the trucks and supplies in charge of the motor pool. Follow our trail through the bush with all men that can be spared." He hesitated. "What a damned foul-up! I hope no one hears of this!"

Even before full dawn I was on my way to join the battalion. Just as I reached them, a patrol came in with a few enemy wounded. One, a shirtless Japanese, had a shiny .30-caliber bullet protruding from the muscles of his shoulder. It looked to be loose, so I attempted to pluck it out. He flinched, giving me a dirty look.

At that point Mac spotted me. "Chuck, bring that Japanese over here, we've got an interpreter."

I leaned over the seated Japanese soldier, spoke, and beckoned with my finger for him to get up. He ignored me.

Our A & P (ammunition and pioneer) officer was a big bruiser and impatient. He booted the enemy in the rear. The

Japanese turned angrily, to say in perfect English, "What's the matter?"

I began to laugh as I called back to Mac, "We don't need an interpreter for this one."

The prisoner admitted to being a pilot at the Japanese airfield, but would not tell us where he had learned his perfect English. I suspect he was a transplant from California.

I often thought of the consequences if anyone had fired at the trucks when they were in the center of the battalion. What a donnybrook that would have been with about seventy armed Japanese dumped into the middle of the pot!

CHAPTER 30

We found the road a dead end about five miles farther on. Two trucks stood just off the road, rendered inoperable by the enemy. (The distributors were smashed.) Within days they were again serviceable. The trucks were copies of 1937 Chevrolets, with long flatbeds. Their fuel was alcohol, made at the sugar mill north of Dumaguette. The Japanese had converted the town of Bias's sugar plant to the manufacture of alcohol. This product was of a poor grade with little power—the truck engines emitting a weak *put-put-put*ting sound accompanied by a disagreeable odor. Two large generators on wheels had been abandoned, power for the two radios lying nearby; they had been destroyed. The generators were of four hundred volts, worthless to us.

From this point the battalion began to climb a steep, narrow ridge, moving forward two miles before receiving mortar fire. The terrain ahead was rough, the escarpment a long, gradual climb. On each side lay huge valleys, the sides of which were almost vertical. The Dumaguette Valley was to our right, deep, perhaps two miles across with a slow-moving stream far below. To our left was another vast valley, the bottom of which lay four thousand feet below, with the usual river.

It was difficult to determine the position of the Japanese mortar, but by its sound, we judged it to be about two thousand yards straight ahead. We bulled through, thinning our line as we passed the danger point. Counterfire from the 81mm mortars of Company H finally silenced the enemy.

We managed another mile, driving a few Japanese from their positions, to find a circular hill where we dug in.

Mac and I had been assigned a Filipino guerrilla corporal to be our interpreter, a young boy named Salvadore Dumanado. He had a low, constant, croupy cough that I suspected might be tubercular. Despite his youth, he was pleasant, quick, and smart, anticipating Mac's desires even before he knew them himself. He knew the country and the people, easing our work with the Filipino carrier groups.

All rifle companies worked forward on our narrow front, not gaining much ground. The terrain was favorable to the Japanese; they were well dug in. We consolidated our main battalion position as engineers began building a road uphill to us. Soon we had an ambulance handy, plus other trucks, also a jeep.

An armored Cat dozer came up to our hilltop, only to slide backward to the edge of the cliff. The thin layer of topsoil slid like a carpet on the wet rock beneath. By digging in the wheels of two winch-equipped vehicles, we were able to hold the Cat until the engine was again started. Using the winches and a slow crawl of the Cat, we managed to save it.

Easy Company made a drive along the right flank and I followed closely behind. Suddenly, on a rock escarpment slightly to my left and above, several Japanese popped up to make a bayonet attack as skirmishers. About a dozen were in the line. Their officer, who was in the center of the line, had only a saber, which he waved around his head. One Easy man was trapped on the left edge, for he had climbed up on the high rock with difficulty. When the closest Japanese came at him with his bayonet, he was still climbing, unable to fire his gun. To save himself he jumped over the edge of the cliff, dropping at least twenty feet or more but saving his life; he ended up with only a broken leg.

The antic scene was like a Hollywood movie, but Easy wiped out every Japanese soldier but one. The amazing part was, no one shot at the officer; he was no threat, he had no gun. He hesitated for long seconds as everyone watched. Looking to the right, then to the left, he was thunderstruck.

All his men were gone! He finally turned, running back over the hill. It so surprised us that everyone broke into laughter.

To my right, about one hundred feet away, I saw Lieutenant Paul Wright, recently assigned to Easy, suddenly drop. He was ahead of his men on the right flank, and had been standing upright. Rifle bullets were thick, coming in and going out. He was lying on his back with his feet on a downslope when I ran to him. There appeared to be no blood, but when I opened his cartridge belt, I suddenly became aware of the damage. A bullet had cut his abdominal wall, for his intestines began flowing down over his trousers. There was no medic immediately available because of the heavy firing; I was forced to be a substitute. I could see no perforations or indication of damage to his intestines and decided they must be tucked back in.

Someone came along at that moment and dropped alongside me. He said, "My God! What can you do with that?"

I opened a package of sulfa powder and gently pulled his intestines back, then I sprinkled them liberally with the white powder. I said, "I'm going to tuck them all back in place; they look okay. Get your Carlisle out quick, I'll need it!"

Adding a sprinkle of water to keep the intestines damp, I added even more sulfa powder, then soaked down the Carlisle he handed me. I suddenly felt guilty about the uncleanliness of my hands; I hadn't been able to wash for days.

Spreading out the large bandage, I had the other soldier hold it in place while I unwrapped mine. Between the two huge Carlisle bandages we were able to hold things together. Finally Easy covered us, and a carrying party arrived with a litter. I was thankful that our battalion surgeon, Nathan Somberg, had given us instruction on how to treat wounds. He had said, "Don't let internal organs dry for even a second!"

Many days later Salvadore and I were able to go back to Dumaguette to clean up and check the men in the hospital. Paul Wright was in a separate room. When I opened the door, he saw me and began shouting curse after curse at me. I quietly closed the door, knowing he must be suffering horribly.

At least he was alive, and never appeared on later casualty lists.

Salvadore asked me if I would like to see the library at Silliman University, where Japanese colonel Oie (pronounced O-E-Ay) kept all prisoners until their execution. Entering the thick, stone-walled building, I was horrified. The inside walls of the large library (perhaps thirty by sixty feet) were whitewashed, but every inch, as high as a man could reach, even while resting upon the shoulders of another, was covered with writing. Much of the writing was done using blood for ink, the prisoners lacking pencils and pens. Last wills and testaments, calendars showing the names of men and their execution dates, littered every wall. Hardly a square foot was left for writing.

There were hundreds of names on the walls, all to be executed by Colonel Oie. Outside, Salvadore led me to the seawall where the Japanese cut off the heads of the prisoners after tying their hands behind their backs and making them kneel with their heads forward. Their bodies were then thrown in the water, disposed of by fish and sharks.

Afterward, Salvadore took me to a friend's home where secret photos had been taken of many of the executions from the second floor of an adjoining building. One clear photo was of an Australian pilot, still in uniform, kneeling with his head bared, his hands tied behind him. A Japanese officer, his saber raised overhead, was about to behead him.

I reported this building, requesting that the walls be photographed by intelligence to confirm identification of the men. I doubt it was ever done; I just don't know. I actually blinked back tears when I left the library, my hatred of the Japanese renewed, especially for Colonel Oie. I found out later that it was doubtful he was ever tried for war crimes. The name Oie means "big house." Supposedly, he was an important man in Japan prior to and during the war.

While we stopped to bathe in a stream, we watched a Filipino man sneaking cautiously along the shore, plucking the large banana flowers from plants. Salvadore yelled and the man ran. Salvadore explained, "It's against the law to remove the flowers. They bake up into a delicious meal, but there will be no fruit on the tree."

Our return trip up to the battalion was a cinch, a journey of twelve miles and a climb to four thousand feet, all by jeep.

While traveling, Salvadore told me a little of his association with the Japanese. He had joined the Filipino guerrillas while still going to school. They harassed the enemy from time to time, keeping them bottled up in the areas between Dumaguette and Bias. Unfortunately, the guerrillas were not a formidable force, being poorly trained and led by local politicians. They were easily pushed back by the Japanese forces.

Salvadore had slipped into Dumaguette at night to visit friends and had been caught at daybreak by the JAP (Japanese Auxiliary Police). These were Filipino collaborators recruited by the Japanese for favors and money. He was confined at the Silliman Library to be executed, but it seemed a JAP officer wanted his sister. To save his life she moved in with this collaborator.

Upon our landing at Dumaguette, on Negros, the guerrillas rounded up these traitors, putting them in the local prison. This JAP and Salvadore's sister were both locked up there. I told Mac the story, so when he went into Dumaguette, he took Salvadore to the prison. It was a tearful reunion for them both; she was pregnant.

One of our battalions came across about seventy-five civilians who had gone into the hills with the Japanese. They were collaborators expecting succor from their former friends. The Japanese were soon short of food and finally refused to feed them. Ordered to return to Dumaguette by the Japanese, some refused, so the Japanese raked them with Nambu fire, wounding several. That convinced them—they were forced to walk the twelve miles back to the city.

Fighting near the entrance to a cave, one soldier found $999 in one-dollar bills while searching a dead Japanese. I was informed this cavity contained large amounts of explosives, stored there by the enemy—they were removed by Easy Company. Now we had overrun them.

Our new officer replacements for Easy Company were now in the thick of the fighting. Following are some experiences of Lieutenant William Byers:

On April 25 our unit sailed from Cebu City on LCI's and on April 26 waded ashore at Dumaguette, Negros Island. My Company Commander was now 1st Lt. Clayton Kingston. Whenever my platoon was the lead platoon on our march inland, and Lt. Kingston was walking beside me, he gave advice and moral support for a new officer in a combat position. I always admired him for that.

The second night on the island the Japanese patrols harried us at night by throwing grenades at our foxholes. One landed on the dirt pile I had made from digging it, but I suffered only hearing loss for a while. We continued to follow the enemy as they retreated to the high mountains in the interior of Negros Island. At night the enemy would check out our positions. The company adopted the policy that after dark no one was to leave his foxhole or they could be shot.

After pursuing the enemy further and higher up in the mountains the Colonel assigned me the task of a flanking maneuver. My 3rd platoon was given one light machine-gun crew and one 60mm mortar to make up a reinforced rifle platoon. We were trucked several miles around the end of a large mountain where we met two Filipino guides—we unloaded. We walked several miles to a point on the opposite side of the mountain from our troops. Here I was introduced to a Major Dumanado, a Filipino in charge of some Filipino resistance fighters. He seemed more content to discuss American history than to run the Japanese off the mountain.

The only way up to the top of this mountain was a very narrow trail up the hog-back, with sides that dropped off almost vertically. We knew from the Filipino troops that the Japanese had a machine gun guarding the trail.

In a day or two I took a squad of men and attempted to assault the Jap position. A single shot was fired at the lead man, but it missed. Needless to say we fell back to a safe distance. We had a 2nd Lieutenant observer from headquarters observing the action. I said it was suicide to send men up again as we know there is a machine gun guarding the trail. The Lieutenant observer said to me, "You're not going to let one shot keep you from going up the hill, are you?" I said to him, "Do you want to lead the way?" His reply was, "That's not my job."

I conferred with my veteran soldier, Staff Sgt. Bill Bailey, and he suggested we lay flat on the ground with two BARs and M1s and lay a lot of fire up the trail. When we did this, the Japanese machine gun opened up full blast and the bullets were just a few feet over our heads. I turned to the observer and said, "Now do you think we can go up the trail?" He replied, "No, it isn't possible without a heavy loss of life." I thanked Sergeant Bailey for his combat knowledge of the situation.

The next day four P38s flew over the area, but they came nowhere near hitting the target area.

A few days later my unit was called back to rejoin our company on the other side of the mountain. On the 5th of June I was promoted to 1st Lt.

After my 3rd Platoon rejoined the company we proceeded to pursue the Japanese farther up the mountain. We were to attack Japanese positions about and above our present location. I was ordered to scout the approach using one squad of men, plus my platoon Sergeant Bill Bailey. We carried an SCR 300 radio on this patrol. My lead scout became intimidated when a Jap threw a grenade at him and disappeared into the jungle-like brush. He was already on orders for rotation and he said he could not do the job properly. Sergeant Bailey immediately said, "I'll take lead scout."

Down in the deep valley or ravine we came across a lot of Jap communication wire and stopped to examine it.

Bailey said to me, "I sure don't like the looks of this. We better work this area over with mortars."

I reported what we had found on the radio to my C.O. I said, "What do you want me to do?" Kingston said, "Keep going, but watch your step. We just saw some Japs up above you in the same rocks."

We started to go farther and instantly two large explosions went off exactly where we were. My two scouts Capper and Bailey were in front of me. My squad sergeant behind me was killed almost instantly. My BAR man had a big hole in his forehead. The Filipino boy who was carrying my radio threw it away and ran to the rear, as did the remaining men in the squad. To show what Army training will do, we were always taught never to abandon our weapon, so I picked up the BAR, rifle and radio and headed back for help. At the time the Japanese started raking the area with machine-gun fire. Fortunately, they could not get the fire low enough as it was just above my head. I got about 100 feet back when I heard a noise in the brush to my left. I checked it out and it turned out to be my second scout, Capper. I said, "Where's Bailey?"

He said, "He is dead."

We returned to the company area and reported. Needless to say we had to recover our dead and wounded. Lt. Kingston, the C.O., called artillery and asked for smoke on the Japanese positions. They said we only have 25 rounds so you will have to hurry. Needless to say, we did!

When we got to the wounded man he was conscious, but had a large hole in his forehead, and said he couldn't see. He was able to walk out with help. I never heard from him after that. I promoted Pfc. Capper to Sergeant.

The worst loss to me was Sergeant Bailey. His help to me in making decisions was almost impossible to replace. His courage in volunteering to take lead scout was remarkable. I will always be indebted to him all my life.

After the recovery of the dead and wounded the artillery pounded that position all night. The next day when we climbed the mountain peak there was not a tree standing and no Japs to be found. Too bad we didn't shell it before I had two good men killed and one wounded.

A few weeks later the whole regiment withdrew from the hills and were transported back to Cebu Island in the vicinity of Cebu City. Here we were issued new clothes and other necessities for personal use.

I received new replacement personnel to bring the platoon up to regulation strength. Next we started amphibious training in LCVP's in preparation for the assault on southern Japan.

Thank God Harry Truman had the guts to drop the bomb, thus saving thousands of lives.

CHAPTER 31

I went back to the airfield to catch a ride in an L4 with Lieutenant Mitchell, a pilot of the 245th Field Artillery. He was to show me some of the major Japanese defensive positions. A separate landing strip had been cleared by the engineers for our small aircraft. This was a stupid waste of time. Although the blacktop main Japanese runway was mined, one hour of work would have cleared all the explosives. I walked a short distance along the blacktop strip, to find small circular holes had been systematically dug with a 75mm artillery shell buried nose-up in each hole. A small board had been placed over each detonator, to be pressed down by the wheels of a landing aircraft.

To defuse this minefield was easy. Remove the board and unscrew (counterclockwise) the detonator from the shell. It was perfectly safe; a child could do it if shown how. I had a few minutes before Mitchell finally arrived, so disarmed several. Unfortunately, not nearly enough.

We had to remove the 612 radio in the L4 to compensate for my weight, since these L4s had little horsepower. (I believe only 65.) We flew up to our battalion, then farther up the ridge, where I saw many defensive holes dug by the enemy. All were located to cover large expanses of open mountain. One Japanese soldier ducked into a hole on the top of the ridge; Mitchell reached for a grenade from the small rack on the right overhead. Diving on the enemy he missed the Japanese by a country mile. I could see why both of our L4s had so many bullet patches on them. Any good rifleman should have been able to shoot them down. Still, many Japanese held off shooting at the small craft, knowing they could expect immediate artillery retaliation.

On completion of our search Mitchell decided to buzz the battalion to give me a thrill. He did, but for this stunt got a tongue-lashing from his CO.

On another occasion Lieutenant Lynn, our other pilot, took me up as the battalion progressed farther up the mountain. He and Mitchell had a tent on the airfield with canvas bunks. Mitchell had a pet monkey on a chain tied to his bed. Lynn told me, "That damned monkey jumped over and pissed all over my cot. When Mitchell was gone, I took the critter for a ride. I had a hellish time dropping him from the plane, he was all over me!"

To protect the waterfront of Dumaguette, the Japanese had placed drums of alcohol along the beaches and seawalls. If we had landed at the city's edge, machine-gun fire with tracer bullets would supposedly have punctured the drums, setting them on fire. Upon our assault landing, those troops entering the city from the north thought it strange when they saw Filipinos busy rolling the black barrels to their homes. Soon after that several homes opened bars.

One afternoon, about 3 P.M., Mac received a call ordering us to march back downhill and load up on trucks to pass back to Dumaguette, then go up the Dumaguette Valley to a position directly across from our present location. This meant abandoning our positions to the Japanese, which was utterly stupid. Using field glasses we could see across the valley to the north. It was open country, devoid of enemy.

Mac questioned the regimental executive (the one I had the encounter with about firing the 37mm gun on Bougainville), to find our regimental commander was thoroughly drunk (another of the great-school-on-the-Hudson graduates!).

I had to give Mac credit, as I heard the entire conversation. "Don't you have any say? Don't you have any guts? If he's as drunk as you say, cancel the order. We all know he's nothing but a damned rum-dum!"

Our cowardly regimental exec, afraid for his job, refused.

We spent the remainder of the day and most of the night retreating the twelve miles back to Dumaguette, then crossing to the other side of Dumaguette Valley.

At noon the next day the regimental CO sobered up and moved us back to our old positions. The Japanese had moved in, as we knew they would; we lost more men killed and wounded retaking our old holes.

Mac and I filed charges against the CO, sending the letter up through to Division; from there it was to go to the inspector general's department, Washington, DC. A few days later we heard the letter was opened by the CO at Division, who said to his cronies, "We can't let poor Jiggs be railroaded by that National Guard bunch!" (This came back to us as gospel since the conversation was overheard. Jiggs was the West Point nickname of our regimental CO.)

In an effort to soften up the Japanese positions a Tactical Air Control Party was sent up to us. This captain and his driver had a jeep loaded with radios to direct aircraft when bombing or dispersing napalm in close cooperation with troops. A bombing raid on the ridges was staged, followed a day or two later with a napalm attack. We moved farther up, reaching 4,400 feet before again being stopped. In one of his artillery shoots Mitchell was directing fire from his L4. Getting too close to the explosions' shrapnel took a chunk off his propeller, but he was lucky; he had enough altitude to glide the twelve miles back to the airfield.

An Air Force pilot flying a P38 had a brother in the 164th, so decided to visit him. Since the blacktop runway had never been cleared of mines, a wheel and wing were totaled when he landed. I imagine that was covered up by saying he had to make a forced landing.

Mac received an urgent call from the regimental CO, who had evidently become disenchanted with both his executive officer and the Regimental S-3. He said to Mac, "They are both cowards. I am sending them up to you to inspect the companies on the line, the ones under fire."

When Mac told me what the CO had said, I began to laugh. I noted a grin on his face too; he had little use for either man.

I said, "Let me take the S-3 up to Company G. It's quiet there, but if anyone moves, the Japanese shoot."

He grinned. "I'll take the exec up to Company F; he'll crap in his pants up there!"

We waited impatiently for a half hour; finally our two guests arrived. Stepping from the jeep the exec questioned Mac, who had a smile on his face. "What's the situation?"

Mac told him a bit, but finally couldn't contain himself any longer. "I'll take you up to Company F to see their problems; Walker can take the S-3 up to Company G. Both of those companies are on the line."

The exec gazed around, then turned to the S-3. I noted the squirrelly look that passed between them; they were scared stiff!

"I guess we've seen all we need to here. We'll leave you now; things look well in hand."

"Whoa," Mac said. "The CO told me to take you up to the companies under fire."

He got dirty looks from both men as they ignored him and climbed into the jeep.

This was too much. Smiling, I said, "A bit afraid, are you?" The looks cast at me would have killed an elephant; both remained silent.

The night before we were relieved by First Battalion, we bunched the battalion together in a perimeter to facilitate loading the next morning. Some group left a jeep loaded with radios outside the perimeter. It was blown up by a Japanese, a loss due to criminal carelessness.

When daylight came we returned to Dumaguette for a rest.

I had three days off before I received a call from the regimental exec. "Captain Walker, you will go back up the mountain and take command of the First Battalion."

I should have expected this revenge, but questioned, "Where is the First Battalion CO? Where is his exec?"

"They are both sick."

"How about the line company COs?"

"Never mind them! You will go up there this afternoon and take charge."

So I did, spending nearly another week in the clouds, soaking wet every hour, day and night. The low scud had moved in, visibility was limited to only a few yards. There was no shooting, since there was no visibility. I found the supposed battalion was only about at full company strength. Where were the rest of the officers and men?

(Later I found the exec had lied to me. I was to find that the regimental CO had relieved the First Battalion commander of his duties. This was trouble!)

On my way up to the First Battalion, I had passed by a group of Filipino guerrillas who were supposed to protect the supply line to the battalion. There were about fifty men in this group; they were bunched together on a hill with no prepared positions. One evening a couple of days before we were relieved, furious firing broke out down the mountain where the guerrillas were stationed. The next morning a messenger arrived from their leader. The message read: *Sir, we were heavily attacked by a large group of enemy last night. We have expended all of our ammunition, we are going home.*

It was a good laugh, and typical of guerrilla leadership. I doubted the Japanese had made any attack. The guerrillas *always* wanted to go home!

Finally, ordered to withdraw, I walked the entire twelve miles down from 4,400 feet in sopping-wet shoes that distorted, the leather stretching completely out of shape. My toes slid forward and upon reaching the rear area, I had blisters on the end of each toe. The next day I couldn't walk. Two weeks later I found a bunion growing on each foot.

CHAPTER 32

One of our replacements to Easy Company was Zane
Jacobs. He tells a few of his experiences:

The Regiment had taken a number of casualties in the
Leyte and Cebu actions and all companies were under-
manned. I was assigned to a platoon of Easy with only 18
or 19 men in the entire platoon, my squad having only five
men. [A squad strength is twelve men.] Jack Kachell was
our platoon Sergeant and leader. He was from Arizona, a
Regular Army man.

When I was a raw recruit in '45, I was filled with mis-
information about the enemy we faced. Sergeant Kachell
soon erased that garbage with a 30 minute talk when we
were assigned to his platoon. The next operation on Negros completed the fast forward of what to do, and not do.

In the excitement of landing on Negros Island that first
night, I was dug in on the west side of the battalion
perimeter blocking a road. This road led from the city of
Dumaguette back into the mountains. We were ordered to
hold our fire, expecting our regimental reconnaissance
unit to join us. Shortly, all hell broke lose with our heavy
.30-caliber machine guns on the east side of the perimeter
cutting loose. Just before the firing started we could hear
truck gears grinding as trucks drove through our circle
and exited the west edge of the block. Sergeant Brown
yelled at us to shoot west at random to try to hit the trucks
that had already passed by.

Later, I found that after the enemy trucks went through

our perimeter; a column of Japanese followed behind them on foot. That's when the east road guard finally opened fire.

The next afternoon we came into a semi-cleared area, with a stone fence perpendicular to our line of advance. The coconut trees were in orderly rows with a small shack about 150–200 yards through the trees. My platoon was told to use the wall as cover, for Sergeant Jack Kachell had spotted two trucks near the house, also three Japanese nearby. One enemy soldier appeared to be wounded. We opened fire, but I believe two enemy faded into the jungle without being killed; the wounded man was left behind.

Later, my squad was point for Easy. Going up a ridge near a knob we were hit by Nambu machine-gun fire. Lazono was point scout. He dived across an opening in the underbrush which had been made earlier by an artillery or mortar burst. I was just behind him. A bullet cut across his forehead, temporarily blinding him. I never saw him again after he got off the hill. A big, tall Texan named Hale was our forward BAR man. He stepped into the shell opening and fired at the Nambu position. He had a good shot uphill about 50 yards, stopping the Nambu for a couple of minutes until the dead gunner was replaced. The new gunner cut loose a few rounds and caught one of our men through the ankle which shattered the joint. He was evacuated and never returned to the company. Hale took out the second gunner, then carried his ankle-shot buddy down off the hill.

During those hectic minutes, Utah Christopher, a seasoned veteran of other campaigns, panicked. He scooted around the hill until he came upon me. He was scared and said he was going back down off the hill. I was located about 15 yards below the Nambu by this time, and below its line of fire. When the gun fired bursts I could tell he was depressed as low as possible as he was shooting three or four inches above me from the way the grass and brush was shearing off. I told Chris to calm down and we might figure some way to get through the brush without being seen, and wipe out the gun.

Chris did not buy this and eased down the slope. That raised him into the line of fire and within a couple of minutes after he left me, I heard the Nambu sweep another burst of fire. It caught Chris. The brush and grass must have given his position away as he moved through. I heard the bullet hit Chris. He was soon dead.

About 10 minutes later, Sergeant Kachell came around the other side of the hill. He, or the heavy .30 machine gun knocked out the Nambu. Jack asked me if I knew where Chris was located. I asked about a BAR man named Gower that I thought had also been hit. Gower had gotten down O.K. We dropped about a hundred yards off the hill, and while we were talking, Jack said, "We have to go back up the hill and get Chris out. *We never leave a wounded or dead man!*"

I was not anxious to go back up the hill, but was the only one who knew where Chris was located, so Jack and I went back up to recover him. Chris had taken a .25 caliber round through his chest, from right to left.

About five or six weeks after joining the platoon in Easy Company, we had a cocksure 2nd Looey assigned as platoon leader. Cannot remember this 2nd John's name, but it seems to have started with a B.

He was all spit and polish and evidently didn't like the way we smelled. (There was no chance to wash all those days on Negros Island.) A couple of days after he took over I asked Jack if he had any success in talking to the lieutenant about staying alive? Jack glared at me and told me the lieutenant had been approached. Jack had been read the riot act—so he let it drop. He said there were two things that could happen. The lieutenant would learn and live, or not learn and die.

A couple of days after that we took another hill. Artillery had laid down a good barrage and there were a couple of cleared spots right on the ridge between where we were hunkered down and the next ridge about 250

yards up the mountain. These spots were cleared of brush
and visible to anyone in the trees up near the top. It took
about two or three steps to cross the clearing. I was about
30 yards from one of the clearings and was looking
through the brush up the hill when the Lieutenant, with a
swagger stick in his hand, came up the path. He headed
along the ridge toward the other squad on the other side of
the clearing.

When he got close I spoke to him, and tried to warn him
to duck down-slope when he crossed the clear area. *Mr.
Know It All* stopped and told me that when he wanted to
hear from a Private, he would ask me, and did I know to
keep my mouth shut until then. I just said, "Yes Sir!" He
took about 10–12 steps and started across the clearing.
One .25 caliber shot got him (250 yards) in the kidneys.
He got a one way ticket. We never heard from him again.

The next day we took that knob again. A bunch of
Japanese charged up the hill to us in a Banzai. We got over
a dozen of them, but the guy carrying the sword never got
hit; he made it off the hill. An Easy man about 30 feet
from me was hit by a bullet that detonated one of the hand
grenades he was carrying on the strap across his chest.
That blew his chest open. I took my grenades off and stuck
them in my belt after that.

I saw the lieutenant get hit, but never knew his name. I
remember Walker sprinkling him with sulfa.

I was about 20 feet off the trail and downhill from an artillery observer attached to our outfit; he was watching
down the trail. Suddenly he cut loose with his Tommy gun.
When I turned about 45 degrees to my right to see why he
was shooting, I saw he had taken out three Japanese soldiers about 50 feet down the hill, just below us.

This second try to take this same hill brought a flurry of
mortar fire down upon us. All the rounds were landing on
the forward edge of the ridge about 75–100 yards from
our line. Captain Walker, called for artillery fire to silence
the incoming from about 300 yards up the ridge. Within
about 10 minutes there was no more incoming, and the

Captain was talking with Jack Kachell about why the mortar was falling away from our men, and on one spot on the hill. Jack asked for volunteers by pointing to me and two other men in the squad to go have a look. We discovered a cave entrance with a huge amount of small arms ammunition and explosives inside.

The captain was made aware of this, and knew that if a lucky hit had entered the opening, the hilltop we were on would have erupted. Volunteers were asked to empty the cave of explosives and bring some into our perimeter. Three of us took turns, carefully passing out the boxes of explosives while looking for booby traps. We rotated each ten minutes because of the heat and difficulty. In addition to the ammo there were several items of a personal nature which we figured belonged to at least three or four of the enemy. All ammo and souvenirs were moved before sunset.*

*Author's note: Kingston was CO of Easy at the time. Walker, although still a captain, was battalion exec. Lieutenant Charles Ross took over as CO of Easy after Company E returned to the island of Cebu.

CHAPTER 33

I noticed that whenever a chow line formed at Easy, nearly every man was accompanied by a Filipino child he had more or less adopted. They even ate from the soldiers' mess kits. Word came down that this feeding of civilians was prohibited, but the order did little good. A hungry child is still a hungry child. Our garbage cans were plundered by the kids for anything they could take home to their parents. Food was hard to come by.

Our so-called Gray Locker Fund came through. Officers had paid $10 months ago and were to receive six quarts of tax-free liquor each. The original six officers had agreed that if they were no longer with the company at the time the bottles arrived, the survivors would inherit the booze. I was presented with thirty-six quarts, as the surviving officer. It was a problem easily solved; thirty-five quarts were turned over to the noncoms for distribution to the men; I kept one quart and celebrated my luck at surviving. Because I was off-duty, I drank it all in one night; you can guess the rest!

Early one evening Mac notified me I was to take a small task force around the island to cut off Japanese suspected of crossing to the opposite side. I was to leave at dawn the next morning, accompanied by Easy Company, a battery of 105mm guns from the 245th Field Artillery, 175 Filipino guerrillas, plus a long-range radio. I was unable to obtain much information that night, but at the city docks the next morning it all came together. Our transportation was an LSM (landing ship medium) and an LCI.

Immediately after appearing at the docks the artillery

loaded their prime movers with guns and men onto the LSM; Easy men with their supplies boarded the LCI. There was a short wait for the guerrillas, who were commanded by a Major Luboton. They and their food supply, which was stored in several large, heavy bags, was loaded onto the open-decked LSM. My jeep and trailer, heavily loaded with rations, also went onto the LSM.

Approaching the south shore of Cauiton Point on the west side of Negros Island at 5 P.M., both landing craft struck a sandbar nearly one thousand feet from the beach. By judicious transfer of water ballast they edged over and reached shore. Dropping ramps, all men, guns, and Army gear were quickly unloaded. The guerrillas moved inland about two hundred yards and sat. The artillery immediately looked for firing positions facing inland. Easy immediately began setting up a perimeter defense.

The skipper of the LSM came ashore to look for me. I could see he was worried. "Captain, the food for those guerrillas is still on board my boat. The tide is going out fast; if I don't get out in the next few minutes I'll be stuck here. I sure don't want to lose my craft to Japanese if they cross the island."

"Wait! I'll see they get it off immediately."

Approaching Major Luboton, I said, "Gather some of your men and get your rations off the LSM. The skipper must leave within the next few minutes."

The major looked toward me, but not at my face. He had his eyes on my captain's bars. I could see he was trying to intimidate me and take command. I scotched that.

"You have five minutes to get your rations off the LSM before it leaves for Dumaguette. If you don't get them off, I have no intention of feeding your men. You will get damned hungry!"

He looked at me, and then said plaintively, "My men are hungry and tired. They haven't eaten since breakfast."

I blew up. "I haven't had any breakfast, nor has Easy Company, yet we work. It's up to you!"

From the look on his face I knew he felt insulted, but what

an impossible man! A Filipino politician made an instant major. I had eight years of service under my belt and I was only a captain. Somehow I knew he would buck me all the way, but finally, reluctantly, he got his rations ashore.

The next morning I had Lieutenant Charles Ross take a patrol up the river toward the mountains. His patrol was accompanied by an artillery forward observer party for fire support if needed. The first message I received from him was startling: "This jungle is loaded with leeches. They are on every leaf and bush along the river. They swell up in your shoes to the size of a spoon, also around your beltline and neck."

I reported this by radio to Dumaguette. Late that afternoon an L4 pilot flew over, dropping a carton of worthless DDT powder.

The next morning I received a radio message saying everyone in our task force with over eighty rotation points would be picked up in two days to be returned to the United States.

I contacted Major Luboton, thinking he would like to be a part of this force, asking for a runner to go inland and pass a message to Lieutenant Ross. He supplied a man to whom I gave two days' rations, and a letter to Charles. (Ross was beyond our radio contact now.)

The next morning the major came over with the messenger. It seemed he had gone out a day (so he said) and being tired, returned to his unit without delivering the message. I knew that if he had pursued only one day he would have easily contacted the patrol.

I was angry and pulled my .45 Colt. I told him I would give him one more chance. If he failed, I would kill him. Would you believe it, that SOB had the nerve to ask for more rations!

I told him that if Ross wasn't back *tonight* with his patrol, he was a dead man. I would see to it! He left, with no rations.

Charles Ross was back with his patrol that night. I never saw the Filipino again.

The next afternoon a boat arrived to take the rotation men

back to Dumaguette. Meanwhile, by radio I received a complete roster of those qualified to go home. I was left with very few men. In fact, all of the artillery officers were now gone, leaving only a warrant officer in charge. He came to me, saying, "I've hardly enough men to fire the guns if trouble comes."

A day or two later another LSM came to take out the remaining artillery with their guns and prime movers. Easy Company and the guerrillas walked south to cross another river; trucks were waiting for them there. My jeep driver, my interpreter, and I remained. I was to recheck the area and be picked up soon.

Just across the Cauiton River an influential Filipino gentleman invited me to his wedding anniversary. His family was large, with twenty-two sons and daughters, all of whom were present at the time. Both he and his wife were gracious hosts—his children, young and old, were wonderful, vivacious people. They had come from many islands for this celebration; I was envious and excited to see such a family relationship. A family of twenty-two children was almost too much to believe.

My interpreter began a lucrative trade with our surplus C rations. After trading one can of C rations for each chicken, he even managed to find a woven cage that fit in our now empty jeep trailer. All told we had about thirty-five to forty chickens. His prize was a huge fighting cock, which he said held great promise.

When our open-decked LSM finally arrived, the lieutenant in command almost had conniptions.

"You mean I've come all of these miles just to pick up you two and a jeep?" He shook his head, obviously put out. He was a good host, though, inviting me to eat with him at his mess table.

CHAPTER 34

We arrived back in Dumaguette after dark. Upon my arrival no questions were asked; it was as if this expedition had never taken place. It seemed that soon after we had left for the west side of the island, the powers that be had found the Japanese had headed north, up the island, instead of crossing to our side.

Two days later I was directed to go around the lower end of the island by coastal road. I was to hire labor and put the road to Cauiton Point back in shape. Stopping here and there, using my interpreter, I had no trouble finding men who wanted employment. I was even able to find responsible supervisors. A few days later I took my roster of men and their hours to the CIC (Counter Intelligence Corps) office to get money to pay their wages. There were no questions asked; they gave me wads of money in a brown paper sack. They seemed unworried about the expenditure; I signed no receipts or formal papers. It was easy to see how corruption could creep into the ranks if every military office operated this way.

In a room adjoining the office they had about six number-five Underwood typewriters. Also sitting around in this room were six attractive teenage mestizo girls, evidently hired as typist-secretaries. I took the opportunity to sit at one of the typewriters to write a brief note to my wife. The girls crowded around to watch; evidently none could type, and were astounded that I could. These girls were not hired for their office abilities; there was more going on here than met the eye. I wondered, How do GIs get such cushy CIC jobs?

Elements of the 77th Division, together with a parachute outfit, entered Dumaguette to take over the reins from us. We were to return to Cebu Island, north of Cebu City, to an area near Sibulan.

It took a full day to pay off the Filipinos working on the south road around the island. They had done a remarkable job clearing the jungle away from the road. The road was now not only passable, but a scenic drive all the way to the river just short of Cauiton Point.

I was the last vehicle of the battalion to leave Negros. Up the island about eight miles from Dumaguette was an LCM landing. The trip across to Cebu was brief; it took only a half hour to cross.

The west coastal road leading north was of macadam with numerous potholes. It seemed there was a dog resting on the road every few miles. Evidently they liked the warmth of the blacktop in the early sun. They acted as if they owned the highway, refusing to move for our jeep.

Crossing over east to Cebu City, we again swung north about twenty-five miles to Sibulan. This town had been a leper colony prior to the war, but most of the diseased people had moved away to avoid the enemy.

Inland about two to three miles we found our bivouac area, a former Japanese camp. It had a large nipa building about thirty by ninety feet, more than adequate for a battalion headquarters. Tents for the companies were already set up, since the battalion had arrived a day or two previously. On a side hill, just across from the large building, the A & P section had set up a row of small officer tents. An electrical cable had been tied to the front pole of each tent, the huge generator parked just across the road.

Mac and I shared the tent farthest from the road; the next tent held a Servel kerosene refrigerator we had purchased in Dumaguette. It functioned as a communal cooler; even some critical medical supplies were stored inside.

We reverted to a training status with replacements, but had more casualties there. Two men found a tape-measure mine and began playing catch with it. When it was caught by one of the men, it exploded. They had been warned and warned!

One evening a dump truck driver from the engineers stopped alongside the road. He accosted me: "I've got a load of mixed cement that's setting up fast. I've got to dump it somewhere mighty soon."

"Where was it supposed to go?"

"To regimental headquarters of the One Hundred Sixty-fourth Infantry."

I didn't know the location of our regimental headquarters, but knew our men liked to play basketball. A concrete court would be an asset. So I said, "Just dump it over there on that level ground."

As he raised the hoist I passed the word, and several men showed up with form lumber and trowels. It was only a six-yard load, but it was a start. Our A & P officer made connections with the cement plant north of Cebu City the next morning. A few days later we had a basketball court of concrete, regulation size. I later found the load of cement was for the floor of Colonel Mahoney's private mess tent. The Regimental S-4 called me later and gave me hell!

We were sleeping soundly one rainy night when we heard a sudden whooshing sound; our tent was gone. We were fully exposed to the rain, our cots were tipped over, and the tent next to us was on fire. At first I thought of a mortar round, but changed my mind when I heard cursing all down the line of officer tents. Each tent was flat on the ground and it was raining heavily.

The engineers had been graveling the road into our area and the driver of one truck had forgotten to lower the hoist on his vehicle. The truck box caught the heavy electrical wire high above the road, ripping down the entire row of tents. I felt sorry for that driver; he caught hell!

Our Servel refrigerator operated with a kerosene flame, and being tipped over, set the tent on fire. Fortunately it was raining hard enough that the slowly burning tent was no problem.

• • •

Mac finally opened his thoughts to me; we became friends. He had reached the point where he was able to put his fears aside. He finally agreed with my tenet: Do your best, forget the rest. (Of course, no leader forgets his mistakes.)

Some days later he was briefly hospitalized. When he came back he never mentioned the past, but I noticed a new self-confidence and camaraderie. He had questioned me about fear. I told him that the more combat a soldier goes through, the less he worries. I mentioned Colonel John Gossett. The men almost worshiped him because he was a leader with confidence, and he instilled confidence in everyone. After all, combat leadership is the one important factor in combat performance.

We still had the two generators we had picked out of caves above Cebu City, so we hunted up more concrete to build a volleyball court. Both courts were illuminated at night and saw plenty of action.

While eating supper one evening, someone said, "Look at that!" There was a monkey atop one of our floodlight poles on the volleyball court. The animal casually unscrewed one of the large bulbs, dropping it to the pavement. Those high-wattage bulbs were almost impossible to obtain, so I shot the monkey. It turned out to be the pet of the motor pool bunch. The mechanics were not happy with me.

Every town had its own special building for cockfights, since fighting the birds was legal. Hearing that I had a fighting cock, the officers took it upon themselves to scheme up a fight. I was to be the financial loser, since they had found a ringer. They came up with the owner of a champion rooster and had the man bring his bird around one evening. At the time I had a few dollars on hand, but was suspicious. I agreed to the cockfight, but wouldn't allow them to put knives on the legs of the fighters.

When they dropped the birds to the ground, they went at it. Because the champion rooster was faster, it seemed he would soon be the winner. However, time was in the larger bird's favor. My rooster (actually, I should say he belonged to my interpreter) pinned down the other bird by sheer weight and stamina. In a few more seconds he would have killed it. The Filipino owner quickly grabbed up his bird and ran some distance away. My loser friends, out a few bucks, wanted to see the conclusion; they were angry at the owner of the other fighter. Poor man, he explained that if his bird was defeated too badly, it would never fight again. This didn't mollify a few of the officers; they wanted blood.

Our bird was well fed each day, and was kept tied by a small string to the front stake of Mac's and my tent. Each morning as the sky lightened, he stood proudly and proclaimed the start of another day.

Finally Mac laid it on the line. "That darned bird has got to go! No more of that four A.M. crowing!"

It was turned over to the battalion cooks for the officers mess. The large bird looked grand as it came from the oven. Everyone waited expectantly for the first bite, only to find the bird so tough it couldn't be eaten. It was like chewing rubber!

Our First and Third Battalions were commanded by experienced majors who had been in combat for two and a half years. To our chagrin two West Point lieutenant colonels arrived to take over command of the battalions. In an attempt to gain our support the new CO of the Third Battalion hosted a party for the various battalion staffs. It was held in the second story of a schoolhouse about fifteen miles south of our camp. When Mac and I arrived, the large room on the second floor was crowded; somehow that colonel had found about ten girls to entertain us. The music came from an old upright Victrola phonograph that needed an occasional winding and changing of records. Mac and I participated at the bar until I became bored and took up post at the phonograph. Looking at the girls I realized they were all prostitutes. Where on earth did that colonel find them? Where did he have this type of connection?

When the record ended, I was about to turn it over when

the former CO of the First Battalion shouted drunkenly to me, "Hey, play that record over again!"

We were not the best of friends and his demand irritated me, or it may have been the drinks I'd had. Smiling, I broke the 78 RPM record over my head. He came at me, leading with his chin. He flew backward about fifteen feet and out the open side door, to tumble down the eighteen to twenty steps to the ground. He was badly bruised and unconscious.

Captain Hamer, who had been coming up the stairs after taking a leak, puzzled, "What happened to Henry?"

I was savvy enough to make myself scarce after that.

On Saturday night the new First Battalion colonel had his party. It was held at battalion headquarters. The high brass were drinking heavily; I anticipated a blowup, so nursed my beer. Soon vitriolic accusations were made about these two Pointers taking over our battalions without any combat experience. The subject turned to the invasion of Japan, Operation Olympic. The new colonel of the First Battalion was exceedingly drunk and bragged, "Hell, you National Guard and Reserve officers are going to take your lumps. Frank and I are going back on forty-five-day leaves to the States— we're not going to Japan with you."

His buddy Frank drunkenly spoke up. "Hell no! My father-in-law is commandant at Fort Sam Houston. Do you think he's going to allow his son-in-law to be killed in Japan?"

We sober ones were shocked, but I admired Henry when he said, "You damned cowards, they ought to abolish West Point."

That ended the party, but if looks could kill, there would have been two dead West Point lieutenant colonels!

A day or two later these two lieutenant colonels did leave for the States. During my remaining time in the Philippines, and later, in Japan, they never returned to our regiment.

CHAPTER 35

After the dropping of the two atomic bombs (the first on August 6, 1945) we later heard Hirohito and his cabinet announced their surrender on August 14, but the final word came to us on the evening of August 15 by radio. A murmur spread across the wide expanse of our tents, growing in volume to a lion's roar. Our discipline held; there was no firing of weapons. Not so in Cebu City with the ships in the harbor; promiscuous firing there killed several men.

Word came that the Americal Division was attempting to negotiate with the remaining Japanese on the island and accomplish a surrender. This was finally realized after a Japanese officer was taken under a white flag to division headquarters to listen to broadcasts from Japan. After that, his commander, Lieutenant General Sadshi Kataoka, agreed to surrender to the Americal Division. The ceremony was to take place on August 29.

For the surrender affair our regiment was to furnish a full company of men, none less than six feet in height. I laughed about that—who were we trying to impress? What fool had cooked this up? That is, I laughed until I found I was stuck to command that composite company at the surrender.

We left early in the morning, supposed to be there by 10 A.M. The trucks kicked up copious amounts of dust, while the sun did its best to raise the temperature to scorching.

Unfortunately, many of the men felt used, and disgruntled remarks came fast and furious as I attempted to gain a formation. Four or five malcontents became mouthy. I lost my temper and told one to step out to the rear of the column when he ignored my order. My old sergeant from Company H, a burley man, snarled at him, "And if he can't whip you, it'll be my turn to beat the hell out of you!" (These few men were not from the Second Battalion; their behavior indicated a total lack of discipline in their own companies.)

I suddenly felt stupid to have lost my temper this way. I turned to face the troublemakers. "Take a good look at those Japanese across from us. They are standing at attention like soldiers, not bitching a bit. Note that every man in the front rank wears a complete uniform, while others in the rear are nearly naked. They have passed parts of uniforms to the front rank to dress their men fully. Then take a look at some further back, with a leg or arm missing. Where is your pride? You are witnessing something you will talk about for the rest of your lives. You are lucky men!"

I must have said the right thing, since the men looked shamefaced; they turned into soldiers again.

We had been ordered to place a light machine gun fifteen feet to our front, as had the other two companies representing the other regiments in the division. When this was done, cries of apprehension were heard from the Japanese troops. I had objected to this for they had no weapons, having stacked theirs in a pile the size of a house. What stupid senior officer had come up with this idea? Where was the trust on our part? One shot fired and what a melee we'd have!

The ceremony went as planned; General Kataoka came forward with three other generals and an admiral. His samurai sword was handed to the division commander, and the affair was over. After we fell out of formation, the Japanese, all 2,667 of them, loaded into a huge convoy of trucks for transportation to a spot below Cebu City. There, under supervision, they were allowed to build and police their own camp. I was told later that there were several Japanese women among the prisoners. If true, they were probably hospital personnel.

Our vehicles were spaced here and there in the long convoy and our troops did their best to stop the rock throwing by Filipinos along the highway. Once or twice we stopped to stare them down; they backed off. Tired and grimy with road dust, we finally arrived back at the regiment in time for supper.

Although I was battalion exec and no longer associated with Easy, I sauntered over to their headquarters to inquire about my personal property locked in their company safe. It had been a policy that the company clerk kept money and valuables stored for the men in the issue lockbox. I was informed that my old company clerk, Chatterton, in whom I had the utmost trust, upon his rotation had stolen everything within the safe. The theft represented quite an amount, but since the war was over and he was already in the States, probably discharged by now, what would be gained by pursuing him? I lost a considerable amount of Japanese currency and several old silver Filipino dollars dated before 1900. These all came from Japanese pockets.

A day or two before we loaded aboard ship and left for Yokohama, Japan, Mac came up with news.

"Chuck, the quartermaster has stores of beer going to waste. They'll sell it for two dollars a case. Why don't you load up your jeep and trailer with beer? I'll take our bedrolls and other equipment in my rig."

The idea sounded good, so I said, "I'll speak with the battalion staff and see if they want to share. I'm sure they will—how much shall I get?"

Mac laughed. "You should be able to get at least four feet above the sides of the trailer if they'll sell you that much. Tarp it tight like its ammunition. If someone suspects its beer, it will disappear."

I smelled the beer long before I entered the quartermaster's fence. My driver and I gasped in awe at the sheer amount of it rotting away. They had piled cases nearly thirty feet high, so high that the lower cases were crushed. Stale, sour beer ran everywhere. Too make matters worse, the heap was at least seventy feet wide and a city block long! What the men would have given for this beer these feather-headed men had wasted, all stored in an open field, subject to every vagary of the weather.

The noncom in charge told me to take what we wanted. He added, "You'll have to dig deep in the mess to get undamaged cases."

It was true. My driver and I worked like beavers to finally find over 150 cases that appeared okay. We tarped the trailer tightly, adding several cases to the rear seat of the jeep. (When we later arrived in Japan we found the cases stored in the jeep gone. The ship's crew had a way down into the hold and had helped themselves. Thankfully, they must have thought the big load in the trailer was ammo.)

Early on the morning of September 1, we trucked to Cebu City in preparation for our trip to Yokohama. No plans were confirmed, but we assumed we would be assigned to occupation duties. We had no idea what they would be.

CHAPTER 36

On the ninth day we entered the harbor at Yokohama, and what a show! Literally hundreds of ships were crowded in the harbor. We had been constantly worried about our few aircraft carriers; now there seemed to be an overabundance. There were carriers, battleships, cruisers, transports, destroyers, and almost every type of craft that existed.

Judging from the ships' flags, it seemed nearly every Allied country was represented, even vessels from South America.

Slipping into our assigned pier we began unloading troops as quickly as possible. When transportation became available Mac immediately took our men inland. I remained to unload our equipment and battalion gear. A huge warehouse stood on our dock, the large door securely locked by a massive brass padlock. For lack of something to do while we awaited our equipment, inquisitive men found a bolt cutter and the lock turned to cheese. Inside were several brand-new 110-volt generators, which were confiscated as booty. Each company took one (unnecessary, as we later found everything in Japan fully electrified).

It was dark when I had the remaining vehicles assembled and a guide appeared to lead us to our new home. At midnight we arrived at a large building, a former Japanese radar school. Leaving my jeep and trailer near the north door I entered a fully lighted room occupied by our battalion staff. A guard stood just outside the door. My cot with bedroll had been prepared for me, and resting upon it, I began to remove my blouse. Looking around the room I noted the other five occupants seemed to be sound asleep. Strange, I thought, the light is still on. Were they that played out?

I suddenly felt a sharp stab at my arm. Looking down I saw a large red flea. I slapped. Too late—missed it! This building had fleas!

Hilarious laughter broke out; it was Captain Manuel, our Second Battalion headquarters CO. Suddenly all the sleepers cast aside their blankets and sat up; they were fully dressed. Mac, rubbing his eyes, asked, "Where's the beer?"

Tired or not, they piled outside and carried every case into the room. Two or three beers later, they finally slept.

It was shortly after our arrival in Japan that I received an order notifying me I was finally a major in the United States Army.

We were issued a crude map of our assigned district with orders to visit each factory, stopping production of war materials. Each day we pursued these duties, closing plants and inspecting businesses. Our targeted area was predominantly industrial; there we found machine shops and foundries still in full production.

When we closed down a manufacturer, the workers continued to arrive day after day, standing by their machines. We had been told that plans were in place to convert the factories to the production of civilian goods, but those orders never materialized.

I had been assigned a personal interpreter, an elderly, dignified, gentleman teacher from an Episcopal girls' school, located near our radar building. This school had a basement machine shop where the girls were busy machining pistons and connecting rods for Japanese aircraft.

I had been told that lies were a polite way of evasion in Japan and found it to be true. With about eight men I inspected a large prison (I believe it was Sugami Prison) with many prisoners. When we entered the office the women clerks began screaming hysterically, running wildly into the ladies' toilet. Evidently their propaganda machine had labeled us Americans as rapists. We ignored them, my interpreter and I going directly to the warden's office, while my men checked the prisoners and further searched the building.

The warden, after offering us a small cup of tea, denied any knowledge of manufacturing war materials. The few men I sent below returned with explosive shell components, parts from a well-equipped machine shop in the basement. I had the men inspect every prisoner confined, but they found all inmates were Japanese.

We were shocked to discover that every huge stamping press and most other machinery in the factories had been manufactured in the United States.

First Battalion liberated a pistol factory, but kept the workers busy completing the assembly of nearly five hundred Nambu 7.65mm pistols, to be given to the men returning home. A coal mine produced (as I remember) six Canadians captured at Hong Kong. One of these soldiers was Charley Fisher; later we became good friends when I was bush flying in Ontario, Canada. The story of his treatment was horrifying.

From Yokohama to Tokyo the destruction was complete, with miles of nothing, just burned-out or smashed buildings; a few brick smokestacks had survived. Bomb craters were everywhere, with smoke still coming from piles of twisted girders and masonry. It was a macabre sight, mile upon mile of rubble as we journeyed toward Tokyo. Efforts had been made to clear the main highways, as streetcars were already back in operation.

To my surprise I found the Ginza untouched; the downtown jewel of central Tokyo had not been harmed. Certainly just the opposite had happened in Germany: Berlin had been totally destroyed. It was now I began to question our government's motives and strategies, and the political power of big corporations. Going farther north along the coast I ran into oil refineries and storage facilities. They had not been bombed.

A stop at Atsugi Airfield was another mind-blower. True, it had been strafed with bullets, but it had not been bombed.

It was then someone pointed out to me that political power held sway. Even Lever Brothers Plantation on Guadalcanal was rumored to have been the recipient of a large settlement for damages. (If true, the Japanese should have paid. Their bombardments caused nearly all the devastation.)

Dick Hamer and I checked many of the newer Japanese aircraft at Atsugi Airfield. One reasonable copy of a B25 had a 75mm cannon installed in the nose. Another aircraft, one of their latest models, had an in-line engine. Later I found few had been made, but they were very fast.

We watched as American pilots flew old Japanese biplanes for entertainment. Under the surrender terms all propellers were supposed to have been removed prior to our landing.

A second trip to the Ginza showed many items for sale, all at astronomical prices. Our new pay, only 13 yen to the dollar, was MacArthur's sick joke. It would not even buy a package of gum.

We heard rumors of banks being stripped and other devious criminal acts by the high-ups. These were only rumors until it was later disclosed that a quart of cut diamonds showed up in the United States. A Colonel Nickerson (high staff) was supposedly convicted by a court-martial. American newspapers said the diamonds were carried to the United States by a WAC captain. We heard nothing further; it was evidently covered up as usual. Bad press.

For several days I felt like a procurer for the batallion. The job was enlightening as it enabled me to see much of the country and farmland. Due to the dense population the farms were small, more like flower gardens—not a weed to be seen.

I was ordered to travel along a major highway, consulting with police chiefs in the various towns as to allowing our men to visit their cities. My interpreter, as I mentioned, was a dignified, staid, and proper man from an Episcopal girls' school; he became very upset. The first thing each police chief did was to consult with him about setting up a special house of prostitution in their city. While we drank the usually offered small cup of tea, I watched my interpreter squirm. He wished nothing to do with harlotry, and arguments ensued. Sad to say, the policeman always won. Days later, as I probed farther and farther inland, I passed crude signs reading: *Paradise ahead!* Farther along would be a sign pointing directly at a door: *Paradise here!*

U.S. Army engineers running a fuel pipeline to a nearby airstrip ran into a problem. The pipe was put in place, but the next morning before pumping could begin, two miles of it had disappeared. It seemed there were still some hard losers.

It was finally decided that we remaining eight officers of the 164th Infantry could return home; unfortunately, one of our officers was bumped; he had witnessed an accident and had to remain for a court-martial. We were transferred to the 43rd Division for movement to the United States.

As many of us were scheduled to go by train to Atsugi Airfield, I argued with Mac, "It's only a half hour by jeep, let's go the easy way."

"Heck, Chuck, let's take the train. It might be enlightening."

It definitely was. We were crowded in small seats from 8 A.M. until 5 P.M. before arriving at the airport. Japanese train cars are made for people of small stature, not six-footers!

At Atsugi Airfield I was assigned as regimental S-2. Then I was assigned to be in charge of laying out a tent camp for an entire infantry division that was on its way from Europe. Now I was positive every big shot in this 43rd Division was crazy. This was a job for Army engineers!

The second night on the airfield a terrific wind came up. The many, many Japanese aircraft lying about the field were not tied down. They were blown to one end of the field against a huge fence. Nearly all were destroyed.

Thankfully, a ship finally became available and we moved to the docks along with officers of the 1st Cavalry Division. As we were not leaving Japan until the next morning, Mac and I left the ship after 6 P.M., walking over to a nearby subway station. Pedestrian traffic was heavy, but people were moving at a leisurely pace along the sidewalks. We noticed as the people passed down the long, slanted ramps to the subway, however, they speeded up. When we reached the train area, everyone was running at a furious pace. It was comical.

Stopping in the large toilet area I had to admire Japanese ingenuity. Everything was of tile and drained to the multiple bowls that were set flush in the floor. Beside each bowl were two high bricks on which you stood. Along the wall hung a large hose so that caring for the bathroom was reduced to just a squirt of water. There was no privacy.

Back on the ship I received another surprise. I was assigned as mess officer until our arrival in Frisco.

It was now mid-October 1945. As there were so many officers present, I wondered how this had come about. I questioned Mac, but he said he was just as puzzled as me.

I was given rosters of men, and in which compartment they could be found. Any attempt to get workers was doomed. All promised, but none showed up. That is, until the next evening, when the men found this was not a catered trip. By the third day I had more help than I needed. Those who came faithfully ate like kings.

A few days later we went under the Golden Gate Bridge and tied up at pier 51, on the opposite side from which we had left.

Talk about a coincidence. A dockworker struck up a conversation with me, saying, "A lovely girl from Fiji Islands arrived yesterday as a war bride. She asked where she could find her husband, an officer named Digvie. It happened he came in just a day or two before her, telling me he was going to stay at the Mark. I hope she found him." (Digvie was one of our original officers of the 164th Infantry. I wished him well.)

We loaded aboard a Catalina ferry and proceeded to Camp Stoneman. On the third morning we loaded on a train for Fort Lewis, Washington. There, an examining board of brass interviewed Mac, Bill Smith, Henry Brown, and me. They wanted us to stay in the Army, probably because of our efficiency ratings in combat. Mac and Bill agreed to stay, while Henry and I bowed out, signing in the Reserves.

The offer they had made to us was: "We'll allow you a forty-five-day leave in the United States, but you must return to Japan at the end of that time. We will guarantee to ship your families to Japan within six months."

We had been overseas nearly four years, and to date I had had a one-day official leave of absence in five and a half years of service. To offer forty-five days' leave in the United States when we had four months' leave coming and had already lost a month and a half (the maximum leave you could accumulate was 120 days) was a bad joke. Also, the promise concerning our families was phony; we knew the situation in Japan all too well!

After a final physical a doctor told me I had heart problems that should be checked. I thanked him, telling him I had a little girl three years old I had never seen. I wasn't about to sit around Fort Lewis for another two or three weeks.

All chances of getting transportation home seemed slim. The wait at the quartermaster for train tickets was at least two weeks. That evening after supper Henry and I went to the Seattle railroad station for tickets, to be told bluntly to get the hell out of the line. "We sell only to civilians. If you want a ticket, get it from your quartermaster."

After that snide remark I was strongly tempted to drag that smart-assed ticket man through the grill. He had never been near a bullet. Common sense ruled, so Henry and I adjourned to a bar to talk it over. Greyhound was on strike at the time, but about 11 P.M. we heard a loudspeaker announcement from next door. "Jackrabbit Bus Lines leaving for Boise, Idaho, in twenty minutes."

Henry looked at me. "That's closer to home!"

"Let's go!"

Three nights later I was able to phone my wife from Jamestown, North Dakota, while the bus made a twenty-minute stop. She met me at the Fargo bus depot two hours later. I had not seen her for three and a half years. She was as beautiful as ever! An hour later I admired my daughter as she lay asleep in bed. My wife had lived with her folks during the war.

The next morning I awoke to find a small hand pulling the sheet from my face. Then a puzzled voice came, "Mommy, who is that strange man in bed with you?"

AUTHOR'S NOTE

Thirty-five years after the war, I received a phone call from a man who said, "This is Paul Clemens."

I said, "Paul is dead. What are you trying to pull?"

He answered, "Darn it all, Chuck, this is Paul! I heard you say, *Poor Paul is dead! Poor Paul is dead!* I could hear every word you said, but couldn't answer. I had a collapsed lung and a body full of cast iron."

Paul and his wife came up that fall to the annual reunion of the 164th Infantry. Needless to say, we have corresponded ever since. What a wonderful surprise!

After returning to Guadalcanal a few years ago, courtesy of the Colorado Air National Guard, we found the area of Point Cruz completely taken over by the capital city of Honiara. Point Cruz had expanded from a swamp to an industrial area, but mullet still swarmed along the beaches as in the old days.

Everything had changed except the hills, which were now covered with roads, with homes everywhere.

Walking Red Beach, our old landing area, we found a 60mm mortar shell, a live one, badly corroded, but a sign of passed years.

Along the coastal roads were at least two thousand automobiles, all Japanese made. There was even a traffic light at the crossroad just off the edge of Point Cruz.

A new pill is available for malaria control, taken only once a week. While at the Mandana Hotel we saw not a single mosquito. Things have changed dramatically, the prices for everything astronomical!